"The KINGDOM IS AT HAND"

"And as ye go, preach, saying,
THE KINGDOM OF HEAVEN IS AT HAND."
—*Matthew 10:7.*

PUBLISHERS
WATCHTOWER BIBLE AND TRACT SOCIETY, INC.
International Bible Students Association
Brooklyn 1, New York, U. S. A.

4,000,000 Edition

IN HONOR

OF

"A great God,
and a great KING
above all gods."
    –Psalm 95:3.

AND OF

"King of kings,
and Lord of lords."
    –Revelation 19:16.

CONTENTS

"The Kingdom Is at Hand"

"THE KINGDOM IS AT HAND"

CHAPTER I

THE KINGDOM of heaven is at hand!" No such message had ever before been heard on earth. The words electrified the multitude of hearers that lined the stony bank of the Jordan river. The ancient river was still running full from the latter rains of the month, and from the melting snow that fed its upland tributary streams. Springtime had come to Palestine. The April skies gave assurance that the rains of winter had passed and the cold had at last given way to a steady season of warmth to bring all growing things to full fruit. It was a beautiful season for the message of the kingdom of a gracious heaven to blossom forth. In the lowlands the barley was ready to harvest. The flowers were appearing on the earth. The tireless bees were busying themselves in winging from flower to flower, gathering their nectar, and then hastening with their precious loads to crevices in the great rocks, and to hollow trunks of trees, there to store up the scented wild honey. The time, too, of the singing of birds was come. The turtledove had not misjudged its appointed time, but had returned, and its cooing to its mate was heard throughout the land. The fig trees were putting

9

forth their green figs, and the grape vines were running with sap that would soon sprout the tender clusters giving a good smell.

All eyes were fixed on the proclaimer of the unusual message, which sounded like good news. He was a man unusual to behold, as there he stood at ankle depth in the river into which he had backed because of the press of the crowd on shore. He was no man clothed in soft raiment such as is worn in the palace of a kingdom, nor was he any soft, compromising sort of character, suave and yielding, easily shaken like a reed in the wind. Not a drop of wine or strong drink had ever passed his lips. A sturdy man was he, a wild man of the desert from his youth up till this day of his appearing. The people that desired to hear his stirring words were obliged to go out to him into the wilderness of the lower Jordan valley, bordered on the west by the province of Judea. As for the man's raiment, he had a garment made of cheap camel's hair thrown about his body, and this was tightened to his loins by a leather girdle. His food rations were very simple, but very tasty, specially to be mentioned being wild honey and that abundant insect, the locust. What was more delicious than the locust wrapped in honey? For all the world it tasted like the shrimp or prawn that the fishers on the shores of the Mediterranean sea delighted to eat. Whereas shrimp was unclean for eating, according to the law of the great prophet Moses, the locust was decreed to be clean. Despite such limited diet, the man of the wilderness was no weakling, but could lift heavy weights, as he now demonstrated daily.

This strange man appeared to be the introducer of something as new and different as his message, something that easily explained his being at the Jordan river. Because of his practice, those among his listeners who could speak Greek called him the *Baptistés* or, commonly interpreted, the baptizer or immerser. And why did he lower the bodies of those who became his disciples beneath the waters and then raise them out again? What did this submerging completely in water symbolize? He only could explain. Before submitting themselves to be immersed, the candidates confessed their sins.

Those that came to the *Baptistés* were Jews according to flesh and blood. They felt a greater responsibility toward Almighty God than did the nations or Gentiles. By birth they had been born into a covenant tie with the Most High God of heaven. This covenant had been made between Him and the fathers of their nation through that mighty prophet Moses about fifteen hundred years previous. Neither they nor their fathers had kept their part of the covenant faithfully, but had broken the God-given laws of the covenant. For that reason they were now a subject people in their own homeland under the hateful yoke of Imperial Rome. According to the baptizer, an event of world importance was at hand, of heavenly origin, and those who felt their sinfulness against the law covenant of God with their nation desired to be found clean and in right standing when the event should occur. Therefore the baptizer preached the baptism of repentance for the forgiveness of sins against the holy covenant. In earnest tones he cried out: "Repent ye: for the kingdom of heaven is at hand." Their burial in water meant to say that they wanted to be dead to sin. Their being raised out of the water told of their coming forth to a clean life henceforth as regards God's covenant, a reformation of their lives unto obedience to His perfect law. Thus they would be prepared to meet the coming King.

This baptizer had a special attractiveness for the God-fearing ones among the Jewish nation. For well over three centuries no prophet had been sent by God to their nation, and here at last a man appeared that had a prophetic mission from God for them. About eight centuries before that the prophet, Isaiah by name, uttered these inspired words: "The voice of one crying in the wilderness, Prepare ye the way of the Lord, make his paths straight. Every valley shall be filled, and every mountain and hill shall be brought low; and the crooked shall be made straight, and the rough ways shall be made smooth; and all flesh shall see the salvation of God." Now, in this baptizer, the people found a man lifting up his voice in the wild gorge of the Jordan and seeking to prepare the way of the people to meet the coming Representative of their God. The news spread like wildfire. Excited multitudes left the villages and cities, even the holy city of Jerusalem, to see and hear this baptizer. From the province of Judea and all the region round about the river they came, and many heard him and were baptized.

The prophet Isaiah had not foretold the name of the one whose voice should be heard crying, but the man now on the scene evidently fulfilling the office was named John, or Jehohanan. The name was of prophetic significance, for it means "Jehovah is gracious". His father gave him the name under special instructions from Jehovah God through His angel Gabriel. John's father was named Zacharias and was a priest. At the time that Zacharias was doing service within the temple at Jerusalem the angel appeared, announced the gracious gift from Jehovah of this son and foretold the son's work, and added: "And thou shalt call his name John." Why did not John enter in upon the priesthood in the steps of his father? John was now thirty years old. That was the age when the son of a priest, after five years of probationary service, was qualified to be registered fully as a priest. Why was John not up at Jerusalem mingling with the leaders of the Jews' religion, Judaism, and offering up animal sacrifices for sin, instead of being out in the wilderness baptizing repentant Jews for the remission of sins? *Why?* Because John the Baptist did not resist the directing power of the spirit of the Most High God upon him. Also John's own unflinching declarations to the religious leaders showed that his place was properly out in the wilderness, and not among the religionists who bragged of having Abraham as their forefather.

Many of the strictest of the Jewish religionists, namely, the Pharisees, as well as their rival religionists, the Sadducees, came to John for baptism. When he saw them he gave his view of their religion, saying: "O generation of vipers, who hath warned you to flee from the wrath to come? Bring forth therefore fruits meet for repentance: and think not to say within yourselves, We have Abraham to our father: for I say unto you, that God is able of these stones to raise up children unto Abraham. And now also the ax is laid unto the root of the trees: therefore every tree which bringeth not forth good fruit is hewn down, and cast into the fire. I indeed baptize you with water unto repentance: but he that cometh after me is mightier than I, whose shoes I am not worthy to bear: he shall baptize you with the holy [spirit], and with fire: whose fan is in his hand, and he will thoroughly purge his floor, and gather his wheat into the garner; but he will burn up the chaff with unquenchable fire." John's language was plain enough. He considered religion as chaff, fit only to be burned with fire that could not be quenched until the chaff was burned to ashes. Unless they, instead of putting on the deceitful show of religion, now produced fruits in keeping with their repentance symbolized by water baptism, they would get the ax. Their claim to be the fleshly descendants of Jehovah God's friend, Abraham, would not count. There was certain to be a purge shortly, and it would be better for them to be baptized with the holy spirit than with fiery destruction.

Hearing John denounce the sanctimonious Pharisees and Sadducees, religionists well known to devour widows' houses and at the same time to make long prayers for a cloak, many asked: "What shall we do then?" John replied: "He that hath two coats, let him impart to him that hath none; and he that hath meat, let him do likewise." Among those coming to him for baptism were the despised publicans, men who acted as agents or who even bought the privilege to gather taxes for the greedy Roman government, and that from their own Jewish brethren, their own nation. "Master, what shall we do?" And John said to them, "Exact no more than that which is appointed you." Even soldiers, off duty, went with the throng to John. Such soldiers were being used to hold down the *Pax Romana,* the peace of a Roman world-organization backed by an adequate military force. They also had a problem, and asked: "What shall we do?" John's pointed answer was: "Do violence to no man, neither accuse any falsely; and be content with your wages." Deeds of justice and mercy were fruits consistent with their profession of repentance.

In the hearts of the common people John's message of the nearness of the Kingdom aroused a great expectation, the coming of the Messiah, whom the Greek-speaking Jews called *Christ.* Many persons of John's nation began

wondering whether he himself was the Christ.
They overlooked that John was of the tribe of
Levi, the priestly tribe, and not of the royal
tribe of Judah. But John humbly confessed he
was merely the forerunner of the King, one who
should be far greater than John. Therefore his
message continued to ring out: "The kingdom
of heaven is at hand." Little did John worry if
the substance of his proclamation came to the
ears of Pontius Pilate, the governor of the Ro-

man province of Judea, or to the ears of the tetrarch, Herod Antipas, governor of the neighboring province of Galilee. Herod could hardly have missed hearing the report concerning John's astounding message. A *kingdom* at hand? Well, if it was a kingdom of *heaven,* Herod was little concerned. He was interested in kingdoms of this earth. He well remembered how his father, Herod the Great, had gotten unduly disturbed when, about thirty years before, several magicians or astrologers came to his palace at Jerusalem and asked about the birth of a new "king of the Jews". Those "wise men" claimed they had seen his star in the east signaling his birth. When those magi disappeared without disclosing to King Herod where or if they had located the supposed "newborn king", then he acted on the suggestion that the Jewish religious heads had given him. He sent his soldiers posthaste to the city of Bethlehem and had all the babes two years old and under slaughtered, among them most likely the baby king-elect.

No, Herod Antipas was not disturbed as his father had been. If though, instead of a heavenly kingdom, John were preaching as a critic of Herod's private affairs, especially of his being in love with the wife of his half-brother, Herod Philip I, the tetrarch of the near-by province of Iturea, and coveting her for his wife, that would change the face of things. It would be a prison offense for the baptist if he should make any damaging comment when Herod Antipas robbed Philip of his wife, Herodias, the mother of that delightful dancer, Salome. Why should John criticize, if the Jewish high priests, Annas and Caiaphas, had nothing critical to say about it in public? Foxy Herod Antipas could easily appease these religionists in other ways by trying to appear as a good proselyte to Judaism, although he was in fact an Edomite hypocrite.

Simply for fear of any man John could not quit preaching. He must continue preparing the way of the Lord God until the mighty Representative of Jehovah God should come. To enable John to identify him and thereafter point him out to the people, the Lord God, who sent John to baptize, said to him: "Upon whom thou shalt see the spirit descending, and remaining on him, the same is he which baptizeth with the holy [spirit]." Six months passed. The summer was drawing to a close, and the dry season would soon be over. The great Jewish celebrations of their seventh month, the national atonement on the tenth day of the month, and the week-long feast of tabernacles from the fifteenth to the twenty-first days inclusive, had brought a sense of release from sin and of restoration to the favor of Jehovah God and his goodness. According to the Roman calendar the month of October had set in. Shortly the shepherds would cease to abide in the fields, keeping watch by night over their flocks in the open country.

According to the historian Luke, in the third chapter of his sacred record, John began preaching and baptizing in the fifteenth year of the reign of Tiberius Caesar as emperor of the Ro-

man Empire. Tiberius was the stepson of the
famed Caesar Augustus. During the old age of
Augustus, Tiberius, then over fifty years of age,
remained almost entirely in Italy, from the beginning of A.D. 11 to the time of the emperor's
death in A.D. 14. During those four years Tiberius held the position of joint-emperor rather
than that of a possible heir to the throne. Nevertheless, the reign of Tiberius is not to be calculated from the time of his close association with
Augustus in the business of imperial government. Rather, it is reckoned from the date of
becoming actual heir to the throne at Augustus'
death on August 19, A.D. 14. Hence the fifteenth
year of Tiberius' reign coincided with the year
29, in which year John the Baptist entered upon
his prophetic work.

In this year 29, after six months of intense
activity, the baptizer had the desire of his eyes
fulfilled: the sign from heaven was revealed to
him. One day John saw a man from Galilee approaching him. John recognized him. It was his
own second cousin, the son of Mary, his mother's cousin. It was the carpenter from Nazareth,
named Jesus. Checking by his own age, which
was a half year more than that of his second
cousin, John knew that this Jesus had just attained the age of thirty years. John watched the
approach of that figure of Jesus, stamped by
human perfection. He could not do otherwise
than admire it and think, "Behold the man!"
Still, why should Jesus come to him, a preacher
of baptism unto the remission of sins? John

knew the circumstances of Jesus' birth. Jesus
had been born by the operation of God's spirit
and was the Son of God. At Nazareth he had
increased in wisdom and stature and in favor
with God and honest men, and he led a life of
absolute purity and sinlessness. What did Jesus
now want John to do? He could make no royal
announcement respecting Jesus unless he saw
the sign.

There is no record that any of John's disciples
or other interested persons were present to witness what now took place there at the Jordan
river. To John's surprise, this perfect one, Jesus, asked to be baptized. John insisted against
Jesus' immersion. He did not understand its
purpose or meaning. It did not seem right, and
John said: "I have need to be baptized of thee,
and comest thou to me?" But Jesus stood firm in
his request, and said: "Suffer it to be so now:
for thus it becometh us to fulfil all righteousness." Then John consented in obedience to the
one who he knew was his superior. They both
stepped well out into the Jordan river, and
John dipped Jesus backwards beneath the water
and then raised him out again. Jesus was praying, but not confessing sins, while this righteous
act was being done toward him.

Then the miraculous sign came. "And Jesus,
when he was baptized, went up straightway out
of the water: and, lo, the heavens were opened
unto him, and he saw the spirit of God descending like a dove, and lighting upon him: and lo
a voice from heaven, saying, This is my beloved

Son, in whom I am well pleased." Jesus saw this visible manifestation of God's holy power peaceably coming down on him as with the innocence of a dove, and he heard the heavenly voice declaring that he is an approved Son of God and well beloved. John, too, saw and heard. Not just then, but about forty days later John testified to his disciples: "Behold the Lamb of God, which taketh away the sin of the world. This is he of whom I said, After me cometh a man which is preferred before me: for he was before me. And I knew him not: but that he should be made manifest to Israel, therefore am I come baptizing with water. . . . I saw the spirit descending from heaven like a dove, and it abode upon him. And I knew him not: but he that sent me to baptize with water, the same said unto me, Upon whom thou shalt see the spirit descending, and remaining on him, the same is he which baptizeth with the holy [spirit]. And I saw, and bare record that this is the Son of God."

CHAPTER II

TESTING THE KING'S INTEGRITY

HE baptized Jesus did not remain with John nor discuss his future operations. The active force that had streamed down from heaven upon Jesus filled him. Under its power he sought solitude. He struck out for deep in the wilderness, unarmed and without any equipment or provisions. What of the wild animals that haunted that lonely country? Jesus felt no terror of them. Strangely, they did him no harm, were they snakes, or scorpions, or lions. It was as if the prophecy of Jehovah God was applied to him which said: "I will make with them a covenant of peace, and will cause the evil beasts to cease out of the land: and they shall dwell safely in the wilderness, and sleep in the woods." Out here in the wilderness this Son of God had no man-made place to lay his head at night. Nor did he live like John on wild honey and locusts. He fasted. Under these conditions he lived for forty days. Familiar with the Holy Scriptures, Jesus' perfect memory recalled how the prophet Moses, the writer of the first book of the Holy Scriptures, once fasted for forty days high up in the mountain of Sinai and received the laws of Jehovah God. To the same mountain the prophet Elijah, fleeing from murderous queen Jezebel, resorted, fasting during the forty-day journey. Also, there was that giant-killer, David, who was obliged to take refuge in the wilderness of Judea; it was when King Saul of Israel pursued after him as after a flea in the wilderness.

Out in the wilderness David received training to become the ruler of the nation of Israel. Hard pressed by Saul, he turned his heart and mind to his only Helper and Deliverer, Jehovah God, and he composed a number of psalms of entreaty and thanksgiving amid that forbidding wilderness. Now Jesus, likely in the same wilderness through which David roamed as a fugitive, turned his heart and his meditations to God his Father. He saw ahead the enemies he must face on leaving the wilderness, enemies more vicious and deadly and venomous than the wild animals of this wilderness. David's prayer in one of his inspired psalms of the wilderness may have come to the mind of Jesus: "Teach me to do thy will; for thou art my God: thy spirit is good; lead me into the land of uprightness." (Psalm 143:10) For that very purpose of instructing his Son, Jehovah anointed Jesus with His holy spirit and opened to Jesus the heavens, not by splitting the skies wide-open or opening a window in them, but by causing him to perceive and understand the things of heavenly meaning. Some of those things he had inquired about when he visited the temple of Jerusalem as a boy of twelve. Under such spiritual illumination from heaven Jesus occupied the

forty days of his wilderness fast with studying
over his Father's will as it was prophetically
foretold in the Bible and as agreed upon before
he came down from heaven to become man.
That heavenly agreement his Father's spirit
now caused Jesus to remember clearly.

Not unexpectedly, Jesus' meditations were
broken in upon by an enemy. A great Serpent
was out there in the stony wilds. It was the great
deceiver. This one presented himself before Jesus, at the close of the forty-day fast when the
pangs of hunger gnawed at Jesus' vitals. How
he appeared to Jesus is not unveiled; but the
hungry man recognized him as Satan, whose
name designates him as the *opposer* of Jehovah
God. At what appeared to be Jesus' weakest
moment the tempter came to him and sought to
stir up in him the spirit of this world, "the lust
of the flesh, and the lust of the eyes, and the
pride of life." His sly, devilish tactics are made
bare to us. "And when the tempter came to him,
he said, If thou be the Son of God, command that
these stones be made bread. But he answered
and said, It is written, Man shall not live by
bread alone, but by every word that proceedeth
out of the mouth of God. Then the devil taketh
him up into the holy city, and setteth him on a
pinnacle of the temple, and saith unto him, If
thou be the Son of God, cast thyself down: for
it is written, He shall give his angels charge concerning thee: and in their hands they shall bear
thee up, lest at any time thou dash thy foot
against a stone. Jesus said unto him, It is writ-

ten again, Thou shalt not tempt the Lord thy God."

Jesus turned back the Devil's twists to Bible scriptures which did not harmonize with the meanings of other scriptures. He did not apply the Scriptures selfishly. Never would he use the miraculous power committed to him for the relief and benefit of himself and make a god of his belly. He refused to make a foolhardy but awe-inspiring demonstration of himself at the temple in order to win the admiration and applause of the populace and draw a large following after himself. Such were not the ways to prove either to himself or to others that he is the Son of God. His obedience to the true sense of his heavenly Father's Word would prove his sonship and that he was determined to hold on to that blessed relationship. If the slanderer, the Devil, thought to stir up doubt in his mind regarding his sonship to God, the Devil had certainly failed. He met a double defeat in trying to move Jesus from his position of subjection as a Son to the will of the Father. Sonship meant the obligation to please the Father. Disobedience meant a forfeiture of a place in God's household, as in the case of Satan the Devil.

One more test remained within Satan's ingenuity to try. This was the most pretentious and spectacular. If Jesus was destined to be a king, then this test would be the one Satan thought most enticing and suited to overcome this Son of God. By powers or means which have not been disclosed to us moderns in these days of the marvels of television, Satan the Devil made a panorama of all the worldly governments flash before Jesus in all their outward glitter and impressiveness. "And the devil, taking him up into an high mountain, shewed unto him all the kingdoms of the world in a moment of time. And the devil said unto him, All this power will I give thee, and the glory of them: for that is delivered unto me; and to whomsoever I will I give it. If thou therefore wilt worship me, all shall be thine." What an opportunity for global domination such as even Emperor Tiberius himself did not wield! Ah, but the wielder of such domination must be subject to the same invisible power that dominated the throne of Tiberius, namely, Satan the Devil. Satan must be the god of the aspiring global ruler. If Jesus came to fulfill the prophecies of Hebrew Writ concerning the ruler that should reign "from the river unto the ends of the earth", here was the chance for him to have it immediately and its glory, without any suffering. The only cost was that the Son of God must deny his own Father as God and must worship Satan as such.

Jesus saw distinctly that the question then for settlement was, Who is God, the "god of this world" or Jehovah? Satan was not disposed to part with his world domination. He was not agreeable to handing over the control of the governments on this globe to Jesus merely to have him deliver them over to his Father. If Jesus would accept the present political and governing powers of earth, it must be on the terms that would not lose for Satan the Devil that one thing. Rather, it must enhance the Devil in the eyes of all living creation and must enable him to hurl further defiance and reproach into the face of Jehovah. A contest for domination was now on. Satan's world domination was pitted against Jehovah's domination over all the universe. Whose domination would Jesus now choose, Satan's or Jehovah's? Who would be winner, and who loser, by Jesus' choice? Whose offer would appeal to Jesus, that of Satan or that of Jehovah God as presented in those prophecies of His written Word which Jesus had been studying with new enlightenment during these past forty days? Not for a moment did Jesus waver from the side of the rightful domination, nor even consider Satan's offer.

"And Jesus answered and said unto him, Get thee behind me, Satan: for it is written, Thou shalt worship the Lord thy God, and him only shalt thou serve." Satan could offer Jesus the rulership as a man over all the earth and over sinful, dying subjects; but only Jehovah the Most High God could offer Jesus the "kingdom of heaven". Jesus had been called to that kingdom when the holy spirit of God descended upon him. When he presented himself for baptism by John in the Jordan river he knowingly and willingly committed himself to an unswerving devotion to the universal domination of Jehovah God. He would never go contrary to his conse-

cration to the cause of Almighty God which that
baptism symbolized. He would not even tolerate
the presence of the chief opposer of his God.
'Be gone, Satan. I turn my back on you, and set
Jehovah God always before my face as the One
whom I worship and serve and obey regardless
of rewards of rulership over others. It is only
right and proper to worship and serve Him. All
others who make bids for worship toward themselves are mimic gods and are wicked opposers
of the universal Sovereign, Jehovah my God.'

With that the great Serpent, who wanted to
get his coils around Jesus and devour him like
a dragon, slunk away. Then Jesus' fast was
broken without violating his Father's law by
any self-service; which indicates that the fast
was according to God's will, and not self-im-
posed by Jesus. "Then the devil leaveth him,
and, behold, angels came and ministered unto
him." The victory of maintaining his integrity
toward his Father in the face of the most prob-
ing temptations was more sustaining than the
material food now ministered to him by angels.
The eternal life of the Son of God was nour-
ished by his uncompromising obedience to the
word proceeding out of the mouth of God far
more than by the bread of physical nourishment
provided by these heavenly messengers. His decision for unquestioning obedience to the true
God, Jehovah, whose law he quoted to meet the
temptations of the Devil, the Son of God must
continue to hold throughout all his days in the
flesh on earth; for the Devil had "departed from

him for a season" only. Where temptation and persuasion failed, coercion and intimidation must be used; so the Devil thought after these his first defeats.

That fortieth day of Jesus in the wilderness, how crucial it was for the interests of humankind! How greatly those faithful decisions he made affected the destiny of all persons of goodwill! How immensely they determined the course of things now happening in this twentieth century! The train of consequences that follows from Jesus' triumphs of faith and obedience in that wild solitude has borne priceless blessings, and it will yet bring in everlasting good things to all seeking truth and life in a new world of righteousness. In the light of the fires of those temptations in the wilderness we get an intimate, heart-revealing close-up of the One chosen by the Most High God to care for the interests of all men of good-will who will live in the new world. The searching tests there caused to stand out sharply that Jehovah's anointed One is the safe one to whom to entrust the highest welfare of the people, and that his rule is certain to be one bringing obedient men into harmony with the Fountain of eternal life, the true and living God.

The outcome of the tests causes our every confidence to be fixed in the Son of God respecting all our good hopes for the future. Only one such as he is worthy to be the Ruler in the "kingdom of heaven". His kingship alone is of divine right. His rule is sure to be for the vindication of the name of the Universal Sovereign, Jehovah God, and for the everlasting unity and peace of all the universe. Every consideration of this tried and tested Son of God argues the importance of our examining his human connections, his singular course on earth, and also the foundations on which his Government rests, and the benefits which will make his kingdom shine above any government that has yet existed or may exist in the postwar era. By such examination we shall know why we do wisely to come over onto the side of his kingdom now.

IMPORTANT: The foregoing chapters quote from the Bible and base themselves upon the historical account as given in the books of Matthew, chapters 1 to 4; Mark, chapter 1; Luke, chapters 1 to 4; and John, chapter 1. Hereafter, unless otherwise indicated, the King James Version or Authorized Version of the Bible will be regularly quoted from, first the book thereof being named, and then the number of the chapter being given, and thereafter the number of the verse in the chapter, as illustrated on page 23, lines 21-24. If any other version of the Bible is quoted from, the name of such version will be given after the verse citation.

CHAPTER III

INTRODUCING THE KING

"THE kingdom of heaven is at hand!" The anointed King himself, Christ Jesus, has taken up the proclamation. John the Baptist's voice has been stilled from announcing the King by his imprisonment in one of the dungeons of Herod Antipas, the governor of Galilee. John's public activity lasted only about a year, or about six months after his baptism of Jesus, but it accomplished its purpose. It called attention to the presence of the long-awaited King, and it introduced to the King a people prepared for him as the royal representative of the Lord God. Everything was just as the angel Gabriel had foretold to John's father: "Many of the children of Israel shall he turn to the Lord their God. And he shall go before him in the spirit and power of [Elijah], to turn the hearts of the fathers to the children, and the disobedient to the wisdom of the just; to make ready a people prepared for the Lord." And at John's birth his father's tongue was loosed by the inspiration from God and he said: "And thou, child, shalt be called the prophet of the Highest: for thou shalt go before the face of the Lord to prepare his ways; to give knowledge of salvation unto his people by the remission of their sins, through

the tender mercy of our God; whereby the day-
spring from on high hath visited us, to give light
to them that sit in darkness and in the shadow of
death, to guide our feet into the way of peace."
—Luke 1: 16, 17, 76-79.

While Jesus was away in the wilderness John
carried on his work with greater conviction than
ever that the Kingdom was at hand. He looked
forward to a great joy, that of pointing out the
King to his baptized disciples, who continued to
grow in number. Once he had introduced the
King, then John knew his work must decline.
As he said respecting Jesus: "He must increase,
but I must decrease." While Jesus refused to
accept a kingship at the hands of the Devil, so
John refused to pretend to be Christ the promised King or to engage in any competition and
run ahead of him; he would not be an antichrist.
A test on this very point came to John, when
the Jews sent priests and Levites from Jerusalem to ask him, "Who art thou?" "And he confessed, and denied not; but confessed, I am not
the Christ. And they asked him, What then?
Art thou Elias? And he saith, I am not." "Art
thou that prophet?" By this they meant the one
whom the prophet Moses said God would raise
up unto his people and who should be like Moses
but greater than he, and whom it would mean
destruction for anyone to disobey. John answered No.

"Then said they unto him, Who art thou? that
we may give an answer to them that sent us.
What sayest thou of thyself? He said, I am the

voice of one crying in the wilderness, Make straight the way of the Lord, as said the prophet Esaias. And they which were sent were of the Pharisees. And they asked him, and said unto him, Why baptizest thou then, if thou be not that Christ, nor Elias, neither that prophet?" (John 1: 19-25) To those men who practiced religion according to the "most straitest sect" of Judaism John did not introduce the King. They were undeserving. They did not believe John's baptism was ordained from heaven, but was of men, and they did not believe his witness as to the "kingdom of heaven". To the shame of those unrepentant religionists, the despised publicans and harlots were honest enough to believe John and to turn to righteousness and prepare to receive the King.—Matthew 21: 23-32.

Among those who came and were baptized to become the disciples of John were a number of Galileans. One was a certain Andrew, the son of Jonah; and another was a certain John, the son of Zebedee. Both men were fishermen; in fact, partners in the fishing business along Lake Tiberias, the lake named from the shoreside city of that name, but more commonly known as the sea of Galilee. John had a brother named James, and Andrew had a brother named Simon. All four men were keenly interested in the coming of the Messiah or Christ. On a day when these men were absent, just the next day after the delegation of priests and scribes interviewed John, he beheld Jesus approaching, coming from his forty-day experience in the wilder-

ness. Jesus was making a revisit or back-call
upon John. Since John was sent to make ready
a people prepared for the Lord God, then Jesus
must come to John and seek first among his disciples those to associate with himself. At Jesus'
approach, John cried out to the disciples near
by: "Behold the Lamb of God, which taketh
away the sin of the world. This is he of whom I
said, After me cometh a man which is preferred
before me: for he was before me." Then John
declared him to be the One anointed with the
spirit of the living God and through whom there
was to be a baptism with the holy spirit. *Anointed* is *Messiah* in Hebrew and *Christ* in Greek.
Whether any of John's disciples thereupon attached themselves to Jesus is not recorded.—
John 1: 28-34.

The next day Andrew and John were standing
with John the Baptist when Jesus came along.
Turning toward Jesus, John the Baptist said:
"Behold the Lamb of God!" It was now Andrew
and John's move, and they began following
Jesus. "Then Jesus turned, and saw them following, and saith unto them, What seek ye?
They said unto him, Rabbi, (which is to say,
being interpreted, Master,) where dwellest
thou? He saith unto them, Come and see. They
came and saw where he dwelt, and abode with
him that day: for it was about the tenth hour."
What was discussed at their study together of
the old Hebrew prophecies is not reported, but
that home Bible-study was convincing to Andrew and John. Andrew was fired to service.

"He first findeth his own brother Simon, and saith unto him, We have found the Messias, which is, being interpreted, the Christ. And he brought him to Jesus. And when Jesus beheld him, he said, Thou art Simon the son of Jona: thou shalt be called Cephas, which is by interpretation, A stone." By interpretation into Greek *Cephas* is *Petros,* or Peter. This Simon Peter thereupon followed Jesus, and Jesus was pleased to have him do so.—John 1: 35-42.

These events were taking place in the lower Jordan valley, opposite the city of Jericho, and near where the river flows into the Sea of Salt, or Dead sea. The rainy, wintry season was now at hand, and Jesus desired to go north to the province of Galilee, where he had been brought up and had worked as a carpenter. "The day following Jesus would go forth into Galilee, and findeth Philip, and saith unto him, Follow me." Philip came from the Galilean city of Bethsaida, just north of the sea of Tiberias. The two fisherman brothers, Andrew and Peter, were from the same city. Unable to keep the good news to himself, Philip hunted up a certain Nathanael. Another name for this Nathanael seems to be Bartholomew, which name means "son of Tolmai". How did Philip approach Nathanael? With these rousing words: "We have found him, of whom Moses in the law, and the prophets, did write, Jesus of Nazareth, the son of Joseph." "And Nathanael said unto him, Can there any good thing come out of Nazareth? Philip saith unto him, Come and see." Philip did not mean that Moses and the other prophets had declared that Jesus would come from Nazareth and would be the son of Joseph. He meant that the One whom all the prophets foretold now proved to be this Jesus of Nazareth, the so-called "son of Joseph". Was that so? Nathanael must come and see for himself.

Jesus, to whom in the mountain of temptation all the kingdoms of the world were shown in a moment of time, saw this honest searcher drawing near and then said to him: "Behold an Israelite indeed, in whom is no guile!" "Nathanael said unto him, Whence knowest thou me? Jesus answered and said unto him, Before that Philip called thee, when thou wast under the fig tree, I saw thee." Such penetrating vision of Jesus convinced Nathanael. "Nathanael answered and saith unto him, Rabbi, thou art the Son of God; thou art the King of Israel." This is the first recorded confession by any of Jesus' disciples of his being the promised King of Israel. "Jesus answered and said unto him, Because I said unto thee, I saw thee under the fig tree, believest thou? thou shalt see greater things than these. And he saith unto him, Verily, verily, I say unto you, Hereafter ye shall see heaven open, and the angels of God ascending and descending upon the Son of man."—John 1:43-51.

From then on Jesus began to increase. John the Baptist started to decrease as many of his disciples began following the One to whom John bore witness. John had the joy to know that those whom he had prepared by his instruction supplied the first disciples to Jesus. (John 3:26-30) The five above-named men were destined to become members of Jesus' group of twelve apostles or "sent-forth" ones. In the following year, A.D. 30, after the spring passover feast, John fell under the wrath of Herod Antipas of Galilee and was imprisoned by him.— John 2:12-25; 3:1, 2, 22-31; 4:1-3.

"From that time Jesus began to preach, and to say, Repent: for the kingdom of heaven is at hand." It was in Galilee of the Gentiles that this message went out first from the lips of the King, carrying forward the message where John in prison was forced to leave off. "Now after that John was put in prison, Jesus came into Galilee, preaching the gospel of the kingdom of God, and saying, The time is fulfilled, and the kingdom of God is at hand: repent ye, and believe the gospel." Jesus carried this message even into the synagogues where the people congregated on the sabbath days in the various cities.—Matthew 4:12-17; Mark 1:14, 15; Luke 4:14, 15.

Did those Jews, did even Jesus' disciples, understand what this startling announcement meant? What kind of government was this to be, this "kingdom of heaven"? Was it to be a government simply of heavenly origin but with its king visibly ruling on earth? or was it to be a government ruling from heaven? What should the Jews expect to gain from such a government, and what relationship did they expect to have with it? Why were they in expectation of a new government, so that this message of the "kingdom of heaven" took a strong grip on any of them? Important questions these, and they can be answered satisfactorily only by looking at the ancient background of the Jews. We can do this by turning back the pages of the Bible to the account of their first forefathers.

For the moment the attention is drawn most to the chief spokesman for the "kingdom of heaven". He appears to be the one upon whom heaven has smiled to make him the royal ruler in that government whether with seat in heaven or upon earth. Is he conducting a political campaign by his publicity work for the Kingdom? Just exactly who is he? Is he of the right stock for the King? and what is his past? There seems to be some uncertainty or contradiction as to whence he is, and it is important to have this settled in order to make sure whether he meets the requirements for the high office. Philip spoke of him as the foretold one, but said he was "Jesus of Nazareth, the son of Joseph". Nathanael, however, lifted him to the sublime level and said he was "the Son of God" and hence the "King of Israel". How could both Joseph and God be the father of this Jesus? If Joseph was his father, then he was, like any other man, a descendant of the first human sinner, Adam; and how could he be specially "THE Son of God"?

Evidently to the minds of these disciples there was no difficulty about such questions of Jesus' descent, due to the information he gave which completely satisfied them and met the predictions of sacred prophecy. Two of the sacred historians of Jesus' life were inspired to supply us today this information. The one historian, Luke, in chapter three of his record, verses 34-38, gives that part of the ancestry which reaches back from Abraham to "Adam, which was the son of God", as follows: 1. Adam. 2. Seth. 3. Enos. 4. Cainan. 5. Maleleel. 6. Jared. 7. Enoch. 8. Mathusala. 9. Lamech. 10. No'e. 11. Sem. 12. Arphaxad. 13. Cainan. 14. Sala. 15. Heber. 16. Phalec. 17. Ragau. 18. Saruch. 19. Nachor. 20. Thara. 21. Abraham. These names are spelled or pronounced according to the Greek in which Luke wrote, and not according to the Hebrew in which the book of Genesis and 1 Chronicles were written. According to Genesis chapters 10 and 11, and 1 Chronicles, chapters 1 to 3, the Cainan who appears 13th in Luke's account is an insertion and should be omitted.

Historian Matthew's record of the origins of Jesus, that is, his apparent human genealogy, begins with Abraham. Therefore, let us now compare the ancestry lines given by Matthew and Luke from Abraham down till they appear to meet in Jesus, in two columns side by side, as below: (1 Chronicles 1-3 is also taken into account.)

Matthew 1: 2-16	Luke 3: 23-34	Matthew 1: 2-16	Luke 3: 23-34
21. Abraham	Abraham	24. Judas	Juda
22. Isaac	Isaac	25. Phares	Phares
23. Jacob	Jacob	26. Esrom	Esrom

Matthew 1: 2-16	Luke 3: 23-34	Matthew 1: 2-16	Luke 3: 23-34
27. Aram	Aram	53.	Melchi
28. Aminadab	Aminadab	54. Jechonias	Neri
29. Naasson	Naasson	55. SALATHIEL	SALATHIEL
30. Salmon	Salmon	56. ZOROBABEL	ZOROBABEL
31. Booz	Booz	57. [Hananiah, according	
32. Obed	Obed	to 1 Chronicles 3: 19, 21]	
33. Jesse	Jesse	58.	Rhesa
34. David	David	59.	Joanna
35. Solomon	Nathan	60. Abiud	Juda
36. Roboam	Mattatha	61. Eliakim	Joseph
37.	Menan	62.	Semei
38.	Melea	63.	Mattathias
39. Abia	Eliakim	64.	Maath
40. Asa	Jonan	65.	Nagge
41. Josaphat	Joseph	66. Azor	Esli
42. Joram	Juda	67.	Naum
43.	Simeon	68.	Amos
44.	Levi	69. Sadoc	Mattathias
45.	Matthat	70. Achim	Joseph
46. Ozias	Jorim	71. Eliud	Janna
47. Joatham	Eliezer	72. Eleazar	Melchi
48. Achaz	Jose	73. Matthan	Levi
49. Ezekias	Er	74. Jacob	Matthat
50. Manasses	Elmodam	75.	Heli
51. Amon	Cosam	76. Joseph	Joseph
52. Josias	Addi	77. JESUS	JESUS

Both genealogies above agree that, according to the flesh, Jesus was a descendant of Abraham (21), and Isaac (22), Jacob (23), and Juda (24), and hence was an Israelite or Jew. Both agree also that he was a descendant of

King David (34), and hence he can be rightly called "the Son of David". But after David the two genealogies part company, Matthew's account running through King Solomon, and Luke's through Nathan. But the two ancestral lines meet again in Salathiel (55) and Zorobabel (56), so that Jesus held fleshly descent from both King Solomon and David's other son Nathan.

Whereas Luke gives a full unbroken line, Matthew makes many omissions in the line he follows, selecting only certain prominent ones in the line, just as when God's angel addressed Joseph (76) and said: "Joseph, thou son of David," although about 40 generations came in between David (34) and Joseph (76).—Matthew 1:20.

Does Jesus trace his descent from King David through Joseph (76) as his direct father? If so, then Jesus was actually the son of Joseph. But it is to be noted that when Luke introduced the genealogy of Jesus he tells of the event which marked Jesus' thirtieth birth-anniversary and says: "Now when all the people were baptized, it came to pass, that Jesus also being baptized, and praying, the heaven was opened. And the holy [spirit] descended in a bodily shape like a dove upon him, and a voice came from heaven, which said, Thou art my beloved Son; in thee I am well pleased. And Jesus himself began to be about thirty years of age, being (*as was supposed*) the son of Joseph, which was the son of Heli." (Luke 3:21-23) Luke knew that it was only a human supposition that Jesus was begotten of Joseph, because Joseph was Jesus' foster-father.

It is plain, therefore, that Matthew's account gives the family tree according to the side of Jesus' foster-father Joseph, while Luke gives Jesus' ancestral line according to his human mother, the Jewish virgin named Mary. Women are not mentioned in the genealogical tables, which, according to the custom of the time, were kept in the public registry of the city of Bethlehem and were open for consultation by the citizens to determine their ancestry. Mary was actually the daughter of Heli (75), and, according to Matthew's account, Joseph was actually the son of Jacob (74). But Joseph married Heli's daughter, Mary, and became son-in-law to Heli. Thereby he legally became the "son of Heli", and Luke lists Joseph as such. In so doing, Luke does not contradict Matthew. Thus Jesus could be the fleshly son of the Jewish virgin and at the same time be "the Son of God". Yet how?

Jesus in the flesh was "the Son of God". This was not because his mother Mary was a descendant of the first man, which man was originally "Adam, which was the son of God". (Luke 3:38) Adam was the son of God because he was created immaculate and sinless or perfect by Jehovah God. Adam, however, committed willful sin in the garden of Eden before ever becoming a father of children. For that reason Mary was a descendant, not of the immaculate Adam, but of the sinner Adam; and she was born in sin as the daughter of the imperfect Jew, Heli, who begot her. To this effect God's Word says: "By one man sin entered into the world, and death by sin, and so death passed upon all men, for that all have sinned." (Romans 5:12) Mary was not a daughter of God by any begettal by Him. There was no need for any immaculate conception of Mary in order for her firstborn son, Jesus, to be the Son of God. The fact that Jesus did not have a human father is responsible. How it came about is explained by Luke before he gives the registered genealogy of Jesus, as follows:

It appears that Mary's mother was a member of the tribe of Levi. Her sister, that is, Mary's aunt, married within the tribe of Levi and had a daughter named Elizabeth, who became the mother of John the Baptist by Zacharias her priest-husband. Mary's mother, on the other hand, married out of the tribe by marrying Heli, a man of the tribe of Judah. Thus Mary was born into the tribe of Judah, but her cousin Elizabeth was of the tribe of Levi. About six months after the angel Gabriel's appearance to the priest Zacharias and the conception then of John the Baptist, this is what happened, as we let Luke tell it: "And in the sixth month the angel Gabriel was sent from God unto a city of Galilee, named Nazareth, to a virgin espoused to a man whose name was Joseph, of the house of David; and the virgin's name was Mary.

"And the angel came in unto her, and said, Hail, thou that art highly favoured, the Lord is

with thee: blessed art thou among women. And
when she saw him, she was troubled at his saying, and cast in her mind what manner of salu-
tation this should be. And the angel said unto
her, Fear not, Mary: for thou hast found favour
with God. And, behold, thou shalt conceive in
thy womb, and bring forth a son, and shalt call
his name JESUS. He shall be great, and shall be
called the Son of the Highest: and the Lord God
shall give unto him the throne of his father
David: and he shall reign over the house of
Jacob for ever; and of his kingdom there shall
be no end. Then said Mary unto the angel, How
shall this be, seeing I know not a man? And the
angel answered and said unto her, The holy
[spirit] shall come upon thee, and the power of
the Highest shall overshadow thee: therefore
also that holy thing which shall be born of thee
shall be called the Son of God. And, behold, thy
cousin Elisabeth, she hath also conceived a son
in her old age: and this is the sixth month with
her, who was called barren. For with God nothing shall be impossible.

"And Mary said, Behold the handmaid of the
Lord; be it unto me according to thy word. And
the angel departed from her." Immediately
thereafter Mary left Nazareth in the province
of Galilee, where Joseph lived, and went south
into the province of Judea to the city where
cousin Elizabeth lived. "And Mary abode with
her about three months, and returned to her own
house."—Luke 1: 26-56.

It is agreed to by the historian Matthew that all this took place before Mary the virgin was joined to her espoused Joseph in marriage. He writes: "Jacob begat Joseph the husband of Mary, of whom was born Jesus, who is called Christ. . . . Now the birth of Jesus Christ was on this wise: When as his mother Mary was espoused to Joseph, before they came together, she was found with child of the holy [spirit]. Then Joseph her husband, being a just man, and not willing to make her a public example, was minded to put her away privily. But while he thought on these things, behold, the angel of the Lord appeared unto him in a dream, saying, Joseph, thou son of David, fear not to take unto thee Mary thy wife: for that which is conceived in her is of the holy [spirit]. And she shall bring forth a son, and thou shalt call his name JESUS: for he shall save his people from their sins. Now all this was done, that it might be fulfilled which was spoken of the Lord by the prophet, saying, *Behold, a virgin shall be with child, and shall bring forth a son, and they shall call his name Emmanuel,* which being interpreted is, God with us. Then Joseph being raised from sleep did as the angel of the Lord had bidden him, and took unto him his wife: and knew her not till she had brought forth her firstborn son: and he called his name JESUS." (Matthew 1:16-25) In that manner Joseph became Jesus' foster-father, and Jesus was supposed to be the carpenter Joseph's son.—Matthew 13:55.

The name *Jesus* was God-given. It does not mean *Savior*, as generally thought. *Jesus* is the Greek form for the Hebrew name *Jeshua*, or the full form of the name *Jehoshuah*. Therefore *Jesus* means *Jehovah the Savior*, so that the name of this Son of God was in itself a witness to Jehovah God as well as testifying to the unusual work that Jehovah would use his Son Jesus to do. "He shall save his people from their sins." The remainder of the Scriptures shows that this does not mean that he would save merely Jews or the people of whom he became a member by birth as a Jew, nor does it mean a so-called "universal salvation" of all. It means that those who would become his people, his "sheep", by taking the steps marked out in the Holy Scriptures, and who would remain his people by a faithful following of him as their King, these he would save, by the grace of Jehovah God. Said Jesus later: "I am the good shepherd: the good shepherd giveth his life for the sheep. I am the good shepherd, and know my sheep, and am known of mine. . . . and I lay down my life for the sheep."—John 10: 11, 14, 15.

Did this One named *Jesus* come first into life through the Jewish maiden Mary? Or did he have existence before becoming born as a man? The unerring Scriptures answer that he existed countless time before ever the first woman was created on our earth. At the time of his beginning of life he was created by the everlasting God, Jehovah, without the aid or instrumentality of any mother. In other words, he was the first and direct creation of Jehovah God. As such he was Jehovah's *only begotten* Son. He was the start of God's creative work, and all that would next be brought into existence would be after-creations. Jehovah God could use this only begotten Son to create such other things, because this Son was the direct offspring of the Almighty One and hence was a mighty one, or a god. This Son of God was the first one to hear God speak, and God spoke to the Son concerning the creative work. Thereafter Jehovah God used his Son as his Word to speak to the future intelligent created ones. He became called "The Word" or "The Word of God".

The historian, the inspired apostle John, introduces Jesus to us by relating something of that One's antehuman existence, as follows: "In the beginning was the Word, and the Word was with GOD, and the Word was God. The same was in the beginning with GOD. All things were made by him; and without him was not any thing made that was made.* In him was life; and the life was the light of men. And the light shineth in darkness; and the darkness comprehended it not. There was a man sent from God, whose name was John. The same came for a witness, to bear witness of the Light, that all men through him might believe. He was not that Light, but was sent to bear witness of that Light. That was the true Light, which lighteth every man that cometh into the world. He was in the world, and

* See the book *"The Truth Shall Make You Free"*, pages 45-48.

the world was made by him, and the world knew
him not. He came unto his own, and his own received him not. . . . And the Word was made
flesh, and dwelt among us, (and we beheld his
glory, the glory as of the only begotten of the
Father,) full of grace and truth. No man hath
seen GOD at any time; the only begotten Son,
which is in [or, which leans upon] the bosom of
the Father, he hath declared him." (John
1:1-14, 18) The reader will notice in the above-
quoted record that no mention is made by the
apostle of any "holy ghost" or "holy spirit", nor
of any so-called "third person".

That there may be no misunderstanding of
the apostle John's words as to Jesus' relationship to Jehovah God, both Jesus and another of
his apostles testify. In Hebrew *Amen* means
truth; and Jesus gave true facts about himself
when he said: "These things saith the Amen, the
faithful and true witness, the beginning of the
creation of God." (Revelation 3:14) That Jesus
was such "beginning" of God's creatures and
that afterward God used his first creation in the
producing of all other creations, the apostle
Paul writes this concerning Jesus: "Who is the
image of the invisible God, the firstborn of every
creature: for by him were all things created,
that are in heaven, and that are in earth, visible
and invisible, whether they be thrones, or dominions, or principalities, or powers: all things
were created by him, and for him: and he is before all things, and by him all things consist."
—Colossians 1:15-17.

Mary, a creature, was not and could not be the mother of God the Creator, nor of "The Word" whom God used to create all other things. At most, Mary could be only the earthly mother of the *Son* of God, and could be such only for the time that he was a man on earth. The life-force of Jesus as "The Word" in heaven was transferred from heaven to the ovum or egg-cell in the womb of the unmarried Mary, and thereby she was blessed with the privilege of supplying Jesus' human body. It was a perfect body, because its life was not from the sinner Adam, but was the original life of the Word from the great Life-giver Jehovah God. The holy spirit or active force of Jehovah God kept that body of Jesus holy and free from sin and imperfection, even though nurtured in the womb of the virgin daughter of the sinful Adam. (Hebrews 7: 26) Hereby Jesus could serve as "the Lamb of God, which taketh away the sin of the world".

A divine miracle occurred when Jesus was "made flesh". He was not an incarnation in flesh, but *was* flesh, a human Son of God, a perfect man, no longer a spirit, although having a spiritual or heavenly past and background. That the heavenly Word of God divested himself of everything as a God-like spirit except his life-force and that he lowered himself to become no more than a perfect man, his inspired apostle bears witness, writing: "Let this disposition be in you, which was also in Christ Jesus, who, though being in God's form, yet did not meditate a usurpation to be like God, but divested himself, taking a bondman's form, having been made in the likeness of men; and being in condition as a man, he humbled himself, becoming obedient unto death."—Philippians 2:5-8, the *Emphatic Diaglott* translation; also *American Standard Version*.

Jesus did not grasp covetously after being superior to Jehovah God, nor even equal to Him in power and glory. Jesus consented to being lowered even beneath what he was as a spirit creature in heaven under the Most High God Jehovah. The Word or Son of God knew that for ever the Lord God Jehovah is and remains all-highest, without equal by any other persons. "To whom then will ye liken me, or shall I be equal? saith the Holy One." (Isaiah 40:25) Only the religious trinitarians are presumptuous enough to claim, without Scripture basis, that two other persons are equal with Jehovah God; but Jesus does not himself claim to be one of such persons. For his humble course Jesus has been exalted even higher than he was before becoming a man, even next to God himself. If Jesus had been equal with God before being "made flesh", then Almighty God could not have further exalted Jesus, because that would have required that Jehovah exalt Jesus higher than Jehovah himself, an impossibility and most unreasonable!

The genealogy of Jesus the Messiah or Christ as "the Son of God" is therefore proved by the Scriptures beyond even the Devil's contradiction. But why should such great care be taken to preserve that genealogy of Jesus according to the flesh? Because it must be demonstrated that the Son of God was born as a man into the tribe of Judah, and that he was a descendant of King David and also of the patriarch Abraham, "the friend of God." This was Jehovah God's loving provision for us that we might know with added certainty that this is the foretold Son of God, the One chosen of God to be the King in the "kingdom of heaven". This genealogical evidence was God's way to safeguard us against being deceived by any religious antichrist or any political antichrist, or counterfeit Christs.

Many of such antichrist sort or counterfeit Christs were foretold to appear, especially in our century marked as it is by global war and by the fruitless efforts of men to maintain total peace under a global government. (Matthew 24: 6, 7, 24) If we follow any, let us follow the only true and God-sanctioned King, the One having real *divine right*. Therefore, to establish that God is true, and hence in our own interest also, let us turn back in the illuminated pages of the Bible and determine why the King of the new world of righteousness was obliged to become "the son of David, the son of Abraham". (Matthew 1: 1) Primarily may our effort be with a desire to vindicate the Word and the holy name of the one true and living God, "whose name alone is JEHOVAH."—Psalm 83: 18.

CHAPTER IV

THE FIRST KINGDOM PROMISE

BRAHAM, the forefather of the new world Ruler, was not a king. Leading a wanderer's life amid the kingdoms of this world, this patriarch sought no kingdom of his own. He adopted that very life of a sojourner who was in but not of this world's organization because he believed that in due time a perfect kingdom would be set up by the sole true Source of all valid government, namely, the Supreme Ruler, Jehovah God. In fact, Abraham as the faithful forefather of the promised King in the "kingdom of heaven" was himself a figure or type of the Lord God Most High.

The "kingdom of heaven" could have no other origin or source than a heavenly one. Its founder must be heavenly, that is to say, higher than man and invisible to man. Jehovah God is the One who first promised such kingdom, and he is its Founder, being the exclusive One that could provide it for the blessing and salvation of humankind. Jehovah God is the great Creator of all things, visible and invisible, throughout the endless universe. He is greater than all his works, and as Supreme One he rules over them and they are all at his disposal. He is rightfully The Universal Ruler, The Universal Sovereign, and he alone exercises absolute universal domination over all his works. His universal sovereignty is beyond the reach of any creature to usurp, to take out of the divine hands by violence, aggression or any other means. Any living creature in heaven or in earth that fights against the divine universal domination and does not willingly choose to come under it must and will justly be blotted out of existence by the Universal Ruler.

The Almighty God is the Rightful Ruler. For that reason he is The *Theocrat,* which title means God-Ruler. His Government is a *Theocracy,* which means a government under the immediate direction and administration of the Most High God. His rule and the organization that he creates are *Theocratic,* and the living creatures in His organization must be subject to the Theocratic rule if they would continue to live and enjoy his boundless blessings. His Theocratic rule binds all the obedient universe in one. Submission to such rule is the only way that permanent 'peace on earth to men of goodwill' can ever be brought about.—Luke 2:14, *Douay.*

Jehovah God is not the Founder of the kingdoms of this world nor the One responsible for them. It is a libel upon God and a reproach to His name for religious clergymen to solemnly teach that such worldly kingdoms are "ordained of God". (Romans 13:1) The Kingdom or Government that He has ordained is the one that he covenanted for in the garden of Eden after humankind began its opposition to Jehovah's Theocratic rule.—Genesis 3: 15.

When God created this earth and placed the perfect man and woman in its garden of Eden, he gave no instructions to them respecting a kingdom. He did not install them as a king and queen, either as regards their yet unborn children or as regards the lower animal creation. Genesis 1: 28 reads: "And God blessed them, and God said unto them, Be fruitful, and multiply, and replenish the earth, and subdue it: and have dominion over the fish of the sea, and over the fowl of the air, and over every living thing that moveth upon the earth." This mandate stated their privileges and duties from God. Hence it was their Theocratic commission as his children and servants. As long as they lovingly fulfilled their commission to subdue the earth to an Edenic state and to fill it with their righteous-born offspring, they would be carrying out the divine mandate. So doing, they would abide as members of Jehovah's universal organization and would be the visible part of that organization. Also their children, who should have a righteous start in life in Eden, would be members of the visible section of the Creator's universal organization.

Prior to the man and woman's creation, God's intelligent organization was made up entirely of his spirit sons, the heavenly sons of God. It was then entirely heavenly and was *above* in relation to the earth. Jehovah's only begotten Son, The Word, was the Chief One in that heavenly organization. Through him Jehovah God created the first human pair, saying: "Let us make man in our image, after our likeness." (Genesis 1:26) For this reason the perfect Adam was the "son of God". He was such by or through God's organization under God's only begotten Son, The Word. When the sinless man and woman in Eden were assigned their duties and were set to work, they were taken into God's universal organization as his earthly children. At the same time that they were the visible or earthly members of His universal organization, they were also its children through The Word. The organization was as a great mother to them, and in such a capacity the universal organization of God's holy creatures was God's "woman" or "wife".

Just as Adam was first in being created and was the head of the human family, and as Eve was given as a wifely helpmeet and cleaved to him, so Jehovah was before his organization of intelligent creatures. Likewise, that holy organization is subject to him as Theocratic Head and serves all his good purposes, cleaving to him in a oneness that comes from harmony with him. It is in a state of holy wedlock with its Creator and God. Any creatures that get out of harmony with the Theocratic Husband of the organization and rebel against the divine will are divorced from the organization. Their final end is destruction; for there is no everlasting life outside of union with God inside his universal organization. From this beautiful viewpoint the

Lord God speaks consolingly to his universal organization, at Isaiah 54:5, 6, and says: "For thy Maker is thy husband; Jehovah of hosts is his name: and the Holy One of Israel is thy Redeemer; the God of the whole earth shall he be called. For Jehovah hath called thee as a wife." —*Am. Stan. Ver.*

Why, then, at Eden did the Supreme Ruler make a covenant with his "woman" (or universal organization) to set up a kingdom over the earth? Because rebellion against His Theocratic rule broke out in that garden of delight, and the Theocracy which had there existed passed away. By opening up the Holy Scriptures God lifts the veil to reveal what took place in the invisible part of the righteous world which then functioned at and about the earth. It was this: For the good of humankind Jehovah God, the great Husband, took out of his holy organization or "woman" certain heavenly creatures, spirits, and placed them over the perfect Adam and Eve as an invisible heavenly organization. The higher part of the "mother" organization thus provided safeguard and instruction for the lower part or lower members of the organization. She must mother all her children, even the least. The one that Jehovah placed at the head of the special invisible organization over man was named Heylel or Lucifer, which name means "bright-shining one". His rank or office was cherubic. Because of his appointment over humankind's interests he was called the "covering cherub". Those under him in the invisible organization were holy angels. Being spirit and hence higher and invisible to man, Lucifer and his organization of angels formed a local *heavens* over humankind.

The perfect Adam and Eve, being formed of the dust of the earth, made up the earthly organization. Together, that heavens and earth constituted a distinct "world" in this sector of Jehovah's universe. Both parts thereof being then righteous, it was a righteous world and was also a part of God's universal organization. It was the first world that man knew.

Far different from the action that was to beautify God's only begotten Son, Lucifer became highminded and set out to exalt himself higher than God's appointment. This he attempted to do by trying to turn that righteous world from a Theocratic world into a world of his own, subject to him as the god to be adored and as a ruler independent of the Universal Theocrat, Jehovah God. Lucifer purposed to become a demon god and to substitute for the Theocracy over earth a demonocracy, or rule of demons. Humankind he would turn out of the pathway of God's perfect righteousness. The starry angels under himself he would seduce and transform into demons. The pride of life to which Lucifer then yielded to launch off on this wicked course must lead to his eventual fall into humiliation and annihilation. The great Inspirer of prophecy says: "How art thou fallen from heaven, O Lucifer, son of the morning! how art thou cut down to the ground, which didst weak-

en the nations! For thou hast said in thine heart,
I will ascend into heaven, I will exalt my throne
above the stars of God: I will sit also upon the
mount of the congregation, in the sides of the
north: I will ascend above the heights of the
clouds; I will be like the Most High. Yet thou
shalt be brought down to hell [the grave, *Sheol*],
to the sides of the pit."—Isaiah 14: 12-15.

Referring to his universal organization as a
lofty mountain towering into the skies, Jehovah
further said to Lucifer, who aimed to be king of
his own rock: "Thou hast been in Eden the
garden of God; . . . Thou art the anointed
cherub that covereth; and I have set thee so:
thou wast upon the holy mountain of God; thou
hast walked up and down in the midst of the
stones of fire. Thou wast perfect in thy ways
from the day that thou wast created, till iniquity
was found in thee. . . . Thou hast sinned:
therefore I will cast thee as profane out of the
mountain of God: and I will destroy thee, O
covering cherub. . . . never shalt thou be any
more." (Ezekiel 28: 12-19) Lucifer, profaning
himself by unfaithfulness and by making Satan
the Devil out of himself, was divorced or cast
off from Jehovah's faithful universal organization or "holy mountain".

With the cunning of the serpent in Eden
which he then used, treacherous Lucifer deceived Eve. He made her think that Jehovah's
Theocratic law was wrongly framed and did not
apply to her and that its penalty of death was
misstated. He enticed her to disobey the divine

law and to eat the forbidden fruit in the paradise of Eden, assuring her it was no mortal offense. Then by sinner woman Lucifer brought pressure upon her husband, Adam, who knew the law of God. Drawn on with lust for the woman, Adam ate of the tree of the knowledge of good and evil with her. They were both now transgressors, more so Adam, the woman's responsible head. It was useless for them to try to hide from the great Lawgiver and Judge, Jehovah God. Though knowing all things, he granted all the culprits in the garden an open hearing. The evidence pointed to Lucifer, now symbolized by his agent the serpent, as the instigator of man's revolt against God's law and universal domination. Forthwith Jehovah passed judgment on the Serpent, the "Shining One" whose light had failed. God said: "Because thou hast done this, thou art cursed above all cattle [beasts being made to be taken and destroyed], and above every beast of the field; upon thy belly [symbolizing greed and selfishness] shalt thou go, and dust shalt thou eat all the days of thy life: and I will put enmity between thee and the woman, and between thy seed and her seed; it shall bruise thy head, and thou shalt bruise his heel."—Genesis 3:13-15.

Thus God debased the satanized Lucifer from his lofty organization to the level of a crawling snake and sentenced him to death. Though execution of the sentence should be deferred till God's due time, yet his extended existence would not result in securing his grip on life; it would be an eating of life-less dust. Also, God did not purpose himself to execute the treacherous Serpent, but to use his Son, the offspring of his "woman" or holy organization. This Son or Seed of God's "woman" would have such hatred of iniquity and all workers of iniquity that he would never compromise but would destroy completely that old Serpent, Satan the Devil.

God's words foretold that Satan the Serpent would form an organization, a "seed", yet there would be those of God's universal organization who would not yield to Satan's seductions but would remain immovably on the side of Jehovah God and within his holy organization. Between these two organizations God would put undying hatred, hostility, enmity. Out from his holy universal organization, or "woman", Jehovah would bring his Seed, armed with all power in heaven and earth. Although Satan and his seed would strike in the back and would persecute this Seed at the heel, yet this mighty Overcomer would crush the head of the Serpent under his heel and wipe out the Serpent and his seed.

Jehovah's pronouncing of sentence next upon Eve and her husband, Adam, proves that God did not mean that Eve was "the woman", neither any of Eve's daughters, not even excepting the Jewish maiden Mary. Adam and Eve, by reason of their violation of Jehovah's Theocratic law, were dismissed from the organization of Jehovah's children, and now Jehovah's universal organization consisted only of spiritual or heavenly creatures and hence was "above" as respects man. It was from this organization that still cleaved to God faithfully as his "wife" and remained free from sin and sin's author Satan, yes, it was from the body of this "woman" that the great Husband, Jehovah God, would bring forth •the holy Seed. The Seed is undefiled by sin and able to destroy the leader in sin, the invisible demon, Satan the Devil. A human mother could never produce such a Seed, a spirit Seed.

Jehovah's declaration of purpose was a covenant toward his "woman" or faithful organization. It was in fact a Kingdom covenant, because the Chief One, who is primarily The Seed, would be the King or Theocratic Governor in the "kingdom of heaven". This royal feature of the covenant became more plain and evident in the days of Jehovah's dealings with Abraham. This covenant was also the first prophecy to humankind. It was uttered by God without any human agency, and is most dependable and sure of fulfillment. Although it was a unilateral or one-sided covenant, declared without first securing consent or agreement of any creatures, yet says Jehovah God: "So shall my word be that goeth forth out of my mouth: it shall not return unto me void, but it shall accomplish that which I please, and it shall prosper in the thing whereto I sent it." (Isaiah 55: 11) His covenant must prosper to the bringing forth of the Seed; and the destruction of the Serpent and his seed merely waits till the coming of the Seed and the setting up of his kingdom.

That explains why Almighty God has permitted Satan and all his wicked brood to continue existing and practicing iniquity; for they must have free hand to bruise the heel of the Royal Seed and to test his integrity to God by pain, trial, opposition and persecution. But God's Word is sure that the Seed must endure the painful ordeal and must defeat the enemy's cruel intentions. The Seed of God's "woman" never will depart wickedly from under Jehovah's universal domination, but will fight for it and destroy all rebels against it. Thereby the Seed, who receives the "kingdom of heaven", will vindicate the word and name of Jehovah God, which name and word the old Serpent, Satan the Devil, has brought under reproach.

Jehovah's likening of the perfidious Lucifer to a groveling serpent showed that now Lucifer had been expelled from God's universal organization as a rebel. This does not mean Lucifer was not permitted to carry on further activity in the heavens and to have contact with the other creatures there. Having succeeded in taking over man and woman, Lucifer next proceeded to steal the world, the heavens thereof as well as the earthly members thereof. He used his influence upon the organization of angels over which God had placed him as covering cherub. Many of these, if not the organization *in toto,* deserted to the side of the rebel. The way of Satan the Devil toward world domination now seemed open, God not interfering. As Adam and Eve brought forth offspring Satan meant to extend his domination over them. He would make it hard for any of these to break loose and to go over onto the side of the Universal Sovereign, Jehovah God. In this way the heavenly organization over man became demonized and the human inhabitants of earth became corrupted. Thereby the whole world became corrupt. The righteous world which humankind first knew ceased and was no more. Nevertheless, Jehovah's covenant in the garden of Eden gave certain promise that a world of righteousness will be recreated, restored, for the vindication of Jehovah's universal domination or sovereignty.

Adam and Eve were driven out of the garden of Eden to meet the penalty for sin: "In the day that thou eatest thereof thou shalt surely die." (Genesis 2:17) In the very 24-hour day that they ate Jehovah the Judge sentenced them and they lost all right to everlasting life, thus being rendered as dead in His sight. Before a thousand years from then should pass they must return to formless non-existence in earth's dust from which they had been taken, for "one day is with the Lord as a thousand years, and a thousand years as ONE DAY". (2 Peter 3:8) While they were slowly dying in sin and imperfection, they brought forth many children, both girls and boys, but not by the divine mandate given to them while perfect in Eden. (Genesis 5:4, 5) Their firstborn son, Cain, became filled with the ambition to be or to play the part of the 'seed of the woman', according to his under-

standing thereof, and killed his brother Abel.
God's favor was upon Abel because of his righteous faith in the Edenic covenant. That made
Cain feel Abel was his rival for the honor which
seemed due to Cain as the firstborn of the human family. God cursed the murderer Cain to
be a "fugitive and a vagabond" all the rest of
his days, but he did not authorize anyone on
earth to execute death upon Cain. There was no
righteous person on earth whom God could
dignify to act as executioner for Him. "Nod"
means "flight" or "wandering"; and Cain "went
out from the presence of the Lord, and dwelt in
the land of Nod, on the east of Eden". (Genesis
4: 15, 16) Cain's wife, one of his father's daughters, went with Cain to Nod.

Cain's ambitions revealed themselves further: he built and organized a city over which
to rule, the first city reported to exist on earth.
"And Cain knew his wife; and she conceived,
and bare Enoch: and he builded a city, and
called the name of the city, after the name of
his son, Enoch." (Genesis 4: 17) It was not built
to honor Jehovah or His name, but to provide
security from harm and to satisfy Cain's "pride
of life" with a sense of rulership. His great-
great-grandson Lamech turned out to be a murderer like himself. These city dwellers went in
for livestock-raising, and instrumental music,
and the heavy industries with copper and iron,
doubtless forging, among other things, arma-
ments.—Genesis 4: 18-24.

John Immerses the King-elect.—Chapter 1.

Jehovah's Anointed Destroys the Totalitarian Giant.—Chap. 9

Another line of Adam's descent ran through his son Seth, born after the assassination of the man of faith, Abel. Seth had a son, Enos. His day is noteworthy. In what way? In that men, who had multiplied considerably by then, organized religion, which religion Satan the Devil introduced in Eden to bring about man's fall. Enos' fellow men had no faith in God or in his Edenic covenant, but began calling either themselves or their false gods by the name of Jehovah. The record, at Genesis 4: 26, in the Hebrew, says: "Then there was a beginning to call upon the name of Jehovah." Five generations after Seth his descendant Enoch was born. Unlike Cain's son Enoch, Seth's descendant of that name did not choose to walk with the men of his day in their organized religion, but "Enoch walked with God". He had faith in Jehovah's covenant and hence was righteous in God's sight and was made Jehovah's prophet.

By Enoch was given God's first prophecy through a man. This prophecy was based upon the Edenic covenant, and its substance is given at Jude 14, 15, which reads: "And to these also Enoch, the seventh from Adam, prophesied, saying, Behold, the Lord came with ten thousands of his holy ones, to execute judgment upon all, and to convict all the ungodly of all their works of ungodliness which they have ungodly wrought, and of all the hard things which ungodly sinners have spoken against him." (*Am. Stan. Ver.*) This foretold of the coming of the King and the destruction of the Serpent and his

seed that a new world of righteousness might
be reset up. The religionists who were calling
creatures by the name of Jehovah and were at
the same time reproaching His name and speaking hard things against Him would have liked
to mete out to Enoch the same deal as Abel got.
Jehovah delivered his faithful servant from
that earthly seed of the Serpent. He translated
Enoch to see a vision of the re-established world
of righteousness, where there shall be no more
death but where the King shall be an "Everlasting Father" to his obedient subjects. While
Enoch was held in the embrace of this entranc-
ing vision, "God took him," and thus Enoch
"was not", and escaped all the pangs of death.
He sleeps in death, awaiting the realization of
the vision under the Kingdom.–Genesis 5:21-24.

OLD WORLD LIQUIDATED

Three generations after Enoch there was
born another man who refused to walk in the
way of organized religion. That man was Noah,
who became known as a "preacher of righteousness". He had faith in the Edenic covenant
and in Jehovah's prophecy through his witness
Enoch. He worshiped Jehovah, and thus, too,
"Noah walked with God." As a witness of Jehovah it was revealed to Noah that God would, in
Noah's day, sweep the whole earth with a flood
and wipe out all the religionists. (Genesis
6:8-17; 2 Peter 2:5) This flood was not to be
the fulfillment of Enoch's prophecy, but was
to be a foreshadowing of the grand and com-

plete fulfillment of that prophecy when God's Seed acts as Jehovah's executioner of the ungodly.

In the days of Noah before the flood men and women were eating, drinking, marrying and giving in marriage, and practicing religion. The history shows they built cities, but there is no record that there were any kingdoms, either city kingdoms or kingdoms over a territory taking in many cities. Hence there is nothing to show that man's invisible overlord, Satan the Devil, appointed any of his mighty spirit demons to serve as special supervisors, as invisible princes over kingdoms. The creation of princedoms in Satan's invisible realm of his corrupt world was as yet without foundation, there being no earthly kingdoms then. One obstacle to this may have been that angels, "the sons of God," came down and appeared in flesh as men and intermarried with the fair daughters of men. Such intermarriage of angels with women did not improve the earthly scene any. Their hybrid offspring developed into "mighty men which were of old, men of renown", but not men for the name of Jehovah. Only Noah and his sons were such. Some time prior to this also many of Satan's demons came down and materialized as "giants". These were Nephilim, fellers or bullies, and they were foremost in filling the earth with violence. The corruption of the human family went on apace, and with it violence increased to fill the earth. The entire "old world", which Satan had created, was a corrupt world, both in its invisible or spiritual part and in its visible or human part.—Genesis 6:1-5, 11, 12.

Then Jehovah God, by an actual demonstration, gave a picture of how he will in due time overwhelm all of Satan's organization, invisible and visible, with destruction, and will restore a world of righteousness and of worship of the true and living God. The great Creator unleashed terrific natural forces to produce a mighty flood. It washed Satan's ungodly earthly arrangement out of existence. The "sons of God" and the *Nephilim* demons escaped with their lives by shedding their human bodies and returning to the invisible spirit realm. The Nephilim rejoined Satan the Devil there and awaited further instructions. The married "sons of God", losing their wives in the flood, were not taken back into the free organization of Jehovah God. Because of their disobedience in Noah's day they were permitted to become "spirits in prison", evidently prisoners of Satan's demon organization. (1 Peter 3:19, 20) Out of human creatures only Noah and his household, eight souls, were saved from a watery grave, and that by means of the ark which Noah built at God's command. These eight were righteous by reason of faith and obedience toward Jehovah God, and with these he gave a new and righteous start to the human family. —Genesis 7 and 8.

When the occupants of the ark came forth therefrom into the purged earth, it was a year and ten days from the time that the first rain in human experience began to fall. Within that time the world of the ungodly perished. "The world that then was, being overflowed with water, perished." (2 Peter 3:6) Outside the ark, the first thing Noah did was to begin family worship of Jehovah. He built no temple, simply an "altar unto the Lord", and on this he offered sacrifices for himself and his saved household.

Except for them the earth was depopulated. Since God "created it not in vain, he formed it to be inhabited", the Creator revived the divine mandate and stated it anew to Noah and his sons. He said to these righteous ones, as he blessed them: "Be fruitful, and multiply, and replenish the earth. . . . bring forth abundantly in the earth, and multiply therein." (Genesis 9:1, 7) This was a prophetic event. It showed beforetime that in the new world of righteousness, governed by the Seed of God's "woman", Jehovah God will issue anew through him the divine mandate to the faithful "men of goodwill" whom he will preserve through the end of this world. When these survivors, pictured by Noah's sons and their wives, bring forth children in righteousness to fill the earth therewith, there will be no Serpent and his vile brood in either heaven or earth. These will have been destroyed down to the last "viper" by the reigning Seed of Jehovah's "wife" in the final battle of Armageddon which will wipe out this world and which was pictured by the deluge of Noah's time.

Noah was not that Seed. He could not be it. He was just a type or prophetic pattern of the Seed; for Satan and his wicked demons were not destroyed by the flood. The Nephilim were merely forced back into the invisible spirit realm. The demon organization was obliged to make a new beginning for world domination. How to overturn the foundation for righteousness which was laid on earth in Noah and his household now became their problem. The Seed of the woman had not yet come. The burning enmity in their hearts fired the demons, from Satan their prince on down, to be on the lookout for the Seed to destroy him on sight, if possible. In conjunction with the divine mandate Jehovah God made a covenant with Noah and his family against wanton bloodshed, saying: "Whoso sheddeth man's blood, by man shall his blood be shed." (Genesis 9:6) But the demons were bent on destroying their foretold enemy, the Seed, even though it meant the flagrant violation of this "everlasting covenant" concerning the sanctity of creature blood.

CHAPTER V

THEOCRATIC KINGSHIP

NOAH was the new father to the future human family, but he could not give them everlasting life. Noah's opportunity to establish a worldly kingdom and to grasp with a firm hand the reins of global domination in the postflood earth loomed large, if he chose to take the chance. However, the suggestion to such a thing could come only from Satan the Devil, him who wanted to make himself a god "like the Most High". Jehovah, the great Theocratic Ruler, had assigned no kingdom to the perfect Adam in Eden, and Noah refused to entertain a suggestion from other sources to set up such a thing. He recognized the Lord God as the Universal Sovereign and himself as only Jehovah's witness and servant in the earth. How, then, did kingdoms of men get started upon earth?

On learning anything of God's purposes Satan, as his opposer, always tries to run ahead of Him in the effort to defeat or forestall His purposes and to deceive men. For a time Jehovah's name was great in the earth by reason of the flood, and his power was feared. His everlasting covenant respecting the sanctity of blood was kept. This situation was not to the

liking of God's enemy. He was bent on world
domination and hence to corrupt humankind
and thus to revive a corrupt world with himself
as the god to be worshiped and feared. On recovering from the upset due to the flood Satan
the Devil reorganized his invisible hosts, the
demons. For the mightier ones or his favorites
among them he planned the office of princes
over world powers in the earth. In progress of
time one of these might become the "prince of
Persia", and another might become the "prince
of Grecia", another "the prince of Rosh, Me-
shech, and Tubal", and so on. (Daniel 10:13, 20;
Ezekiel 38:2, 3, *Am. Stan. Ver.*) Jehovah God
had branded Satan and his servants as a serpent and its seed. Very well, then! Satan the
Devil would organize a huge monstrosity like a
mammoth snake, a dragon. As seven is a number symbolic of spiritual completeness, it should
have seven heads, each head being a prince under Satan. Such is the way the new or reorganized "heavens" of Satan in the postflood
world looked to Jehovah God, and thus he pictured it in his Revelation. The seven princely
heads of the "dragon" have had counterparts in
seven kingdoms or world powers on earth. So
Bible history shows.

Of the three lines of descent from Noah running through Shem, Japheth and Ham, Satan
the Devil seized upon Ham's line to set forward
the scheme of man-made kingdoms on earth.
Nimrod, the grandson of Ham, proved to be
the first to be audacious enough to defy Jeho-

vah, scrap his everlasting covenant and yield to
the temptation for world domination. He was
the first among men to make himself king. The
brief Bible record speaks volumes, though it
says: "And Cush begat Nimrod: he began to be
a mighty one in the earth. He was a mighty
hunter before the LORD: wherefore it is said,
Even as Nimrod the mighty hunter before the
LORD. And the beginning of his kingdom was
Babel, and Erech, and Accad, and Calneh, in the
land of Shinar." (Genesis 10: 8-10) It is certain
that Jehovah God did not authorize Nimrod's
kingdom. He did not anoint or ordain Nimrod
as the "higher powers" on earth to whom the
peoples should be subject as unto an institution
representative of God's will.

King Nimrod was a human power as a
"mighty hunter", but his power was not of God.
Men that lost faith in Jehovah God looked to
Nimrod as a mighty hunter, before, ahead of or
superior to God and in opposition to Him. Nimrod's hunting prowess was won by wanton
slaughter of brute beasts and also of weaker
peoples, in violation of God's everlasting covenant with Noah and all his descendants. Nimrod
turned his subjugated peoples away from Jehovah by setting up the religious cult of worship-
ing a leader and his state, so that man gave
glory to the state ruler and leader rather than
to God. It was at Babel, the beginning of Nimrod's kingdom, that the tower was built to unite
men about a centralized global government, and
there in disapproval Jehovah God confused the

tongue of the ungodly builders. It is Babel, or Babylon, that is used throughout the Holy Scriptures to symbolize the organization of Satan the Devil. Fittingly, therefore, Babylon is pictured as an unclean woman, Satan's woman or wife, the mother of his seed.—Genesis 11: 1-9.

Babylon on earth became the nursing place of organized religion, which is demonism or demonolatry. All of Babylon's kings, from Nimrod on, practiced religion or devil-worship. They were imbued with the same idea as that of the Devil, that of domination in disregard of God and in defiance of his promised Seed of the "woman". This first human kingdom was, therefore, founded by Satan, its god. It was the beginning of his visible organization or corrupt "earth". Satan's revised demon-organization over it made up the "heavens". Together they constituted his world after the flood. That world has continued until now; and it is called "the heavens and the earth, which are now". (2 Peter 3: 7) Its days are numbered and are few now, because the Seed of the "woman" is at hand.

Although Noah lived 350 years after the flood, he had nothing to do with that newly-formed unrighteous world. He continued to be a man of faith and to walk with Jehovah God and to be a "preacher of righteousness". Ten generations after Noah another man of faith in the true and living God was born through the line of Shem. His name was Abram, which was later changed to Abraham, meaning "father of a multitude". He lived about 300 miles southeast of Babylon, at Ur of the Chaldees. By then the "king" idea had spread and there were many such rulers, as the "king of Shinar", the "king of Ellasar", the "king of Elam", the "king of nations", Pharaoh the king of Egypt, and kings of Sodom, Gomorrah, Admah, Zeboiim, and Bela respectively. (Genesis 12: 14, 15; 14: 1, 2) Abraham had faith regarding Jehovah's covenant-promise at Eden and His prophecy by Enoch. He saw the issue, that it was a choice of either these worldly kings or Jehovah's universal domination. When God put him to the test on this issue, Abraham immediately took the side of Almighty God, rather than seek any kingship for himself.

At God's behest Abraham moved out from under the worldly kingdom under which he was born. He became a free rover, under guidance and protection of the Universal Sovereign, Jehovah. Because of this he was accounted worthy to become an earthly forefather of the promised Ruler of the "kingdom of heaven". "Now Jehovah said unto Abram, Get thee out of thy country, and from thy kindred, and from thy father's house, unto the land that I will show thee: and I will make of thee a great nation, and I will bless thee, and make thy name great; and be thou a blessing: and I will bless them that bless thee, and him that curseth thee will I curse: and in thee shall all the families of the earth be blessed." (Genesis 12: 1-3, *Am. Stan. Ver.*) Abraham was sincerely interested in the lasting welfare of the peoples of earth, and he was glad to lend himself to Jehovah God for their blessing.

The above declaration disclosed Jehovah's purpose to bring blessings to humankind. It did not originate with Abraham, but with Jehovah God. Hence it was His unilateral covenant. Abraham could become a party to it by obedience to God's command; and he did so. It is therefore called "the Abrahamic covenant". The promise to make of Abraham a "great nation" showed that Almighty God would give him a seed, although Abraham was then childless at 75 years of age, with his wife, Sarah, just ten years younger. If all the families of the earth were to be blessed in Abraham, then it must be that the "Seed" promised to God's "woman" in Eden would come through this man Abraham. For that reason Abraham was simply serving as a type or prophetic pattern of his Friend and God, Jehovah, forasmuch as the Seed would be Jehovah's Seed in actuality and would be by Jehovah's "woman". Hence the covenant-promise to make obedient Abraham's name great signified that Jehovah God would make his own name great through his Seed. It signified that those honoring and blessing Jehovah's name would be the only ones to receive the blessings from Him and through His Seed.

Twenty-four years later, when Abraham was ninety-nine years old and his wife was eighty-nine and still childless, the Lord said to him: "I am the Almighty God; walk before me, and be thou perfect. And I will make my covenant between me and thee, and will multiply thee exceedingly. . . . And I will make thee exceeding fruitful, and I will make nations of thee, and kings shall come out of thee. . . . As for Sarai thy wife, thou shalt not call her name Sarai, but Sarah shall her name be. And I will bless her, and give thee a son also of her: yea, I will bless her, and she shall be a mother of nations; kings of people shall be of her." (Genesis 17:1, 2, 6, 15, 16) Abraham laughed with joy at the promise, and God commanded that Abraham's son by Sarah should be called "Isaac", which name means "laughter".

. In the light of these divine declarations concerning the offspring of Abraham and Sarah, it becomes clear that the Abrahamic covenant was in reality a Kingdom covenant. It was merely an enlargement upon or extension of the Kingdom covenant Jehovah made to His "woman" at Eden. It took that covenant out of the field of generality and showed that his Seed of the "woman" would travel an earthly course as an offspring of Abraham and Sarah, the Seed thus coming through them and their descendants. Abraham the Hebrew and his offspring through Sarah became the ones for Satan the Serpent and his seed to watch in enmity, to prevent, if possible, even the appearance of the Seed of God's "woman". The demons began by making Isaac the target of persecution, threatening his life. How? Within Abraham's very household and by a member of it.

Fourteen years before Isaac's birth Abraham, with his wife Sarah's consent, begot a son by her maidservant, Hagar, an Egyptian. The son was called "Ishmael". For the thirteen years that followed he was looked upon as Abraham's heir, and especially the heir to the privileges of the Abrahamic covenant. Then, at the divine revelation that Abraham would have an heir by his freewoman, Sarah his wife, that hope for Ishmael faded out, and even Abraham said to God: "O that Ishmael might live before thee!" (Genesis 16:1-16; 17:17,18) Isaac was born at the time foretold, when Abraham was 100 years old and his wife, the freewoman, 90 years old. This was by a miracle of Almighty God, by His spirit or active force, especially since Sarah was far past the age of childbearing.

Certainly Isaac was a child by the promise of God and was born "after the spirit". This is full of meaning, because Abraham was a type of the great Father Jehovah. Hence the aged Sarah pictured God's woman or his universal organization in the heavens above, and she pictured this free organization when it would be *aged* or more than 4,000 years older as reckoned from the Edenic covenant concerning the Seed of the woman. Sarah's miraculous conception and bringing forth of Abraham's son Isaac pictured how Jehovah's only begotten Son Jesus was taken forth, near the beginning of the year 2 B.C., from the universal free organization above, which is God's "woman", and his life was transferred by a miracle from the spirit realm above to the virgin's womb, from whence Jesus was born as a child of the tribe of Judah.

The aged wife, Sarah, well past the time of childbearing, did not picture the young virgin Mary, not yet united to her espoused Joseph. Under divine inspiration the apostle Paul tells us, at Galatians 4:22-31, that Sarah pictured Jehovah's "woman", his loyal spirit organization above and which is free of any bondage or servitude because wholly united to Jehovah. Isaac pictured particularly "the man Christ Jesus", when he was baptized at the Jordan, and the spirit descended upon him and his Father's voice from heaven said: "This is my beloved Son, in whom I am well pleased." This descent of the spirit and this acknowledgment by God before his witness John the Baptist was an instance of begetting by the heavenly Father. Then it was, indeed, that His "woman" brought forth her Seed, her Son "full of the holy spirit".

The ill-feeling that soured the growing Ishmael, Hagar's son, at the birth of Isaac specially burst forth a few years later when Isaac was weaned. In place of rejoicing at the progress of the divine purpose, Ishmael mocked and persecuted his half-brother Isaac, the free child. Observing this, and fearing for her son's life, Sarah urged the dismissal of both Hagar and her son from Abraham's tents: "Cast out this bondwoman and her son: for the son of this bondwoman shall not be heir with my son, even with Isaac." God approved of Sarah's request, saying to Abraham: "In all that Sarah hath said unto thee, hearken unto her voice; for in Isaac shall thy seed be called." (Genesis 21: 1-12) The apostle Paul comments upon this, saying: "Now to Abraham and his seed were the promises made. He saith not, And to seeds, as of many; but as of one, And to thy seed, which is Christ." (Galatians 3: 16) Hence the entire transaction was a prophetic drama. Just how this scene of the persecution against Isaac and the casting out of Hagar and her son was fulfilled in the momentous events some nineteen centuries thence we shall find of intense interest to read in later pages.

Isaac's being made sole heir to Abraham gave great assurance to him. Yet the trial of Abraham's faith relative to the Kingdom covenant was not finished. When Isaac had grown to be a lad or young man, Jehovah's orders came to Abraham: "Take now thy son, thine only son Isaac, whom thou lovest, and get thee into the land of Moriah; and offer him there for a burnt offering upon one of the mountains which I will tell thee of." (Genesis 22: 1, 2) The name of the mountain, Moriah, that was to witness this sacrifice means "Jehovah provides (or points out)". With unquestioning obedience Abraham kept his part of the covenant and journeyed to Mount Moriah with Isaac and built the sacrificial altar. In his mind the question may have been turning round, 'But how can Jehovah God fulfill his covenant, bound up as it is in my only son by Sarah, if Isaac is killed and sacrificed?'

Faith in God answered to Abraham's heart and mind: 'The Almighty God is able to raise the dead. He can fulfill the covenant with a resurrected Isaac.' With this conviction sustaining him, Abraham bound Isaac upon the altar and proceeded to the sacrifice. When he was about to strike his son dead, God's angel called from heaven and bade him halt. Then God provided a ram for sacrifice by a miracle, and confirmed His covenant.

"And the angel of Jehovah called unto Abraham a second time out of heaven, and said, By myself have I sworn, saith Jehovah, because thou hast done this thing, and hast not withheld thy son, thine only son, that in blessing I will bless thee, and in multiplying I will multiply thy seed as the stars of the heavens, and as the sand which is upon the seashore; and thy seed shall possess the gate of his enemies; and in thy seed shall all the nations of the earth be blessed [or, bless themselves]; because thou hast obeyed my voice." (Genesis 22:15-18, *Am. Stan. Ver.*) By himself, who is all-highest and almighty, Jehovah swore to fulfill the Kingdom covenant. This gives unshakable hope and true comfort to all of any nationality whatsoever who await Jehovah's blessings through the Seed of his "freewoman", his universal organization above.

The inspired apostle Paul strongly suggests the meaning of this restoration of Isaac from the very jaws of death, when he writes: "By faith Abraham, when he was tried, offered up

Isaac: and he that had received the promises
offered up his only begotten son, of whom it
was said, That in Isaac shall thy seed be called:
[Abraham] accounting that God was able to
raise him up, even from the dead; from whence
also he received him in a figure." (Hebrews
6:13-20; 11:17-19) It was a resurrection picture, pointing forward to Almighty God's greatest miracle. This seemingly resurrected Isaac
Abraham had the pleasure later on of seeing
happily married to his beautiful grandniece,
Rebekah, and then seeing the marriage blessed
with twin sons. This was assurance that the
covenant birthright would be passed along till
the Seed of the "woman" should come. Before
his death, "Abraham gave all that he had unto
Isaac" as the rightful covenant heir.—Genesis
25:5-8.

TYPICAL KING BY DIVINE RIGHT

One other event in Abraham's career in the
promised land that has a definite bearing upon
the Kingdom covenant and serves to illustrate
its fulfillment must not be overlooked. This took
place in Canaanland before the birth of either
Ishmael or Isaac, and shortly after Abraham
returned from a sojourn in the land of Egypt.
God had not yet given Abraham the land of
Canaan, but let the heathen occupants remain
therein. Therefore Abraham maintained himself neutral toward the affairs of the kingdoms
of the land. He did not intermeddle in their
politics, because he knew he was in a covenant

with God respecting a coming Government
much higher than these Gentile kingdoms.
When four aggressor kings from the north in-
vaded Canaan and five kings of Canaan united
and tried to push back the invaders, Abraham
did not take sides, because it was a fight between kingdoms of this world. None of them
were Theocratic governments. But a test came
to Abraham when the five united kings were defeated and plundered and the four aggressor
kings made off with their booty; for Abraham's
nephew Lot was caught in the tide of battle and
was taken captive, with all his goods.

"And there came one that had escaped, and
told Abram the Hebrew; . . . And when Abram
heard that his brother was taken captive, he
armed his trained servants, born in his own
house, three hundred and eighteen, and pursued them unto Dan." (Genesis 14:13, 14)
Though a neutral with respect to worldly con-
troversies, Abraham displayed that he was not
a pacifist, and so went in pursuit of the captors
of his brother's son. It was not because Lot was
a relative of his by blood-and-flesh ties. It was
because Lot was a man of faith and a righteous
servant of Jehovah God, that Abraham chose
to fight for Lot's deliverance and freedom. The
apostle Peter speaks of Lot as "just Lot" and
"that righteous man", whose "righteous soul"
was vexed at the lawlessness of the wicked.
(2 Peter 2:7, 8) Therefore Abraham felt a responsibility before God Jehovah to do what he
could to liberate his fellow servant of the Lord

God. When it came to an attack by the worldly
enemies upon those who were serving Jehovah
God, then Abraham was not a neutral. Jehovah
showed approval of Abraham's course by blessing him with success against superior enemy
forces. "And he divided himself against them,
he and his servants, by night, and smote them,
and pursued them unto Hobah, which is on the
left hand of Damascus. And he brought back all
the goods, and also brought again his brother
Lot, and his goods, and the women also, and the
people."—Genesis 14: 15, 16.

Now, from a striking event, comes strong con-
firmation that the Supreme One, Jehovah, was
responsible for Abraham's victory and that He
had not ordained those four aggressor kings as
the "higher powers" to whom both Lot and
Abraham should submit their souls; and, further, that Abraham's fight for the interests of
God's people prefigured the course of the Seed
of God's "woman", which is the "seed of Abraham". This event was Abraham's meeting with
the only king then on earth that God approved,
the only Theocratic king then reigning on earth.
The inspired report of this reads: "And Melchizedek king of Salem brought forth bread and
wine: and he was the priest of the most high
God. And he blessed him, and said, Blessed be
Abram of the most high God, possessor of heav-
en and earth: and blessed be the most high
God, which hath delivered thine enemies into
thy hand." Then Abraham gave to Melchizedek
tithes, or the tenth of all the goods he brought

back as the fruits of victory. On the other hand, that Abraham was not seeking to curry favor and protection from any worldly ruler is shown when Abraham refused to accept from the king of Sodom one single thing, "from a thread even to a shoelatchet." Why? Lest the king of Sodom should feel that Abraham was under an obligation to him and owed his wealth and prosperity to that worldly ruler. (Genesis 14:18-24) If that was the case toward Sodom's king, why did Abraham conduct himself differently toward the king of Salem?

Abraham knew that Melchizedek, king of Salem, was at the same time "the priest of the most high God". Therefore, when Abraham paid tithes to Melchizedek, he was ascribing to his Friend, Jehovah God, the victory over the kings of Satan's organization. Also, the blessing that Melchizedek pronounced upon Abraham was inspired of Jehovah and expressed God's approval of Abraham the warrior.

Melchizedek was king of Salem, the name of which city means "peace; prosperity". This was not discordant with his blessing upon the warrior, because the fight of Jehovah's servant had been in the interest of the peace and prosperity of Jehovah's people on earth. The name of Salem's ruler, Melchizedek, means "king of righteousness"; and his blessing upon Abraham was because the warfare was righteous and was for the vindication of Jehovah's name. Melchizedek was not a religionist, but was a priest upon his throne and worshiped the great Theocrat, Jehovah God. He did not inherit his priesthood and kingship from any human source, he was not raised to such office by the democratic or popular choice of his subjects, nor did he take the course of Nimrod and make himself priest and king. Melchizedek was ordained by the Universal Sovereign, the Most High God, and he had no successor on earth. That all this is so, and to show that Jehovah God had raised up Melchizedek to picture the coming King, the inspired apostle writes:

"So also Christ glorified not himself to be made an high priest; but he that said unto him, Thou art my Son, to day have I begotten thee. As he saith also in another place, Thou art a priest for ever after the order of Melchisedec. . . . even Jesus, made an high priest for ever after the order of Melchisedec. For this Melchisedec, king of Salem, priest of the most high God, who met Abraham returning from the slaughter of the kings, and blessed him; to whom also Abraham gave a tenth part of all; first being by interpretation King of righteousness, and after that also King of Salem, which is, King of peace; without father, without mother, without descent, having neither beginning of days, nor end of life; but MADE LIKE UNTO THE SON OF GOD; abideth a priest continually."

"Now consider how great this man was, unto whom even the patriarch Abraham gave the tenth of the spoils. . . . it is yet far more evident: for that after the similitude of Melchisedec there ariseth another priest, who is made, not after the law of a carnal commandment, but after the power of an endless life. For he testifieth, Thou art a priest for ever after the order of Melchisedec. . . . Inasmuch as not without an oath he was made priest: (for those [Levitic or Aaronic] priests were made without an oath; but this [priest] with an oath by him that said unto him, The Lord sware and will not repent, Thou art a priest for ever after the order of Melchisedec:) by so much was Jesus made a surety of a better testament. For such an high priest became us, who is holy, harmless, undefiled, separate from sinners, and made higher than the heavens."—Hebrews 5:5,6; 6:20; 7:1-4, 15-17, 20-22, 26.

The inspired writer above tells us that the king-priest Melchizedek, who had no successor and whose death is not reported, was a type of the Seed of God's "woman", Christ Jesus. This shows further that the Edenic covenant and also the Abrahamic covenant were in fact Kingdom covenants, and for this reason it was fitting that Abraham meet up with Melchizedek. In explaining the picture the apostle Paul quoted above from Psalm 110. To make clear that Jehovah's King of righteousness and peace will not be a pacifist when it is God's due time for him to reign, Psalm 110:4-6 says to the Lord Jesus Christ prophetically: "Jehovah hath sworn, and will not repent: Thou art a priest for ever after the order of Melchizedek. The Lord [according to the original unemended Hebrew text: JEHOVAH] at thy right hand will strike through kings in the day of his wrath. He will judge among the nations, he will fill the places with dead bodies; he will strike through the head in many countries."—*Am. Stan. Ver.; Rotherham,* footnote.

By such prophetic previews recorded in the Bible the evidence keeps on adding up that God's promised King would be a heavenly King and that his kingdom is not to be a measly tiny "State of Vatican City", on Italy's boot, having diplomatic relations with kingdoms of this world. It must be the "kingdom of heaven", which is "not of this world". For that cause Abraham left his homeland at Ur of the Chaldees and wandered from place to place, having no political relations with any of the kingdoms of this world. He and his faithful son Isaac and grandson Jacob looked ahead by faith to the setting up of the heavenly government of the Seed of Jehovah's "woman". Testifying to that effect, Hebrews 11:13-16 reads:

"These all died in faith, not having received the promises, but having seen them afar off, and were persuaded of them, and embraced them, and confessed that they were strangers and pilgrims on the earth. For they that say such things declare plainly that they seek a country. And truly, if they had been mindful of that country from whence they came out, they might have had opportunity to have returned. But now they desire a better country, that is, an heavenly: wherefore God is not ashamed to be called their God: for he hath prepared for them a city." Also Psalm 105:13-15 says of them: "When they went from one nation to another, from one kingdom to another people; he suffered no man to do them wrong: yea, he reproved kings for their sakes; saying, Touch not mine anointed, and do my prophets no harm."

That all those putting their trust in the Kingdom covenant should ascribe their protection, salvation and benefits to the Most High God, Jehovah said to Abraham after putting the four aggressor kings to rout: "Fear not, Abram: I am thy shield, and thy exceeding great reward." (Genesis 15:1) Abraham experienced the fulfillment of that divine guarantee to the day of his death. Those who today take their stand for the heavenly kingdom of Jehovah's King-Priest after the order of Melchizedek, the Seed of Abraham, are likewise "strangers and pilgrims" in an alien land, being in this world but "not of the world". Like Abraham, they may be sure that Almighty Jehovah is their protective shield against the aggressive kingdoms of this world whose enmity they incur. All the blessings which Jehovah God has within His power will be their "exceeding great reward" through the Theocratic Government of his beloved Son.

CHAPTER VI

THE TYPICAL THEOCRACY

HE covenant which the Ruler of the universe made with Abraham was renewed with Abraham's heir Isaac, and then with Isaac's heir Jacob, namely: "In thee and in thy seed shall all the families of the earth be blessed." (Genesis 26:1-5; 28:10-16) This showed the route that the ancestral line was taking leading down to the human birth of the royal Seed. When Jacob was blessed with twelve sons, through which one of these would the regal privileges of the covenant run? Only Jehovah God, the Originator and Founder of the Kingdom, could determine and show this.

For a time it appeared that the covenant privilege would proceed through Jacob's firstborn son, Reuben, according to the prevailing law of primogeniture or senior right of the firstborn son. Then when Reuben showed himself disqualified, it seemed that the covenant honors were transferred to Joseph, Jacob's firstborn by his beloved second wife, Rachel. However, in the things of God, human laws based upon the flesh and its seeming rights are not the deciding factors. That which decides is the will and pleasure of the One who exercises universal sovereignty or domination, the One from whom all rightful power and authority flow. All kingdom rule on earth from other sources, though permitted by Jehovah God to operate for a time, is not authorized or ordained by him. All such must at last give way to the only everlasting government that He has ordained to rule this globe.—Daniel 7: 9-14, 22, 27.

The mystery or sacred secret which was known only to Jehovah was disclosed at his chosen time. That was when Jacob lay dying down in the land of Egypt and surrounded by his twelve grown-up sons. Then the divine choice must be revealed for the guidance of Jacob's survivors. Under God's direction and inspiration Jacob pronounced a blessing upon each son. Beginning in the order of their birth, Jacob blessed Reuben, then Simeon and Levi. Their blessings showed they were not the chosen ones. Then came Judah for his blessing. The name *Judah* means *praise*, and was given to this son in praise of Jehovah. (Genesis 29: 35) Although Jacob's fourth son in order, he was blessed with this divine blessing:

"Judah, thou art he whom thy brethren shall praise: thy hand shall be in the neck of thine enemies; thy father's children shall bow down before thee. Judah is a lion's whelp: from the prey, my son, thou art gone up: he stooped down, he couched as a lion, and as an old lion; who shall rouse him up? The sceptre shall not depart from Judah, nor a lawgiver from between his feet, until Shiloh come; and unto him

shall the gathering of the people be. Binding
his foal unto the vine, and his ass's colt unto the
choice vine; he washed his garments in wine,
and his clothes in the blood of grapes: his eyes
shall be red [flashing] with wine, and his teeth
white with milk."—Genesis 49: 8-12.

This blessing settled the question: the Kingdom privilege would reside in the tribe of
Judah. The blessings upon all the other tribal
patriarchs did not crowd in upon or take away
from that divine assignment to Judah. Through
him must come the Lawgiver and to him must
the people of good-will come and be blessed
with permanent peace, *Shiloh* meaning *Peace-
ful One*. He is to be the unconquerable King,
like a lion, whom it means destruction for all
enemies, Satan and his seed, to stir up to wrath
by their incessant opposition to Him. Before
him all those gaining life in Jehovah's universal organization in heaven and in earth will
bow. They will praise him as the Seed whom
Jehovah ordained from the body of His "woman". He will drink the wine of the joy of the
Lord God, and his glorious reign will be with
great joy to "men of good-will".

Concerning Jehovah's decision at this critical
time it was written: "Reuben the firstborn of
Israel . . . was the firstborn; but, forasmuch
as he defiled his father's bed, his birthright was
given unto the sons of Joseph the son of Israel:
and the genealogy is not to be reckoned after
the birthright. For Judah prevailed above his
brethren, and of him came the chief ruler; but

the birthright was Joseph's." (1 Chronicles 5:1, 2) *Israel* was the new name given to the patriarch Jacob for his faithfulness to God's covenant, and means "ruling with God". For this reason Jacob's descendants by his twelve sons were called "the children of Israel", or simply "Israel", as a nation. The historian writes: "All these are the twelve tribes of Israel: and this is it that their father spake unto them, and blessed them; every one according to his blessing he blessed them." (Genesis 49:28) It was a blessed people.

Along the pathway, however, the Serpent was lurking, eager to fasten his vicious fangs in the heel of the Seed. Out of spite of the divine blessing and its connection with the Seed, that old Serpent, Satan the Devil, hated the twelve tribes of Israel. He thought he now had them where he could effectively deal with them and destroy them and that hated hope of the Seed. Should the Seed prove to be this whole Israelite nation, then he would wipe out the nation or corrupt it beyond God's use. They were then in the land of Egypt, realm of the Pharaohs. Egypt was the first world power, although Nimrod's kingdom of Babel was older. The fact that in the devastating world famine all the nations came down to Egypt for food enhanced its importance as the first world-power in ancient time. According to Satan's scheme of organization of the invisible demons, he appointed a demon 'prince of Egypt' to be one of the heads of the dragon organization. During

Egypt's dominance on earth this demon prince
was the chief one under Satan. All the Egyptians practiced religion under this invisible
prince and worshiped the demons. Egypt's
monuments, obelisks, pyramids, tombs, and
temples, and accompanying hieroglyphics and
paintings, show this.

The Israelites were worshipers of Jehovah,
the God of Abraham, Isaac and Jacob. During
the time that their brother Joseph was the
prime minister of Egypt's Pharaoh, they were
officially protected in the province of Goshen.
Immediately when this official bar was removed
at Joseph's death Satan, through his 'prince of
Egypt', saw to it that a Pharaoh came to the
throne to oppress them.

By a decree ordering all Israelite boy babies
to be killed at birth, Satan's representative
Pharaoh thought to have the males die out in a
generation's time and all Israelite women be
forced to marry demon-worshiping Egyptians.
Like Herod's decree against the babes of Bethlehem, Pharaoh's measure was calculated to destroy as a babe any boy born to be the Seed.
As to obeying this decree that violated God's
everlasting covenant of the sacredness of blood
the Israelites did not recognize Egypt's rulers
as the "higher powers" to whom to be subject
and to murder the little innocents. They obeyed
God and spared their babies. Due to such faith
and faithfulness Moses, the third child of Am-
ram and Jochebed, was born and preserved
alive. Ironically, this boy was even adopted into

Pharaoh's household and reared to manhood there, but only after he had been taught by his parents concerning the God of their forefathers.—Exodus 1:1-22; 2:1-10.

Moses was not of the royal tribe of Judah, but of the tribe of Levi. Aaron was his older brother by three years. Moses was no pacifist, but when he was forty years old he slew an Egyptian taskmaster who was brutally oppressing an Israelite slave. The Israelites, dulled by more than forty years of 'Nazified' oppression, did not rally around Moses as a promising deliverer, and he was obliged to flee to the land of Midian to await a day of God's choosing. (Exodus 2:11-25) For forty years Moses was a shepherd for his father-in-law, and then Jehovah's angel appeared to Moses in the burning bush at the foot of Mount Horeb. Through the angel God commanded Moses to return to Egypt and to lead his brethren, the Israelites, forth from their bondage. When Moses asked what he was to say when they asked who commissioned him as deliverer "God said unto Moses, I AM THAT I AM: and he said, Thus shalt thou say unto the children of Israel, I AM hath sent me unto you. And God said moreover unto Moses, Thus shalt thou say unto the children of Israel, Jehovah, the God of your fathers, the God of Abraham, the God of Isaac, and the God of Jacob, hath sent me unto you: this is my name for ever, and this is my memorial unto all generations."—Exodus 3:13-15, *Am. Stan. Ver.*

Right after revealing his name to Moses Jehovah stated his purpose respecting the Israelites. This associated his name *Jehovah* with his purpose and showed that his name *Jehovah* stands for or implies his purpose toward his creatures. The name *Jehovah* literally means "He causes to be", that is, causes for a purpose.

By his proper credentials Moses, with his brother Aaron as mouthpiece, won the confidence of his brethren in Egypt and then appeared before Pharaoh to demand the immediate release of the Israelites from Egypt. Pharaoh obeyed his god, the Devil, and refused to grant Jehovah's demand. Through Moses Jehovah then brought nine plagues upon all the land, the first three afflicting the Israelites as well as Pharaoh's subjects. *Ten,* as a number, symbolizes earthly completeness; and the tenth plague completed the series of plagues and was foretold to bring the death of all of Egypt's firstborn ones. By this plague it was now to be demonstrated who are the "higher powers". Are they Pharaoh and his demon backers or are they Jehovah God and his Word, his only begotten Son? (Doubtless the angel that appeared to Moses in the burning bush was the Word, the Son of God.)—Exodus, chapters 5-11.

The smiting of the firstborn in Egypt was announced to the Israelites as scheduled to take place shortly after the spring equinox, namely, on the fourteenth day of the first month of their year, or Nisan 14. For them it was to be a "passover" night. God's angel of destruction would pass over the Israelite houses and spare their firstborn if they would obey His instructions to do the following: On the evening of Nisan 14, which day began at sunset according to the Israelites, they must slay an unblemished male lamb that was selected four days earlier, and must sprinkle its blood on the beams about their doors. They must then go into their houses for the night, the lamb's flesh must be roasted with its bones unbroken, and then the household, including any sojourning strangers with them, must eat of the lamb, together with bitter herbs and unleavened bread. They must eat thereof standing, their feet shod, loins girded, and staff in hand, all ready to leave the houses and march out of Egypt at God's signal.

Midnight of Nisan (or Abib) 14 came. Silently the tenth plague stole throughout Egypt, and Pharaoh's firstborn and all his subjects' firstborn expired. The Israelite firstborn were passed over by Jehovah's angel. That same night Pharaoh, crushed, ordered all the Israelites to get out of Egypt with all their movable property. That day of Nisan 14 was exactly 430 years after Abraham left Mesopotamia, crossed the Euphrates river and entered the Promised Land, so becoming a party to Jehovah's covenant concerning the Seed in whom all human families are to be blessed. It was 400 years after Ishmael began persecuting Abraham's son and proper heir, Isaac. (Exodus 12: 1-51; Galatians 3: 17; Genesis 15: 13, 14) In order to memorialize this deliverance of His people in vindication of His name, Jehovah commanded that the Israelites celebrate a passover feast each year thereafter on its anniversary date.

On passover night Jehovah was not through with making a name for himself by display of superior power over Satan and the first worldpower, Egypt. Jehovah led his enemies into a trap when he led the escaping Israelites under Moses to the western shores of the Red sea and the vengeful Pharaoh and his chariots and hosts bore down upon them in pursuit. Then Jehovah opened the jaws of the trap by parting the waters of the Red sea and permitting his chosen people to pass through dryshod and reach the Arabian shores opposite. Driven on by blind hate and deluded by Jehovah into thinking the way safe for them also, the chariots and cavalry of Pharaoh charged into the sealane. When the last of them had raced in, Jehovah's power sprang the trap shut, and the watery walls billowed over them all, baptizing them in retributive destruction. Safe on Arabia's shores, the witnesses of Jehovah's "strange act" of deliverance sang his praises as a free nation. "Then sang Moses and the children of Israel this song unto Jehovah, and spake, saying, I will sing unto Jehovah, for he hath triumphed gloriously: the horse and his rider hath he thrown into the sea. Jehovah is my strength and song, and he is become my salvation: This is my God, and I will praise him; my father's God, and I will exalt him. Jehovah is a man of war: Jehovah is his name. . . . JEHOVAH SHALL REIGN FOR EVER AND EVER."—Exodus 15:1-18, *Am. Stan. Ver.*

By that victory song God's prophet Moses led the Israelites in openly declaring that Jehovah is the Universal Sovereign, despite the mightiest kingdom on earth; and that He is the rightful King of his covenant people, Israel. By the blood of the passover lamb slain in Egypt this Universal King brought the Israelite nation into a covenant with himself through his mediator Moses. In the third month after their leaving Egypt Jehovah inaugurated or dedicated this covenant with them. It took place at Mount Horeb, or Sinai, where he had told Moses the Israelites should worship Him.

When they reached the mountain God instructed Moses to say to the Israelites: "Ye have seen what I did unto the Egyptians, and how I bare you on eagles' wings, and brought you unto myself. Now therefore, if ye will obey my voice indeed, and keep my covenant, then ye shall be a peculiar treasure unto me above all people: for all the earth is mine: and ye shall be unto me a kingdom of priests, and an holy nation." (Exodus 19:4-6) The Israelites told Moses to assure the Lord God that they would keep His covenant that they might become this "kingdom of priests, and an holy nation". Then God dedicated the covenant by giving to them the Ten Commandments, and thereafter many other regulations and statutes and ordinances related to those Commandments and based upon them. For such reason it became known as "the law covenant" with Israel.

Under this covenant arrangement the people of Israel became organized according to God's law and rule, and became a Theocratic nation. They became a typical Theocracy. That is, their twelve tribes, united under the law and rule of the great Theocrat Jehovah, were a type or prophetic pattern of the Theocratic Government which it is Jehovah's purpose to set up for the blessing of all the families and nations of the earth. That future Theocratic Government is the stated "kingdom of priests, and an holy nation", which Jehovah said the Israelites might become if they faithfully kept His covenant with unbreakable integrity toward him.

Diligently search all the laws and provisions with which God inaugurated the law covenant, and you will be impressed with the fact that he appointed or ordained no human king over the nation of Israel. Moses was not their king, and he did not assume to be such. Jehovah was their King, invisible, immortal. As long as they remained obedient to his covenant they could be called "Jeshurun", meaning "upright one". Moses declared: "Jehovah came from Sinai, . . . And he was king in Jeshurun, when the heads of the people were gathered, all the tribes of Israel together." (Deuteronomy 33:1-5, *Am. Stan. Ver.*) When the king of Moab hired an unfaithful prophet to curse the Israelites, God turned the curse into a blessing and caused Balaam to say instead: "Behold, I have received commandment to bless: and he hath blessed; and I cannot reverse it. He hath not beheld iniquity in Jacob, neither hath he seen perverseness in Israel: the LORD his God is with him, and the shout of a King is among them." —Numbers 23:19-21.

Israel's King invisible set up a priesthood for them in the family of Aaron, Moses' brother. Aaron became the high priest. Moses was told to anoint Aaron with holy anointing oil when inducted into that sacred office, and Moses did so. The rest of the tribe of Levi outside of Aaron's sons were appointed to be the servants and helpers of the priesthood as Levites. The priests must offer the various sacrifices for Israel at God's holy altar. Aaron, however, was not like Melchizedek, who was a priest upon a royal throne, a priest-king. Aaron as high priest was not made king. Aside from Moses the prophet and mediator, Aaron was Jehovah's chief representative in Israel, and he must teach them carefully the laws and commandments of the great Theocrat, Jehovah their King.

In behalf of his worship God commanded the construction of an altar of copper and also a tabernacle with a "holy of holies", in which "most holy" compartment the sacred ark of the covenant or testimony should be deposited. This sacred gold-covered chest had a golden lid or mercy seat, on which were mounted two golden cherubim. Before the mercy seat the high priest must sprinkle the blood of atonement sacrifices on the yearly atonement day. The ark contained the stone tablets of the Ten Commandments and other sacred articles. The preparation of all things for the tabernacle worship was made entirely by the consecrated hands of Israelites. On the first day of the second year after coming out of Egypt, namely, on Nisan 1, the tabernacle and all its furniture were set up and Moses anointed Aaron high priest.—Exodus, chapters 35-40.

Besides the annual passover feast, Jehovah ordained other feasts for his covenant people. The next day after passover was to be kept as a sabbath or rest day, and the next day after that, or Nisan 16, the high priest of Israel must offer to the Lord an omer's measure of the first-ripe barley harvest of the Promised Land as the "firstfruits unto the Lord". Beginning with that day and counting fifty days would bring the Israelites to the date of the next feast, known as the "feast of weeks". Centuries later it came to be called the feast of Pentecost by Greek-speaking Jews, for *Pentecost* means *fiftieth* (*day*). On that day the high priest must offer to the Lord two wave loaves made from the firstfruits of the wheat harvest. In the seventh month of the year, on the tenth day, the atonement sacrifices must be offered for the whole nation of Israel. Five days later, on the fifteenth day of the seventh month, the week-long feast of tabernacles or feast of ingathering must begin to be celebrated. It commemorated their dwelling in tabernacles or tents in the wilderness while on their journey from Egypt to the Promised Land. It also marked the ingathering of the final harvest of the year, and was the most joyful celebration of all the year. To all of these feasts the strangers of goodwill, of whom a great multitude came along with the Israelites out of Egypt, were welcome, provided they were first circumcised.—Exodus 12:48,49; Leviticus 23:4-44; Deuteronomy 16:1-17.

As further blessings to his covenant people the all-wise Theocratic Ruler of Israel appointed to them the observance of a weekly sabbath day. Also, in behalf of the land that he promised to give them he declared a larger sabbath of a year's length, as follows: "Six years thou shalt sow thy field, and six years thou shalt prune thy vineyard, and gather in the fruit thereof; but in the seventh year shall be a sabbath of rest unto the land, a sabbath for the LORD: thou shalt neither sow thy field, nor prune thy vineyard. That which groweth of its own accord of thy harvest thou shalt not reap, neither gather the grapes of thy vine undressed: for it is a year of rest unto the land."—Leviticus 25:1-7.

Besides that, Jehovah distinguished the laws of his covenant by providing an additional sabbath thereto every fiftieth year, a jubilee year of freedom from bondage. "Then shalt thou cause the trumpet of the jubilee to sound on the tenth day of the seventh month, in the day of atonement shall ye make the trumpet sound throughout all your land. And ye shall hallow the fiftieth year, and proclaim liberty throughout all the land unto all the inhabitants thereof: it shall be a jubilee unto you; and ye shall return every man unto his possession, and ye shall return every man unto his family. A jubilee shall that fiftieth year be unto you: ye shall not sow, neither reap that which groweth of itself in it, nor gather the grapes in it of thy vine undressed. For it is the jubilee." (Leviticus 25:8-12) In every fifty-year period, therefore, Israel would enjoy seven seventh-year sabbaths and one fiftieth-year jubilee sabbath, making eight year-long sabbaths to the God-given land of Israel. The count of years to calculate these sabbath years was to begin as soon as they entered this land.

All such regulations respecting the tabernacle and priesthood and the feasts and sabbaths were no mere ritual or system of public entertainments and diversions for the people. Jehovah, the Giver of Theocratic law, does nothing purposeless or with idle intent. All these features of his perfect law were of high significance, forecasting good things and grand times to come for all "men of good-will" through the promised Seed of the Greater Abraham. As it is written: "There are priests that offer gifts according to the law: who serve unto the example and shadow of heavenly things, as Moses was admonished of God when he was about to make the tabernacle: for, See, saith he, that thou make all things according to the pattern shewed to thee in the mount." "For the law having a shadow of good things to come, and not the very image of the things [not the perfect representation of the realities]." (Hebrews 8: 4, 5; 10: 1) "Let no man therefore judge you in meat, or in drink, or in respect of an holyday, or of the new moon, or of the sabbath days: which are a shadow of things to come; but the body is of Christ." (Colossians 2: 16, 17) Those things of Israel's law covenant were simply typical, and Israel under Jehovah was a typical Theocracy. Since it was not the real thing, it and its typical covenant were established to endure only until the coming of Christ.—Galatians 3: 17-19.

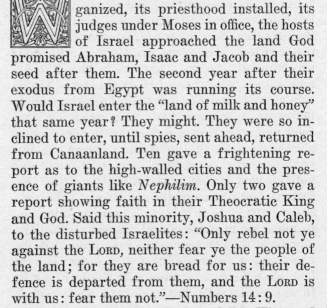

CHAPTER VII

THEOCRATIC JUDGES

ITH the Theocratic nation now organized, its priesthood installed, its judges under Moses in office, the hosts of Israel approached the land God promised Abraham, Isaac and Jacob and their seed after them. The second year after their exodus from Egypt was running its course. Would Israel enter the "land of milk and honey" that same year? They might. They were so inclined to enter, until spies, sent ahead, returned from Canaanland. Ten gave a frightening report as to the high-walled cities and the presence of giants like *Nephilim*. Only two gave a report showing faith in their Theocratic King and God. Said this minority, Joshua and Caleb, to the disturbed Israelites: "Only rebel not ye against the LORD, neither fear ye the people of the land; for they are bread for us: their defence is departed from them, and the LORD is with us: fear them not."—Numbers 14:9.

The Israelites forgot their invisible King and Deliverer, they listened to defeatist propaganda, and their faith failed them. They expressed fears for their wives and their children, and refused to follow their Leader Jehovah God into the land of promise. The tribe of Levi and its priesthood were not represented in this disturbance. They had been separated from all the other tribes unto the tabernacle service. Joseph's offspring had been divided up into the tribes of Ephraim and Manasseh to make up for taking Levi's tribe out. There was no spy from the tribe of Levi among those twelve spies.

In displeasure Jehovah declared that out of the twelve non-Levitical tribes only the children under the age of twenty years would survive the wilderness journey to enter the land with Joshua and Caleb. All the others would die in the wilderness. The spies had searched for forty days. Accordingly they shall all wander for forty years, "each day for a year," until the responsible faithless generation was dead. Those Israelites did not stand fast for freedom from fear of man and for faith in Jehovah God. —Numbers 14:10-38.

The inspired writer Jude makes this comment: "I will therefore put you in remembrance, though ye once knew this, how that the Lord, having saved the people out of the land of Egypt, afterward destroyed them that believed not." (Jude 5) This truth completely disproves the religious doctrine of so-called "universal salvation" and warns us against the religious attitude of "once saved, always saved". Having gotten into the way of His salvation, we must be on guard against provoking the God of our salvation to our own undoing. "Take heed, brethren, lest there be in any of you an evil heart of unbelief, in departing from the living

God. While it is said, *To day if ye will hear his voice,* harden not your hearts, as in the provocation. For some, when they had heard, did provoke: howbeit not all that came out of Egypt by Moses. But with whom was he grieved forty years? was it not with them that had sinned, whose carcases fell in the wilderness? And to whom sware he that they should not enter into his rest, but to them that believed not? So we see that they could not enter in because of unbelief. Let us therefore fear, lest, a promise being left us of entering into his rest, any of you should seem to come short of it. For unto us was the gospel preached, as well as unto them: but the word preached did not profit them, not being mixed with faith in them that heard it. For we which have believed do enter into rest: . . . let us labour therefore to enter into that rest, lest any man fall after the same example of unbelief."—Hebrews 3: 12, 15-19; 4: 1-11.

For us to submit to Theocratic rule, direction and organization it always requires faith in the great invisible Ruler, the Universal Sovereign, Jehovah God. As in Eden, Satan the Serpent always tries to stir up unbelief or lack of faith by evil thoughts or evil reports respecting the great Theocrat and thereby to foment rebellion against His Theocracy. By reason of the Israelites' outburst of unbelief toward the close of the forty years of wandering in the wilderness, Moses was provoked into an act of impatience. He exceeded his authority when the miracle of bringing forth water out of the rock at Meribah was performed. "And the Lord spake unto Moses and Aaron, Because ye believed me not, to sanctify me in the eyes of the children of Israel, therefore ye shall not bring this congregation into the land which I have given them." (Numbers 20: 1-13) Shortly thereafter Aaron died, and his son Eleazar was nominated and appointed by Jehovah God to be high priest in Aaron's stead. Looking forward to Moses' death, Jehovah appointed faithful Joshua to succeed him. God instructed Moses to give Joshua the charge as such successor before all the congregation of Israel. (Numbers 20: 23-29; 27: 15-23) Joshua was not made king of Israel, but a judge and commander. He was of the tribe of Ephraim. Over a thousand years later, when the Hebrew Scriptures were translated into Greek to form the Septuagint Version of the Scriptures the name of Joshua was translated *Jesus*.—Acts 7: 44, 45; Hebrews 4: 8.

In the fortieth year of Israel's wilderness journey they debouched onto the plains of Moab on the eastern side of the river Jordan. There they camped, opposite the city of Jericho on the other side of Jordan. On the first day of the eleventh month Moses was inspired to deliver to Israel his farewell speech and its warnings and blessings as set forth in the book of Deuteronomy. Prophetically he warned them against taking up religion, which is demonism. He said: "For these nations, which thou shalt possess, hearkened unto observers of times, and unto diviners: but as for thee, the LORD thy God hath not suffered thee so to do. The LORD thy God will raise up unto thee a Prophet from the midst of thee, of thy brethren, like unto me; unto him ye shall hearken; according to all that thou desiredst of the LORD thy God in Horeb in the day of the assembly, saying, Let me not hear again the voice of the LORD my God, neither let me see this great fire any more, that I die not. And the LORD said unto me, They have well spoken that which they have spoken. I will raise them up a Prophet from among their brethren, like unto thee, and will put my words in his mouth; and he shall speak unto them all that I shall command him. And it shall come to pass, that whosoever will not hearken unto my words which he shall speak in my name, I will require it of him." That Prophet to come greater than Moses was Jesus Christ. The law covenant was made with the Israelites to safeguard them from religion until his coming.—Deuteronomy 18:14-19; Acts 3:20-23.

Some days later, at God's call, Moses went up alone to the top of Mount Nebo. From that eminence the 120-year-old prophet, whose vision was yet sharp and clear, was permitted to view the "land of milk and honey" that lay across the river Jordan. Then, alone with God, Moses died, as God had said. "And he buried him in a valley in the land of Moab, over against Beth-peor: but no man knoweth of his sepulchre unto this day." (Deuteronomy 34:1-7) As a deliverer and prophet and mediator of the mighty Theocrat,

Moses served as a type or prophetic figure of Christ Jesus the King.

Then Joshua, the son of Nun, took over the command subject to Jehovah God. Under Joshua the hosts of Israel crossed the Jordan river dryshod by a miracle of Jehovah, and entered the Promised Land, Canaan. The heathen Canaanites were terrified at the wonder-working power of the God of Israel. Further miracles followed in the land in behalf of His covenant people. The towering walls of the city of Jericho fell down flat, and from its destruction only a woman of faith and good-will, Rahab the harlot, together with her relationship, was saved. This is that Rahab whom the apostle Matthew lists as the wife of Salmon in the ancestral line of Jesus Christ. (Joshua, chapters 2-6) The city of Ai was destroyed with God's help. The inhabitants of the city of Gibeon, realizing they were under Jehovah's decree of extermination of the demon-worshiping population of Canaan, used strategy to work their way into a treaty of peace and exemption with Joshua and the Israelites. The lives of these Gibeonites were spared, but they were made to be "hewers of wood and drawers of water for the congregation, and for the altar of the LORD".—Joshua, chapter 9.

The Canaanite king of Jerusalem united forces with other city-kings of the land and laid siege to Gibeon. At the appeal of the Gibeonites, Joshua made a forced march, lifted the siege, and routed the combined enemy. While these

demon-worshiping opposers of Jehovah's Theocracy in Canaan were in flight, He miracu-
lously rained down huge hailstones upon them,
slaying more than the Israelites did with the
sword. For light to see to complete the destruction, Joshua prayed that the declining sun and
the rising moon stand still. Wonder of wonders,

"the sun stood still, and the moon stayed, until the people had avenged themselves upon their enemies." (Joshua, chapter 10) Then a still larger combination of Canaanite kings took place. Their hosts were "even as the sand that is upon the sea shore in multitude, with horses and chariots very many". They moved against Captain Joshua, but the Lord delivered them all into his hand and they were smitten, put to flight and destroyed. So the conquest of Canaan proceeded, and shortly thirty-one city-kings were overthrown.—Joshua 11 and 12.

All the above was Theocratic warfare. It was no violation of Jehovah's everlasting covenant made with Noah and applying to all human-kind respecting the sanctity of blood. That covenant said: "Whoso sheddeth man's blood, by man shall his blood be shed: for in the image of God made he man." (Genesis 9:6) Jehovah is the Most High Judge and Executioner of the wicked. He made the faithful Israelites to act "in the image of God" as his executioners. For the destruction of the wicked, therefore, God took the responsibility. The warfare was waged at the direct command of God, who declared war to the death against the Canaanite religionists. (Deuteronomy 20:16-18) Their presence in the land presented a continual danger and snare to the Israelites in their efforts to worship God in spirit and in truth. Moreover, the Canaanites took the side of the Devil in opposing the establishment of the typical Theocracy of Jehovah in that land. God advocated no "good-neighbor policy" with the devil-worshiping religionists. He ordered the destruction of these fighters against his Theocracy. By miracles he helped in their destruction; "for the LORD fought for Israel."—Joshua 10:14.

The invasion of the land was no act of unjust aggression against the Canaanites. The Lord God owns all the earth, and he gave the land to his people according to the covenant he made with Abraham 470 years previous. The Canaanites were unlawful squatters in the territory. Under the divine decree to evict such resisters the Israelites were rightfully taking possession of their God-given land in faith and obedience toward Jehovah. This action was typical of how Jehovah God must take over the entire globe and destroy out of it all religionists and opposers, that his devoted people on earth might live under His Theocratic Government and freely worship him without molestation or hindrance or snares.

After the defeat of the 31 Canaanite kings, but before the land was all subdued, the division of the territory was made among the twelve tribes of Israel. The priests and Levites were given no inheritance in the land. Jehovah God and his service were their inheritance. Cities of refuge, all together six of them, were appointed from among the 48 cities assigned to the priests and the Levites. Any Israelite or stranger unintentionally killing a person without malice might flee from the avenger of blood to these cities and live therein safely; but only after the death of Israel's high priest was he decreed to be free to leave the city of refuge and return to his own.—Joshua, chapters 13 and 20; Numbers 35:1-32.

On entering the land the count of years for calculating the seventh-year sabbaths and the fiftieth-year jubilee sabbath must also begin. There is no doubt that in the life of Joshua and the elders that outlived him these sabbath years were faithfully kept. "And Israel served the LORD all the days of Joshua, and all the days of the elders that overlived Joshua, and which had known all the works of the LORD, that he had done for Israel."—Joshua 24:31.

After Joshua's death Jehovah assigned the foremost position in Israel to the tribe of Judah in order to press the offensive against the remaining Canaanite demonolaters in the Holy Land. In the course of the offensive the city of Jerusalem was taken over, but only partially. Its stronghold or citadel continued to be held and occupied by the heathen Jebusites.—Judges 1:1, 2, 21.

God had promised Israel: "I will not drive them out from before thee in one year; lest the land become desolate, and the beast of the field multiply against thee. By little and little I will drive them out from before thee, until thou be increased, and inherit the land. And I will set thy bounds from the Red sea even unto the sea of the Philistines, and from the [Arabian] desert unto the river [Euphrates]: for I will deliver the inhabitants of the land into your hand; and thou shalt drive them out before thee. Thou shalt make no covenant with them, nor with their gods. They shall not dwell in thy land, lest they make thee sin against me: for if thou serve their gods, it will surely be a snare unto thee." (Exodus 23:29-33) Hence the offensive was renewed and rolled on. Before ever it reached the divinely mapped boundaries, the Red sea on the southwest, the Mediterranean sea on the west, the Arabian desert on the southeast and east, and the Euphrates river on the north, it halted. Why? The Israelites lost their zeal for Jehovah and their faith in him. They became ensnared with religion. In disregard of the warning of their Theocrat, they yielded to flattery and human philosophies and gave in to a "good-neighbor policy" with the remaining Canaanite religionists. Because the Israelites compromised the worship of Jehovah God with the devilish racket of religion, the Lord God did not drive out the residue of religionists from the Promised Land. He left them therein that they might prove a thorn in the side continually to the Israelites, "that through them I may prove Israel, whether they will keep the way of the LORD to walk therein, as their fathers did keep it, or not."—Judges 2:20-22; 3:1-4.

The heathen, whose religion the Israelites imitated or borrowed, did not prove to be advantageous friends to them on religious terms, but committed aggressions against the Israelites and oppressed them. When the Israelites remembered their covenant with Jehovah and appealed to him by repenting and converting to his commandments, then the Lord God raised them up judges to act as leading figures in His deliverance of them. He raised up *Othniel* to liberate them from the oppression by the king of Mesopotamia; *Ehud* to lead the "free Israel" movement against the Moabite king Eglon; *Barak,* together with the prophetess *Deborah,* to break the power over Israel of the Canaanite king Jabin, and his 900 chariots of war under Captain Sisera; *Gideon* to chase out the marauding Midianites; *Jephthah* to regain Theocratic territory and to drive the Ammonites back behind their own borders; *Samson* to slay at his death more than 3,000 Philistine Dagon-worshipers, which was more than all he slew during the twenty years that he judged Israel; and *Samuel* to discomfit the Philistines while the Lord God thundered from heaven, and thus Israelite cities were wrested from Philistine hands. (Judges, chapters 3 to 16; 1 Samuel 7: 3-17; 12: 11; Hebrews 11: 32-34) The deeds of these judges of old provided faint foregleams of the mightier deeds of the greater Judge and Deliverer to come, Christ Jesus, the Seed of Jehovah's "woman".

CHAPTER VIII

HUMAN KING FAILS

HE effect of Israel's repeated yielding to religion and violating their covenant to have no other God than Jehovah their King began to show up in the nation's wrong leanings as to rulership. It led to their desiring to conform themselves to the political nations who made them trouble. This cropped out in the days of Gideon, of the tribe of Manasseh. On his return from whipping the Midianite kings and princes the men of Israel said to Judge Gideon: "Rule thou over us, both thou, and thy son, and thy son's son also; for thou hast saved us out of the hand of Midian." True to God, Gideon recognized the Theocratic government over Israel and replied: "I will not rule over you, neither shall my son rule over you: Jehovah shall rule over you." —Judges 8: 22, 23, *Am. Stan. Ver.*

Abimelech, the son of Gideon by his concubine, was not of the same mind with his father. After his father's death he carried on political wire-pulling with the citizens of Shechem. Then he bought the services of a lot of ward heelers and killed off all the many other sons of Gideon, except the youngest. The way to the throne was now clear. "And all the men of Shechem gath-

ered together, and all the house of Millo, and
went, and made Abimelech king." (Judges
9:1-6) Abimelech's kingdom proved to be most-
ly local and did not catch on to all the rest of
Israel. He came under God's curse, and his
reign of three years was terminated by rebellion against him, and a violent death at the
hand of a woman.—Judges, chapter 9.

Israel's history serves to show that any regular falling away from the recognition that Jehovah is God tends at the same time to dull the
vision of his being the "King of Eternity". (Jeremiah 10:10, marginal reading) The effect of
backsliding was to make Israel impatient at waiting for the heavenly King to produce the Seed
of the "woman", the Seed of Abraham, of the
tribe of Judah. Till now the Israelites had held
back from following the example of the Babylonians in setting up the blood-stained Nimrod
as king. Not so, however, with other peoples.
Even the Edomites, the descendants of Jacob's
twin brother Esau or Edom, set up kings over
them while the Israelites were sojourning down
in Egypt. On this it is written: "And these are
the kings that reigned in the land of Edom, before there reigned any king over the children of
Israel. And Bela the son of Beor reigned in
Edom."—Genesis 36:8, 9, 31, 32.

During the days that the judges ruled in
Israel as visible representatives of the Lord
God, the fact of their having a theocracy in
which the invisible God was their King differen-
tiated them so greatly from all other nations

that it was commented upon. The Israelites had
the Theocratic law of Jehovah and were obli-
gated to do right according to it. "In those days
there was no king in Israel: every man did that
which was right in his own eyes." (Judges
21:25) There was no flaw about such Theocratic rule. The loveliness thereof, when the
Israelites lived in harmony with it, is set forth
in the book of Ruth, which Ruth was an ances-
tress of Jesus according to the flesh. Failure
for such Theocratic rule can never be laid to
Jehovah's account, but must be laid entirely to
the lack of faith and obedience on the part of
his covenant people Israel.

The day finally came regarding which God
had given forewarning in Moses' farewell
speech to Israel, saying: "When thou art come
unto the land which the LORD thy God giveth
thee, and shalt possess it, and shalt dwell therein, and shalt say, I will set a king over me, like
as all the nations that are about me; thou shalt
in any wise set him king over thee, whom the
LORD thy God shall choose: one from among thy
brethren shalt thou set king over thee: thou
mayest not set a stranger over thee, which is
not thy brother." (Deuteronomy 17:14, 15)
What such a move by the Israelites meant in
God's sight came to view when such actually
occurred in Samuel's day. This the inspired
Record shows.

Judge Samuel was old, and the elder representatives of the nation of Israel came to him
at his home town Ramah. They said: "Behold,

thou art old, and thy sons walk not in thy ways: now make us a king to judge us like all the nations." "But the thing displeased Samuel, when they said, Give us a king to judge us. And Samuel prayed unto the LORD. And the LORD said unto Samuel, Hearken unto the voice of the people in all that they say unto thee: for they have not rejected thee, but they have rejected me, that I should not reign over them. According to all the works which they have done since the day that I brought them up out of Egypt even unto this day, wherewith they have forsaken me, and served other gods, so do they also unto thee. Now therefore hearken unto their voice: howbeit yet protest solemnly unto them, and shew them the manner of the king that shall reign over them."—1 Samuel 8: 1-9.

Samuel's detailing of the burden that a visible human king would be to them and of the restrictions it would place upon their liberties and freedom of enterprise failed to dim the glamor of having a man as king. "And the LORD said to Samuel, Hearken unto their voice, and make them a king." (1 Samuel 8: 10-22) At God's direction Samuel the Levite privately anointed Saul of the tribe of Benjamin, pouring a vial of oil upon his head and saying: "Is it not because the LORD hath anointed thee to be captain over his inheritance?" Soon the anointed Saul was brought to public notice as God's choice, at a gathering of all the tribes at Mizpeh. "And all the people shouted, and said, God save the king [(*Hebrew*) Let the king live]. Then

Samuel told the people the manner of the kingdom, and wrote it in a book, and laid it up before the LORD." Even this concession from the Theocratic Ruler did not please all, and there were many discontents. Saul, by virtue of his anointing, was called "the anointed", or "messiah" or "christ". Would he prove to be a faithful picture of the promised Christ the King? or would he be an unfaithful "christ" (or anointed one) abusing his anointing or commission as king? Backward, bashful Saul appeared to make no effort to organize the kingdom of all Israel, but returned home and resumed farming.—1 Samuel 10: 17-27.

A crisis quickly followed from an Ammonite invasion of the land of Gilead, east of Jordan river. The Israelites again appealed for a human king to lead them. God's spirit came upon Saul, and he left the plow and led the Israelites to a victory over the aggressors. This demonstrated to Israel that God was using Saul. "Then said Samuel to the people, Come, and let us go to Gilgal, and renew the kingdom there. And all the people went to Gilgal; and there they made Saul king before the LORD in Gilgal." (1 Samuel 11: 1-15) At this confirming of the kingdom in Saul's hands Samuel addressed the rejoicing people and, in closing, said:

"And when ye saw that Nahash the king of the children of Ammon came against you, ye said unto me, Nay, but a king shall reign over us; WHEN JEHOVAH YOUR GOD WAS YOUR KING. Now therefore behold the king whom ye have

chosen, and whom ye have asked for: and, behold, Jehovah hath set a king over you. If ye
will fear Jehovah, and serve him, and hearken
unto his voice, and not rebel against the commandment of Jehovah, and both ye and also the
king that reigneth over you be followers of Jehovah your God, well: but if ye will not hearken
unto the voice of Jehovah, but rebel against the
commandment of Jehovah, then will the hand
of Jehovah be against you, as it was against
your fathers."—1 Samuel 12: 12-15, *Am. Stan.
Ver.*

It was then springtime, just about the time
of the feast of weeks or Pentecost, when the two
wave loaves of the wheat first-fruits were
offered to God by the high priest at the tabernacle. The rainy season of winter in the Holy
Land had passed about two months before, and
the continuous dry season was due to run yet
four or more months longer. Under this circum-
stance Samuel next said: "Now therefore stand
still and see this great thing, which Jehovah
will do before your eyes. Is it not wheat harvest
to-day? I will call unto Jehovah, that he may
send thunder and rain; and ye shall know and
see that your wickedness is great, which ye have
done in the sight of Jehovah, in asking you a
king." The miraculous storm that followed terrified the conscience-stricken Israelites, and reminds us of the later saying of Hosea the
prophet of God: "Thou saidst, Give me a king
and princes. I gave thee a king in mine anger,
and took him away in my wrath." (Hosea

13:10, 11) Samuel warned the Israelites further, saying: "But if ye shall still do wickedly, ye shall be consumed, both ye and your king." Notwithstanding their having rejected Him as King, Jehovah did not forsake or cast off the Israelites, because his great name was connected with their nation which he had been pleased to make his people, before Egypt and all other Gentile nations. (1 Samuel 12:16-25) What would now determine the fate of Israel's kingdom with its visible head? Not primarily the economic measures that the king took or the military exploits that he did, but how he promoted and cared for Jehovah's worship. Would he rule for the vindication of Jehovah's name?

King Saul early showed whether he would use his position and power in harmony with Theocratic rule. Such rule was still in force in Israel because of their covenant, in spite of the setting up of a kingdom. Whether his son Jonathan would succeed him in the throne was affected by this. After Saul reigned two years, the worst invasion till then by the Philistines befell his kingdom. His subjects were in great distress and terror, Saul and Jonathan being practically the only armed men in Israel. By appointment Saul at Gilgal waited seven days for the prophet Samuel to come down and offer sacrifice. Impatient of waiting further, on the seventh day Saul presumed before God to offer the sacrifice. He thereby usurped the service assigned to the tribe of Levi and was combining the priestly office with the king's office. Just after the sacrifice Samuel appeared. Saul excused his act of running ahead, saying that, because of the dangerous emergency, "I forced myself therefore, and offered a burnt offering." Then came Samuel's prophetic words: "Thou hast done foolishly: thou hast not kept the commandment of the LORD thy God, which he commanded thee: for now would the LORD have established thy kingdom upon Israel for ever. But now thy kingdom shall not continue: the LORD hath sought him a man after his own heart, and the LORD hath commanded him to be captain over his people, because thou hast not kept that which the LORD commanded thee." (1 Samuel 13:1-14) Jehovah God therefore entered into no covenant for the kingdom with undependable Saul. Jonathan his son was now definitely out as successor, and the Lord God purposed to select a "man after his own heart" who was certain to prove an obedient king, trusting and obeying the great Theocrat. In the tenth year of Saul's reign that man was born, at Bethlehem.

Another test of Saul's regard for Jehovah's Theocratic instructions came in due time. Appointing Saul, who was understood to represent the Lord on the throne, Jehovah commanded Saul to destroy the Amalekites. Long previous the Amalekites attacked the Israelites under Moses when marching away from Egypt. After the defeat of the Amalekites "the LORD said unto Moses, Write this for a memorial in a book, and rehearse it in the ears of Joshua: for

I will utterly put out the remembrance of Amalek from under heaven. And Moses built an altar, and called the name of it JEHOVAH-nissi: for he said, Because the LORD hath sworn that the LORD will have war with Amalek from generation to generation". (Exodus 17:8-16) Now in furtherance of that divine purpose, Saul must go and destroy all the Amalekites without sparing, "both man and woman, infant and suckling, ox and sheep, camel and ass." The Lord God devoted everything of the Amalekites to destruction.

As God's executioner King Saul went to slaughter the Amalekites. He came short of this commission. He spared the Amalekite king, Agag, and let the Jews seize upon all the fine livestock of every kind, but "every thing that was vile and refuse, that they destroyed utterly". When Samuel went down to Saul at Gilgal, the prophet asked: "Wherefore then didst thou not obey the voice of the LORD, but didst fly upon the spoil, and didst evil in the sight of the LORD?" Saul explained that the animals were taken for sacrifice to God and that, except for Agag, he had utterly destroyed the Amalekites. Then Samuel said: "Hath the LORD as great delight in burnt offerings and sacrifices, as in obeying the voice of the LORD? Behold, to obey is better than sacrifice, and to hearken than the fat of rams. For rebellion is as the sin of witchcraft, and stubbornness is as iniquity and idolatry. Because thou hast rejected the word of the

LORD, he hath also rejected thee from being king."

As Samuel turned about to leave the entreating king, Saul took hold of the border of Samuel's mantle, only to have it rend. This appeared symbolic, and Samuel said: "The LORD hath rent the kingdom of Israel from thee this day, and hath given it to a neighbour of thine, that is better than thou. And also the Strength of Israel will not lie nor repent: for he is not a man, that he should repent." After conducting the worship of the true Ruler and Strength of Israel, in which worship King Saul joined, Samuel called for captive Agag to be brought. Agag expected Jehovah to revoke his decree of extermination of Amalek. But, as God does not lie or repent, Samuel executed the commission that Saul failed to carry through and Samuel himself put Agag to death. Then Samuel left Saul's presence and never saw him again. "And the LORD repented that he had made Saul king of Israel."—1 Samuel 15:1-35.

The first human king of all Israel failed. The cause was his refusal to obey Theocratic instructions in vindication of the name and word of Jehovah God. In displaying such rebelliousness he was going in the course of the covering cherub Lucifer. He was thus practicing devil-worship. By his stubbornness in this disobedient course he was committing lawlessness and perverseness and an idolizing of himself and his pride. He rejected God's Word and failed to see or appreciate Jehovah's Theocratic or-

ganization. He could not properly sit on the throne of the Lord in Israel. Hence God rejected Saul and his house. God repented, not of His purpose in permitting a kingdom over Israel, but that he had made Saul king. Consistently, then, God let the kingdom go on, but he turned to another man suitable to be made next king.

CHAPTER IX

COVENANT FOR THE KINGDOM

ONATHAN, oldest son of Saul, was a man of faith and was faithful to God and the Theocratic organization. (1 Samuel 14:1-15, 44, 45) However, because of the rebelliousness of Jonathan's father against God's law, Jehovah God could not see fit to make a covenant with King Saul for the throne of Israel. No royal line beginning with Saul could be established, and hence it was not the divine will that faithful Jonathan should succeed to the throne over Theocratic Israel. The "man after his own heart" whom God sought for the kingship must therefore be an Israelite other than Jonathan.

When Jonathan had been a prince under Saul his father for ten years, there was a child born to a man named Jesse at Bethlehem, a city of the tribe of Judah. Bethlehem was destined to become called "the city of David" in commemoration of this child born in it. David was the eighth son of Jesse. He grew to be a shepherd lad tending his father's flock, and also became an expert slinger and a skillful player on the harp. One day he was called in from the field. On arriving home, he beheld the prophet Samuel, who had asked for his appearance. Samuel

at once went to the ruddy, goodly-looking David
and anointed him with oil, as he had done to
Saul over twenty years before. Why? Because
God had sent his prophet to secretly anoint the
successor to King Saul. "And the spirit of the
LORD came upon David from that day forward.
. . . But the spirit of the LORD departed from
Saul, and an evil spirit from the LORD troubled
him." To soothe him in his depression King
Saul hired David to play at court for him, until
the pressing matters of war with the Philistines
caused that David was sent home.—1 Samuel
16: 1-23.

One day David's father sent him to take some
special provisions to his three oldest brothers,
who were at the fighting front face to face with
the uncircumcised Philistines. The battle lines
were in array, when David saw a monstrosity,
the Philistine giant Goliath, stride forth into
"no man's land" and challenge the Israelites to
settle the whole war by a duel between him and
their select champion. This had been going on
for days. No Israelite entered the lists against
Goliath, but all fled back. David's indignation
rose at hearing the giant "defy the armies of
the living God". He expressed his willingness to
fight. The heavy armor which Saul tried on
David proved unsatisfactory. David put them
off. Then he stepped out in advance of the
Israelites and entered upon "no man's land",
with only his shepherd staff and sling, and five
picked stones in his shepherd's bag. King Saul
watched from a distance.

The heavily armored Goliath, with his shield-bearer before him, felt highly insulted at seeing this shepherd stripling put in the field against such a tough bruiser as himself. By all his demon gods he cursed David and threatened to make him carrion for animals. David retorted: "Thou comest to me with a sword, and with a spear, and with a javelin: but I come to thee in the name of Jehovah of hosts, the God of the armies of Israel, whom thou hast defied. This day will Jehovah deliver thee into my hand; and I will smite thee, and take thy head from off thee; and I will give the dead bodies of the host of the Philistines this day unto the birds of the heavens, and to the wild beasts of the earth; that all the earth may know that there is a God in Israel, and that all this assembly may know that Jehovah saveth not with sword and spear: for the battle is Jehovah's, and he will give you into our hand."

Here was a vindicator of God's name, and Jehovah could not fail him now, but sped the stone from David's sling unerringly to the vital spot in Goliath's forehead. Then David cut off the head of the fallen devil-worshiper, while the Philistines fled, with the Israelites in pursuit, smiting them. When David appeared with Goliath's head in King Saul's presence, Jonathan loved him on sight, "as his own soul." He recognized him as the one marked to become the king of Israel. (1 Samuel 17:1-58; 18:1; *Am. Stan. Ver.*) As for Saul, the Devil soon showed him cause to become jealous of David.

Twice Saul tried to spear David while harping soothing music for the king. Failing, Saul next plotted his death. David escaped all such devices and fled for his life. David and Jonathan met secretly thereafter, and made a covenant with each other that David's house in kingdom power would not cut off kindness from Jonathan's house for ever. Because Jonathan stood up for David, King Saul was infuriated and made an attempt upon the life of even his own son.—1 Samuel 18: 5 to 20: 42.

David, the Lord's anointed, became a virtual outlaw in King Saul's realm, and without just cause. It was part of Satan the Serpent's scheme to kill off anyone likely to be the Seed of God's "woman" and so cause Jehovah's Edenic covenant to fail. After temporary refuge in Philistia David "escaped to the cave Adullam: and when his brethren and all his father's house heard it, they went down thither to him. And every one that was in distress, and every one that was in debt, and every one that was discontented, gathered themselves unto him; and he became a captain over them: and there were with him about four hundred men". (1 Samuel 22: 1, 2) From then on mighty men of good-will from a number of the tribes of Israel sought unto the outlawed David: ambidextrous fighters of Benjamin, Saul's own tribe; warriors of Gad with faces like lions and bold enough to force passage "over Jordan in the first month, when it had overflown all his banks"; men of Judah who perceived that God was helping David; and also valorous men of Manasseh. David's following became a "great host".

Even while King Saul's hunt for David continued, Prince Jonathan ventured to visit him in his hide-out to strengthen him, and said: "Fear not: for the hand of Saul my father shall not find thee; and thou shalt be king over Israel, and I shall be next unto thee; and that also Saul my father knoweth." "And they two made a covenant before the LORD: and David abode in the wood, and Jonathan went to his house."— 1 Chronicles 12:1-22; 1 Samuel 23:14-18.

Although David was banned and proscribed, he and his fighter force were never seditious. They never turned their arms against King Saul and his realm. David persisted in looking upon Saul as "the Lord's anointed" and left it up to Almighty God to remove Saul. David did not consider that his own anointing from God authorized him to rise up and overthrow King Saul. Twice, when murder-minded Saul pursued David into the Judean wilderness like a wild goat upon the rocks, David had it within his power to kill his relentless pursuer. He refused to do so, not choosing to 'touch the Lord's anointed' and run ahead of Jehovah God. Repeatedly God delivered David from encirclement by Saul's hosts, and David acknowledged Jehovah as his Savior.—1 Samuel 23, 24, 26.

At last Saul desisted from pursuit, but did not lift the ban off David. When the Philistines prepared war and made their final march against Saul, David and his forces did not join with them in the aggression against Israel's king. At the same time David was estopped as outlaw from helping Saul against Israel's traditional enemies, the Philistines. Disaster faced Saul, and all communication between him and the great Theocrat was cut off. His rebelliousness had been as the sin of witchcraft. Now in desperation Saul went down to the witch of Endor, disobeyed God in not killing her off, and asked the impossible thing, that she should raise Samuel from the dead. The witch got in touch with a demon that pretended to be the dead Samuel and gave a lying but disheartening message to the king. Hopelessly, Saul led his armies into the battle at Mount Gilboa, and he and three of his sons were slain, as the Philistines defeated and routed the Israelites. (1 Samuel 28-31) David mourned bitterly over the death of King Saul and prince Jonathan.

Under God's instruction David returned with his band into Judah to the city of Hebron, about fifteen miles south of his birthplace, Bethlehem. "And the men of Judah came, and there they anointed David king over the house of Judah." He was thirty years old when thus anointed to be king over the tribe of Judah; which fact reminds us of Jesus' anointing with God's spirit at thirty years of age at the Jordan river. (2 Samuel 2:1-4; 5:4; Luke 3:21-23) The adherents of Saul's house put his surviving son upon the throne over the other tribes, and warfare between them and the tribe of Judah followed for a long time. When the cause of Saul's house failed due to lacking God's blessing, the tribes all turned to David. "So all the elders of Israel came to the king to Hebron; and king David made a league with them in Hebron before the LORD: and they anointed David king over Israel." This was David's third anointing. —2 Samuel 5:1-4.

Hebron continued as David's capital for seven years and six months. Then David's obedience to God's decree to push the offensive against the religionists within the boundaries God had marked for Israel led to an important change. The heathen Jebusites still occupied the stronghold or fortress-citadel in Jerusalem, about twenty miles northeast of Hebron. David first proceeded against them. By means of the secret "gutter", or underground passage leading to the water supply of the Jebusite stronghold, David's men under Captain Joab gained entrance into the stronghold, and it was taken. "David took the strong hold of Zion: the same is the city of David. . . . So David dwelt in the fort, and called it the city of David. And David built round about from Millo [the fill-in] and inward." (2 Samuel 5:5-9) David thus made Jerusalem the capital city of the typical Theocracy. Because the king dwelt in the stronghold of Zion, the city's most prominent part, Jerusalem as a whole was also called "Zion". The two names *Zion* and *Jerusalem* came to be applied interchangeably to the Theocratic capital.

Again showing the poisonous enmity of Satan the Serpent against any representative of

the Seed of Jehovah's "wife", the Philistines
tried to unseat David. "But when the Philistines
heard that they had anointed David king over
Israel, all the Philistines came up to seek
David." David, by a miracle of God, defeated
them at Baal-perazim. When they recovered
and again attempted to interfere in the government of the typical Theocracy, God gave David
another victory over the devil-worshipers at
Gibeon. And David's prestige rose.—2 Samuel
5:17-25; 1 Chronicles 14:8-17.

It was a long time since the Philistines' victory at Shiloh in the boyhood days of Samuel.
Ever since their temporary seizure of the ark
of the covenant at that time, the sacred ark had
not known the inside of the tabernacle's holy of
holies. It was kept in the home of a Levite at
Gibeah. King David brought it out of its obscur-
ity there and caused it to be borne amid great
rejoicing to a place on Mount Zion, within a special tent near his palace. But the tabernacle
built by Moses and its altar of sacrifice remained in the high place at Gibeon. As the pro-
cession brought the ark up into the royal city,
the Levites sang this psalm of David:

"Sing unto Jehovah, all the earth; show forth
his salvation from day to day. Declare his glory
among the nations, his marvellous works among
all the peoples. For great is Jehovah, and greatly to be praised: he also is to be feared above all
gods. For all the gods of the peoples are idols:
but Jehovah made the heavens. Honor and
majesty are before him: strength and gladness

are in his place. Ascribe unto Jehovah, ye kindreds of the peoples, ascribe unto Jehovah glory and strength; ascribe unto Jehovah the glory due unto his name: bring an offering, and come before him; worship Jehovah in holy array. Tremble before him, all the earth: the world also is established that it cannot be moved. Let the heavens be glad, and let the earth rejoice; and let them say among the nations, JEHOVAH REIGNETH!"—1 Chronicles, chapters 15 and 16, *Am. Stan. Ver.*

Time passed. David, dwelling in a house of cedar, felt a tent unworthy to cover the ark of God. He told the prophet Nathan of his desire to promote the worship of God in Israel by the building of a glorious temple for the ark in Jerusalem. Then it was that, although not authorizing David to build the temple, Jehovah God made a covenant for the kingdom with this "man after his own heart". By Nathan God sent this covenant message to David: "Moreover I tell thee that Jehovah will build thee a house. And it shall come to pass, when thy days are fulfilled that thou must go to be with thy fathers, that I will set up thy seed after thee, who shall be of thy sons; and I will establish his kingdom. He shall build me a house, and I will establish his throne for ever. I will be his father, and he shall be my son: and I will not take my loving-kindness away from him, as I took it from him [Saul] that was before thee; but I will settle him in my house and in my kingdom for ever; and his throne shall be established for ever."–1 Chronicles 17: 1-15, *Am. Stan. Ver.*

As a covenant for the Kingdom this declaration of the divine will and purpose was directly related to Jehovah's covenant in Eden and to his covenant thereafter with Abraham. His covenant with David left no further uncertainty: the Seed of God's "woman", which seed is also the Seed of the Greater Abraham, Jehovah, must come according to the flesh through the royal line of King David of the tribe of Judah. Hence the Seed would be rightly called "the Son of David", denoting his royal inheritance. The covenant with David was a prophecy, which had only a partial and illustrative fulfillment in the successor of David at his death. The Seed of the "woman" is the One to whom in reality Jehovah is a Father, and the Seed is to Him a son. It is the throne of the Seed that must be established for ever. The Seed is the One whom Jehovah must settle in the divine household for ever and whose kingdom must be forever in Jehovah's Theocracy. The Seed is the One privileged to build the true and abiding house or temple of the Most High God. The Seed is the sole Heir to the covenant for the Kingdom. He is accordingly the Lord Jehovah's Anointed One, the only rightful Ruler in the "kingdom of heaven" in the New World of righteousness.

David's name means "Beloved". He was deeply touched by this loving-kindness of the Lord, and prayed: "And now, O Jehovah, let the word that thou hast spoken concerning thy servant, and concerning his house, be established for ever, and do as thou hast spoken. And let thy name be established and magnified for ever, saying, Jehovah of hosts is the God of Israel, even a God to Israel: and the house of David thy servant is established before thee."—1 Chronicles 17 : 16-27, *Am. Stan. Ver.*; 2 Samuel 7 : 18-29.

When later, possibly during the Israelite captivity to Babylon, it appeared that the Kingdom covenant had broken down, the inspired writer of Psalm 89 drew comfort of its certainty of fulfillment from these d i v i n e unbreakable words: "I have made a covenant with my chosen, I have sworn unto David my servant: Thy seed will I establish for ever, and build up thy throne to all generations. . . . Blessed is the people that know the joyful sound: they walk, O Jehovah, in the light of thy countenance. . . . For our shield belongeth unto Jehovah; and our king to the Holy One of Israel. . . . I have found David my servant; with my holy oil have I anointed him: . . . I also will make him my firstborn, the highest of the kings of the earth. My lovingkindness will I keep for him for evermore; and my covenant shall stand fast with him. . . . My covenant will I not break, nor alter the thing that is gone out of my lips. Once have I sworn by my holiness: I will not lie unto David: His seed shall endure for ever, and his throne as the sun before me. It shall be established for ever as the moon, and as the faithful witness in the sky."—Psalm 89 : 3, 4, 15, 18, 20, 27, 28, 34-37, *Am. Stan. Ver.*

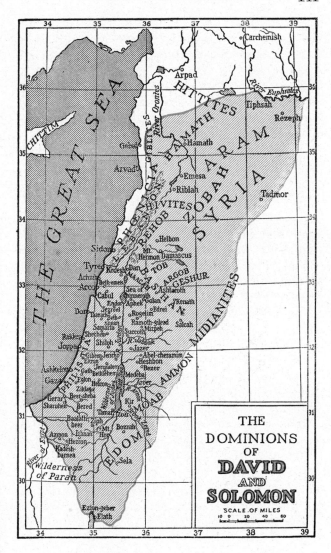

THE
DOMINIONS
OF
DAVID
AND
SOLOMON

SCALE OF MILES

CHAPTER X

PALACE OF THE THEOCRAT

N THE covenant which He made with Abraham, the Lord God foretold that the land he purposed to give to Abraham's seed should be "from the river of Egypt unto the great river, the river Euphrates". When he was leading Abraham's descendants, the children of Israel, to that promised land, he declared that its bounds should be from the Red sea to the Mediterranean sea, upon which Philistia bordered, and from the deserts on the east up to the river Euphrates. (Genesis 15: 18-21; Exodus 23: 31) Since the Kingdom covenant with King David made it fitting that his immediate successor should be a type or a figure prophetic of the coming King, Christ, it was also fitting that the realm of David's successor should reach to the divinely ordained bounds. Then this would be a correct type picturing how the royal Seed of God's "woman" should reign to the very ends of the earth.—Psalm 72: 8.

Feeling his responsibility in this regard, King David was filled with burning zeal on account of the Kingdom covenant. He carried on an offensive against all the unfriendly, troublesome heathen peoples within the boundaries that the Lord had marked, such as the Syrians, Moabites, Ammonites, Philistines, Edomites, and Amalekites. All such he subdued and made tributary. "And Jehovah gave victory to David whithersoever he went. And David reigned over all Israel; and David executed justice and righteousness unto all his people." (2 Samuel 8:1-15) With all the God-given territory brought under Theocratic rule, David could with satisfaction turn over the kingdom to his son and successor.

David's was a hard-fought course. His reign was marked by great difficulties and temptation. In deepest contrition and self-humiliation he passed through retributive punishment and recovered from his sin with Bathsheba, Uriah's wife, and was reinstated in God's favor. Conspiracy and rebellion were hatched against him by his beloved son, Absalom, assisted by the perfidious Ahithophel, David's most trusted counselor. It ended in disaster for the rebels and failed to bring God's Kingdom covenant to nought. Absalom was hung by his own long hair, and Ahithophel hung himself; both were prototypes of an infamous Judas Iscariot and a "man of sin" class. Famine smote the land three years straight until the sin of King Saul against the Gibeonites was properly expiated by David's order. Pestilence cut down at one time 70,000 Israelites due to David's mistake in taking an unlawful census of the population. Nevertheless, the humbled David displayed a right heart-condition toward God, whom he recognized as

the real and invisible King of Israel; and thus
the Kingdom covenant with him stood.—2 Samuel 11-24.

The forty years of David's reign drew near
their close. He was mindful of the special work
assigned to his successor, that of building a
temple to Jehovah's name. At the climax of the
pestilence God's angel indicated where the site
of the temple must be, at Araunah's threshingfloor on the spur known as Mount Moriah running northward from Mount Zion. (2 Samuel
24: 15-25; 1 Chronicles 21 and 22) With zeal for
Jehovah's house, David prepared much building material for Solomon's use. He was guided
of the Lord to make Theocratic arrangements
for the work of the Levites at the temple, and
also for the music and musicians, and he sys-
tematized the course of service of the many
houses of priests. All affairs of the kingdom
were so disposed as to leave them in proper state
for David's successor to take over.—1 Chronicles 21: 28 to 27: 34.

Thereupon the aged David, in the presence of
a representative assembly of all the tribes at
Jerusalem, gave a charge to his son Solomon,
whom God chose "to sit upon the throne of the
kingdom of the Lord over Israel". David said:
"And thou, Solomon my son, know thou the God
of thy father, and serve him with a perfect
heart and with a willing mind: for the LORD
searcheth all hearts, and understandeth all the
imaginations of the thoughts: if thou seek him,
he will be found of thee; but if thou forsake

him, he will cast thee off for ever. Take heed now; for the LORD hath chosen thee to build an house for the sanctuary: be strong, and do it." "Then David gave to Solomon his son the pattern . . . the pattern of all that he had by the spirit, of the courts of the house of the LORD, and of all the chambers round about, . . . also for the courses of the priests and the Levites, and for all the work of the service of the house of the LORD, . . . All this, said David, the LORD made me understand in writing by his hand upon me, even all the works of this pattern." —1 Chronicles 28:9-21.

Then the retiring king addressed himself to all the congregation of Israel, saying: "Solomon my son, whom alone God hath chosen, is yet young and tender, and the work is great; for the palace is not for man, but for Jehovah God [The Theocrat]. Now I have prepared with all my might for the house of my God. . . . Moreover also, because I have set my affection on the house of my God, seeing that I have a treasure of mine own of gold and silver, I give it unto the house of my God, over and above all that I have prepared for the holy house." —1 Chronicles 29:1-3, *Am. Stan. Ver.*

At this royal example of devotion to Jehovah's temple work the princes and people contributed willingly, with perfect hearts, to the temple support. This made King David rejoice, and he said: "Blessed be thou, O Jehovah, the God of Israel our father, for ever and ever. Thine, O Jehovah, is the greatness, and the power, and the glory, and the victory, and the majesty: for all that is in the heavens and in the earth is thine; thine is the kingdom, O Jehovah, and thou art exalted as head above all. Both riches and honor come of thee, and thou rulest over all; and in thy hand is power and might; and in thy hand it is to make great, and to give strength unto all. Now therefore, our God, we thank thee, and praise thy glorious name. . . . give unto Solomon my son a perfect heart, to keep thy commandments, thy testimonies, and thy statutes, and to do all these things, and to build the palace, for which I have made provision."—1 Chronicles 29:6-19, *Am. Stan. Ver.*

This was a royal confession before God and all the nation of Israel that the Most High God, the source of all power and authority, was the true King in Israel. It was a confession that this was a Theocracy. The entire nation, from the king on down to the least subject, were under God's rule and his law covenant. His covenant was the Constitution for the nation, and it was binding also upon Jehovah's regal representative on the throne and upon the high priest in holy office. Hence it is recorded: "And they made Solomon the son of David king the second time, and anointed him unto Jehovah to be prince, and Zadok to be priest. Then Solomon sat on the throne of Jehovah as king instead of David his father, and prospered; and all Israel obeyed him. And all the princes, and the mighty men, and all the sons likewise of king

David, submitted themselves unto Solomon the king." (1 Chronicles 29: 22-24, *Am. Stan. Ver.*) All the covenant people must fear God the Supreme Theocrat and must honor his king, doing so as unto Jehovah.—1 Peter 2: 17.

This was the second time that Solomon was anointed to be king. The first time was in order to forestall a seditious attempt to grab the throne ahead of Solomon. David's son Adonijah ignored Jehovah's appointment of Solomon to succeed his father, and said: "I will be king." Then he had a select assembly held at which he had himself installed as king, the priest Abiathar anointing him. Word of this was quickly relayed to aged King David. Immediately David ordered a coronation assembly, and that Solomon be ridden on the king's mule down to the spring of Gihon just outside Jerusalem and there made king. This was done. "And Zadok the priest took an horn of oil out of the tabernacle, and anointed Solomon. And they blew the trumpet; and all the people said, God save king Solomon [(*Hebrew*) Let king Solomon live]. And all the people came up after him, and the people piped with pipes, and rejoiced with great joy, so that the earth rent with the sound of them." (1 Kings 1: 1-40) Another anti-Theocratic attempt of Satan the Serpent to make disturbance and to bring Jehovah's Kingdom covenant to nought was thus foiled. Jehovah was the Higher Power in Israel and reigned.

After David's death the Lord God appeared to Solomon in a dream and promised, at Solo-

mon's request, to give him wisdom and understanding. Such wisdom early manifested itself
in his judgments toward his subjects; "and they
feared the king: for they saw that the wisdom
of God was in him, to do judgment." (1 Kings
3:4-28) From the very beginning of his forty-
year reign it was a time of prosperity for his
happy subjects. The nation was populous and
could afford to be: there was freedom from
want. "Judah and Israel were many, as the sand
which is by the sea in multitude, eating and
drinking, and making merry. And Solomon
reigned over all kingdoms from the river unto
the land of the Philistines, and unto the border
of Egypt: they brought presents [tribute], and
served Solomon all the days of his life. . . .
and he had peace on all sides round about him.
And Judah and Israel dwelt safely, every man
under his vine and under his fig tree, from Dan
[on the north] even to Beer-sheba [on the
south], all the days of Solomon. And God gave
Solomon wisdom and understanding exceeding
much, and largeness of heart, even as the sand
that is on the sea shore. For he was wiser than
all men; . . . And there came of all people to
hear the wisdom of Solomon, from all kings of
the earth, which had heard of his wisdom."
—1 Kings 4: 20, 21, 24, 25, 29, 31, 34.

That was more than a thousand years before
Christ, or hundreds of years before the first
Greek Olympiad (776 B.C.) and before Rome
was founded (753 B.C.). Solomon's reign closed
in the year 997 B.C.

What distinguished Solomon's rule above all other accomplishments was his construction of Jehovah's temple at Jerusalem. (2 Chronicles 2:1) Hiram of Tyre, an allied king, loved Solomon. He gladly co-operated with him, to the extent permitted, in building this glorious palace of Jehovah, which, according to today's values, cost more than two billion dollars to build. It was in the fourth year after he began

ruling, and in the spring of the year, about a half month after the passover celebration, that King Solomon came to the temple work. As the historian records: "And it came to pass in the four hundred and eightieth year after the children of Israel were come out of the land of Egypt [after the passover celebration], in the fourth year of Solomon's reign over Israel, in the month Zif, which is the second month, that he began to build the house of the LORD." (1 Kings 6:1) The chronicler reports: "Then Solomon began to build the house of the LORD at Jerusalem in mount Moriah, where the LORD appeared unto David his father, in the place that David had prepared in the threshingfloor of Ornan the Jebusite. And he began to build in the second day of the second month, in the fourth year of his reign."—2 Chronicles 3:1, 2.

King Solomon followed the Theocratic pattern given him as to the temple. This was important, because that temple was typical, being a prophetic pattern of a greater, grander temple which it was Jehovah's purpose to build, not made with human hands, nor made of lifeless stones. (Hebrews 8:2-5) The two vital compartments, namely, the holy and the most holy, within the glorious temple were of just twice the size of the like compartments in the tabernacle built by Moses in the wilderness of Mount Sinai.

The work went on smoothly at the temple site: "and the house, when it was in building, was built of stone made ready before it was brought thither: so that there was neither hammer nor ax nor any tool of iron heard in the house, while it was in building." How typical that was of the truth stated by the apostle Paul concerning the true temple: "Let all things be done unto edifying. For God is not the author of confusion, but of peace, as in all churches of the saints." (1 Corinthians 14:26, 33) Even with all such smooth progress, due to well-planned preliminaries, the building was of such magnitude that it took more than seven years to complete. "In the fourth year was the foundation of the house of the LORD laid, in the month Zif: and in the eleventh year, in the month Bul, which is the eighth month, was the house finished throughout all the parts thereof, and according to all the fashion of it. So was he seven years in building it"; or, more exactly, seven years and six months.–1 Kings 6:7-38; 2 Chronicles 3:3-17; 4:1-22.

The temple was completed in the eighth month, Bul, but the record is that the temple was dedicated "at the feast in the month Ethanim, which is the seventh month". The feast of tabernacles or of ingathering, seven days long, was celebrated in the seventh month, Ethanim 15-21; and whether Solomon advanced the time of dedication a month before the temple's completion in order to take advantage of the feast of tabernacles is not certain. The record may mean that he waited till the seventh month of the following year, the eighth year from the time of beginning building. This would allow time for the bringing in of all the things belonging to the temple and for giving the priests and Levites advance training for regular service, which service would be steady, when once begun. (1 Kings 8:51) At all events, the dedication of the temple for seven days led into the most joyful feast of the Jewish year, which made it fourteen days of continuous joy.

"Then Solomon assembled the elders of Israel, and all the heads of the tribes, the chief of the fathers of the children of Israel, unto king Solomon in Jerusalem, that they might bring up the ark of the covenant of the LORD out of the city of David, which is Zion. And all the men of Israel assembled themselves unto king Solomon at the feast in the month Ethanim, which is the seventh month." The priests carried the ark into the Holy of Holies of the temple, with its decorations of cherubim and palms. "There was nothing in the ark save the two tables of stone, which Moses put there at Horeb, when the LORD made a covenant with the children of Israel, when they came out of the land of Egypt." Then, as if in symbol of the fact that Jehovah had taken his seat on his throne amid the cherubim of the ark and those other cherubim decorating the Most Holy, a miracle occurred. "When the priests were come out of the holy place, . . . the cloud filled the house of the LORD, so that the priests could not stand to minister because of the cloud: for the glory of the LORD had filled the house of the LORD. Then spake Solomon, The LORD said that he would dwell in the thick darkness. I have surely built thee an house to dwell in, a settled place for thee to abide in for ever." —1 Kings 8: 1-14.

Thereafter, as the king stood before the altar of the Lord in the temple court, before all the congregation, he spread forth his hands to heaven and prayed that the Lord would continue to fulfill his Kingdom covenant toward the royal house. He entreated that Jehovah God have respect unto this temple palace, of which he had said, "My name shall be there"; and that He regard the prayers of his covenant people that should be offered in it or in the direction of it. Why? "That they may fear thee all the days that they live in the land which thou gavest unto our fathers."—1 Kings 8: 22-40.

Then, to show that the blessings of the temple would not be kept down to just the covenant people but would extend also to all strangers of faith and good-will toward Jehovah God, of whatever nationality, the Lord inspired Solomon to continue praying with these words: "Moreover concerning a stranger, that is not of thy people Israel, but cometh out of a far country for thy name's sake; (for they shall hear of thy great name, and of thy strong hand, and of thy stretched out arm:) when he shall come and pray toward this house; hear thou in heaven thy dwelling place, and do according to all that the stranger calleth to thee for: that all people of the earth may know thy name, to fear thee, as do thy people Israel; and that they may know that this house, which I have builded, is called by thy name."—1 Kings 8:41-43; 2 Chronicles 6:32, 33.

The king's supplication took up entreaty again in behalf of the people of Jehovah's inheritance, that He might "maintain the cause of his servant [the king], and the cause of his people Israel at all times, as the matter shall require: that all the people of the earth may know that the LORD [Jehovah] is God, and that there is none else". (1 Kings 8:44-61) The entire prayer was for the Lord God to make a name for himself and to vindicate his name before all nations. At the finish of the prayer the merciful Hearer of prayer responded with an open token. "Now when Solomon had made an end of praying, the fire came down from heaven, and consumed the burnt offering and the sacrifices; and the glory of the LORD filled the house. And the priests could not enter into the house of the LORD, because the glory of the LORD had filled the LORD's house."

Moreover, after the temple dedication and the feast were over and the people departed on the twenty-third day, Jehovah appeared to Solomon by night and directly assured the king He had heard his prayer. Also if Solomon kept God's covenant faithfully, then a royal successor to him would not fail. But if he and his people forsook God and turned to religion, God would uproot them from their land and he would cast out of his sight this palace built to his name and let it become an astonishing ruin.—2 Chronicles 7:1-22.

CHAPTER XI

REIGNING LINE INTERRUPTED

ID the royal line running from faithful King David continue unbroken until the coming of the Seed in whom the Kingdom covenant finds its complete and everlasting fulfillment? It did. But not all those in the line occupied the throne of the typical Theocracy in Israel. The kingdom ceased to function at the end of 511 years from the time that King Saul began to reign over the chosen nation. For the vindication of Jehovah's name and word He did not cast away the Kingdom covenant he made with David. Though clouded over for hundreds of years, due to the overthrow of the typical kingdom, it burst forth again in all its glory as the sun in the heavens to brighten the hopes of all seeking truth and life.

After dedicating the sacred palace of Jehovah the Universal King, Solomon occupied himself thirteen years in building the palace of the royal family and also the "house of the forest of Lebanon" and also a "porch for the throne where he might judge". At the end of twenty years, wherein he built the temple and his own palace, Solomon directed his efforts to a building program in other cities of the kingdom. —1 Kings 7:1-12; 2 Chronicles 8:1-6.

Solomon's fame spread to all nations of the earth. The queen of Sheba, far distant, heard thereof and undertook a long journey to come and interview him. When she had seen his building works and his kingdom arrangements, and had heard him wisely answer all her hard questions, she was left breathless. Then she said: "Behold, the one half of the greatness of thy wisdom was not told me: for thou exceedest the fame that I heard. Happy are thy men, and happy are these thy servants, which stand continually before thee, and hear thy wisdom. Blessed be the LORD [Jehovah] thy God, which delighted in thee to set thee on HIS throne, to be king for the LORD thy God: because thy God loved Israel, to establish them for ever, therefore made he thee king over them, to do judgment and justice." After receiving her gifts of appreciation, Solomon gave the queen all her desire, and then she returned to the land of Sheba.—2 Chronicles 9:1-12.

It cannot Scripturally be imagined that God bestowed all this fame and wisdom and glory upon King Solomon merely to glorify a man. It must have been, and it was, because all this glory of the kingdom of Israel under the great Theocrat Jehovah was typical. It portrayed in a small degree the glory and wise government and godliness and prosperity that will distinguish the Theocratic Kingdom of the reigning Seed of Jehovah's "woman", Christ the King. Despite all prophetic previews thereof, and the testimony given by the witnesses of Jehovah, 'behold, the half was not told.'

That the glory of Solomon's reign was not the realization in completeness of the Kingdom covenant but was merely typical is proved by the fact that it passed away. Therefore if the Israelites were thinking that The Kingdom was at hand, through which all families and nations of the earth are due to be blessed, they were in for a disappointment. For a successful reign, blessed of the Lord God, these instructions from him as contained in his covenant with his typical people must be fulfilled by the king: "He shall not multiply horses to himself, nor cause the people to return to Egypt, to the end that he should multiply horses: forasmuch as the LORD hath said unto you, Ye shall henceforth return no more that way. Neither shall he multiply wives to himself, that his heart turn not away: neither shall he greatly multiply to himself silver and gold. And it shall be, when he sitteth upon the throne of his kingdom, that he shall write him a copy of this law in a book out of that which is before the priests the Levites: and it shall be with him, and he shall read therein all the days of his life: that he may learn to fear the LORD his God, to keep all the words of this law and these statutes, to do them: that his heart be not lifted up above his brethren, and that he turn not aside from the commandment, to the right hand, or to the left: to the end that he may prolong his days in his kingdom, he, and his children, in the midst of Israel." (Deuteronomy 17:14-20) The king's chief concern must be to inform himself on the Theocratic law and to continually meditate upon it and faithfully perform it and thus to put foremost the worship and service of the Lord God Jehovah.

King Solomon multiplied to himself many wives as well as horses and chariots. Regardless of what typical significance this may have, the pressure which these things exerted upon an imperfect man in the wrong direction proved finally too much for wise King Solomon. With reference to Solomon's matrimonial alliances with foreign heathen rulers, Nehemiah said: "Did not Solomon king of Israel sin by these things? yet among many nations was there no king like him, who was beloved of his God, and God made him king over all Israel: nevertheless even him did outlandish women cause to sin." (Nehemiah 13:26) In his old age Solomon weakened, and his non-Israelite wives, who were demon-worshipers, prevailed upon him to turn to the worship of false gods. For this, Solomon came under God's displeasure. Out of respect of his covenant with David God did not take away the kingdom completely from Solomon's family, but took away the greater part of it and turned such over to other tribesmen of Israel to govern. God warned unfaithful Solomon that He would do this after Solomon's death. (1 Kings 11:1-14) There is nothing to show that Solomon repented of his course or that the book of Ecclesiastes was written by him after such repentance.

God's decree of kingdom partition went through. At the beginning of the reign of Rehoboam, son of Solomon, the Israelites sent a delegation under Jeroboam of the tribe of Ephraim to ask for a lightening of their burdens. Rehoboam listened to bad advisers and gave a harsh, threatening answer. At this, ten tribes of Israel revolted against the royal house of Solomon and made Jeroboam king. Only the tribe of Benjamin remained loyal to the tribe of Judah and its royal line of David. When Rehoboam set out to bring the rebellious tribes back under his scepter, Jehovah God made known his disapproval to the king. Two kingdoms now appeared in the land, that kingdom of Judah under Rehoboam at Jerusalem, and the kingdom of ten tribes of Israel under Jeroboam at Shechem in Mount Ephraim.—1 Kings 11: 26-43; 12: 1-33.

In his law covenant with Israel the great Theocrat had expressly forbidden that any religion or demonism should be interwoven into the kingdom. Because King Saul erred in this respect God let him be slain and he forfeited the crown for his family. (1 Chronicles 10: 13, 14) For like reason God rent the united kingdom from Solomon's royal house. If Jeroboam avoided this besetting sin of religion, then he might be blessed in his reign over the northern kingdom of ten tribes. If he obeyed, then, said Jehovah, "I will be with thee, and build thee a sure house, as I built for David, and will give Israel unto thee. And I will for this afflict the seed of David, but not for ever." Yes, "not for ever," because Jehovah purposed a reunion of all Israel under the Seed of his "woman" in due time.—Ezekiel 37:15-28.

King Jeroboam, however, did not trust in God's offer. Fearing that his subjects would return to the house of David if they kept on going up regularly to Jerusalem to worship Jehovah and celebrate His feasts there, he leaned to his own understanding and violated God's covenant. For political reasons, namely, to make sure his kingdom for himself, Jeroboam turned from the worship of Jehovah, invented the idolatrous worship of golden calves, and appointed a priesthood of religious racketeers. He ordered his subjects to stay away from Jehovah's worship at Jerusalem and to adopt the new state religion. By this step Jeroboam sealed the doom of the new kingdom as well as of his own dynasty. He became notorious ever after as 'Jeroboam the son of Nebat which caused Israel to sin'. (1 Kings 12:25-33; 13:1-6, 33, 34) Nevertheless, a remnant of the ten tribes remained faithful to Jehovah God and declined to take up the religion of the golden calf-idols.

Peace accompanied by God's blessing was taken away from the new kingdom of ten tribes because of religion. The rulership of the nation passed by violence and bloodshed from the hands of one family to another, in quick order. Omri, seventh king, shifted the nation's capital to a new city which he built on a hill. He called it "Samaria". Samaria, therefore, became a symbol of the ten-tribe kingdom of Israel and stood as a rival of Jerusalem.

Omri's son, Ahab, exceeded all previous kings in wickedness. "He took to wife Jezebel the daughter of Ethbaal king of the Zidonians, and went and served Baal, and worshipped him. And he reared up an altar for Baal in the house of Baal, which he had built in Samaria. And [he] made a grove [or, Asherah, symbol of Satan's *woman*]." (1 Kings 16:1-33) "Baal" means "lord, master, husband, owner". Baal was an idolatrous symbol of Satan the Devil as the sun-god. His worship was attended with moral uncleanness and with the sacrifices of living children by fire, suggestive of the religious doctrine of torments in a fiery hell or in a purgatory. In utter detestation of such religious practice Jehovah God said: "They have built also the high places of Baal, to burn their sons with fire for burnt offerings unto Baal, which I commanded not, nor spake it, neither came it into my mind."—Jeremiah 19:5; 7:31.

Jezebel, Ahab's queen, was so wicked as a backer of Baal-worship that God's Word speaks of her as a symbol of Satan the Devil's "woman" or organization, the mother of his wicked seed. She attempted the destruction of all of Jehovah's prophets in Israel, including the prophets Elijah and Elisha, but failed. For all her idolatry and bloody crimes she met a violent death at the hands of King Jehu, whom God instructed Elijah to anoint to act as God's executioner against the Baal-worshipers in the land of Israel.

Jehu destroyed Baal-worship out of Israel for a time. With him in this effort there was associated a right-hearted man, a non-Israelite named Jehonadab (or Jonadab) the son of Rechab. (2 Kings, chapters 9 and 10) However, the calf-worship continued in Israel, and later Baal-worship was resumed. The kings of Israel, in rivalry, fought against their brethren of the kingdom of Judah, and made alliance with heathen nations in that behalf. At length, in vindication of his word and name, Jehovah God brought the kingdom of the ten tribes of Israel to an end, after 258 years of existence.

Jehovah permitted the king of Assyria, the second world-power after Egypt, to rise up in his might and to act as God's executioner against the wicked covenant-breakers and to destroy the kingdom of Israel, in 740 B.C. (2 Kings 17: 1-23) The surviving Israelites, except a faithful remnant that had escaped into the land of the kingdom of Judah, were carried off from Palestine and held captive in the land of Assyria. To take their place in Palestine the king of Assyria transplanted heathen religionists and "placed them in the cities of Samaria instead of the children of Israel: and they possessed Samaria, and dwelt in the cities thereof". Thinking to safeguard themselves from harm, they adopted the name of Jehovah and a religious form of his worship into their devil-worship. From them are descended the Samaritans, with some of whom Jesus came in touch in his days. Jesus' parable of "the good Samaritan" is quite well known.—2 Kings 17:22-41; Luke 10:30-37; 17:11-19; John 4:1-42.

The kingdom of Judah survived that of the other house of Israel by 133 years. Because space does not permit of going into the reigns of the kings of Judah in detail, and because the apostle Matthew does not give the complete list in the genealogy running down from David to Joseph the husband of Mary, we here give a list of the kings of Judah beginning with David, and show also the year B.C. (before Christ) when each began to reign:

YEAR	KING'S NAME	YEAR	KING'S NAME
1077 B.C.	David	826 B.C.	Uzziah
1037 "	Solomon	774 "	Jotham
997 "	Rehoboam	759 "	Ahaz
980 "	Abijah	745 "	Hezekiah
978 "	Asa	716 "	Manasseh
938 "	Jehoshaphat	661 "	Amon
917 "	Jehoram	659 "	Josiah
910 "	Ahaziah	628 "	Jehoahaz
909 "	[Queen Athaliah]	628 "	Jehoiakim
903 "	Joash	618 "	Jehoiachin
866 "	Amaziah	617 "	Zedekiah

607 B.C. Jerusalem destroyed, in Ab, the fifth month

In the above list there is taken into account the six-year reign of Queen Athaliah, the wife of King Jehoram and mother of King Ahaziah. God's covenant with the nation of Israel, and his covenant with David for the kingdom, made no provision for a woman to usurp the place of a man and to rule God's people. By murder Athaliah set herself up on Judah's throne. At the time of installing her grandson Joash as king, the high priest Jehoiada disregarded her sham cries of "Treason, treason!" and commanded her to be killed as a murderess and usurper, a daughter of idolatrous Ahab and Jezebel. High priest Jehoiada said: "Behold, the king's son shall reign, as the LORD hath said of the sons of David."—2 Chronicles 22: 2, 3, 10-12; 23: 3.

Only during the reign of Athaliah did it seem that David was wanting a man to sit upon the throne at Jerusalem. But the sole remaining heir was preserved within the temple precincts six years and then the royal line of David was reinstated on the throne. Thwarted again, Satan the Serpent was determined, if he could not destroy the royal Davidic line, to corrupt the nation to such an extent from its royal head downward as to bring about its destruction. By what means? By that against which Jehovah solemnly warned his people and as a safeguard against which he had provided the law of his covenant, namely, religion. With the king taking the lead in religion, demon-worship quickly spread through the people. Worship at the temple was neglected, yea, the temple was defiled and robbed of many treasures. A time came when it was even shut up and the written copies of the Word of God were lost and unknown.

This was but the effort of Jehovah's great adversary to show that Almighty God could not set up a government upon this earth but what the Devil could corrupt it beyond God's use. It was part of the Devil's scheme to bring world-wide reproach upon Jehovah's name. It was Satan's defiance to Jehovah's universal domination.

Faithful kings appeared in the line of succession, who tried to stem the swelling tide of religion and to set the feet of the covenant people of God firmly in the paths of the pure worship of Jehovah. In their days Jehovah added fresh glory to his name by defeating the demonized enemies of his nation. In Asa's day he gave his endangered people an amazing victory over one million Ethiopians led by the invader Zerah, thereby answering Asa's prayer: "In thy name we go against this multitude. O Lord, thou art our God; let not man prevail against thee." (2 Chronicles 14) In Jehoshaphat's reign, when the combined armies of Moab, Ammon and Mount Seir pressed onward toward Jerusalem, Jehovah smote these enemies of his Theocracy with confusion. He turned their weapons against themselves in gory self-slaughter, while Jehoshaphat's people marched forth from the imperiled city singing: "Praise the Lord; for his mercy endureth for ever." (2 Chronicles 20) In the days of King Hezekiah, eight years after the Assyrian power of the north had overthrown the kingdom of Israel, the Assyrian conqueror Sennacherib threatened Jerusalem with siege and defied Jehovah, God of Hezekiah, to save it. Then, in one night, Jehovah avenged this reproach of his name by smiting 185,000 of Sennacherib's hosts, forcing him to retire into Assyria and to assassination. (2 Kings 18 and 19; Isaiah 36 and 37) Satan's invisible 'prince of Assyria' was thereby given a decided setback. The second head of the Devil's seven-headed dragon or demon organization was abased, and the third head, functioning as the 'prince of Babylon', came into prominence.

Furthermore, Jehovah raised up many prophets to call the notice of his covenant people to their fall away from his covenant and their entanglement and bondage in religion. Among those prophets whose writings have been preserved in the Bible were Hosea, Amos, Micah, Nahum, Zephaniah, Isaiah, Jeremiah, and Ezekiel. By them God sounded warning of the approaching overturn of the typical kingdom by reason of the sin of religion, and that salvation was only by a return to the true, living God and his worship. All the prophets foretold of Jehovah's final triumph over Gentile power and of his restoration or restitution of the Theocratic kingdom in the hands of the promised Seed of the line of David. However, the messages of Jehovah's faithful prophets went generally unheeded. The message-bearers were persecuted and a number of them slain.

In the final days of Jerusalem under her kings a tug of war raged between two ancient powers, "the king of the north" and "the king of the south", as to the controlling influence over the kingdom of Judah. Faithful King Josiah died in a vain endeavor to stay the northward advance of the Egyptian hosts. Then the victorious king of Egypt removed Jehoahaz, the people's choice, from the throne of Jerusalem and made Eliakim, another son of Josiah, king instead, and changed his name to Jehoiakim. Thereafter the king of Egypt met defeat before the Babylonian armies of Nebuchadnezzar in the battle of Carchemish at the Euphrates river. Moving southward, Nebuchadnezzar made King Jehoiakim subject to him and forced him into a treaty as a tributary king. Then in the eleventh year of Jehoiakim's rule in Jerusalem, or in the third year of his reign as a tributary of Nebuchadnezzar, Jehoiakim rebelled and again the king of Babylon came against Jerusalem. Meantime Jehoiakim was killed, and his son Jehoiachin was enthroned. After three months' reign, he surrendered at the arrival of Nebuchadnezzar before Jerusalem. The king of Babylon carried him and many thousands of important and essential Israelites to captivity in Babylon. Among such was the young Judean prince Daniel and his three companions, Hananiah, Mishael, and Azariah. (Daniel 1: 1-7) Before leaving, Nebuchadnezzar put Jehoiachin's uncle, Mattaniah, son of Josiah, upon the throne of Jerusalem and took an oath of allegiance from him. He changed Mattaniah's name to Zedekiah.—2 Kings 23: 28-37; 24: 1-18.

Despite the faithful counsel of the prophet Jeremiah, King Zedekiah rebelled in the ninth year of his reign against the king of Babylon. Then Nebuchadnezzar moved against Jerusalem. An appeal by Zedekiah to Egypt for help brought only temporary relief, for after but a brief retirement before the Egyptian armies the Babylonians came back and closed in on the siege of the doomed city. Zedekiah refused to heed Jeremiah's last-minute counsel to go out to the king of Babylon, as his predecessor King Jehoiachin had done. In the eleventh year of his reign Jerusalem fell and was destroyed, also her temple in which her unfaithful people had been trusting as a charm against disaster. Thousands of survivors were carried off captive to Babylon in that disastrous fifth month of the year 607 B.C. The poor people of the land were let remain in the land. However, these poor could not prevent the fulfillment of Jeremiah's prophecy that there must be a complete desolation of the land of Judah, "without man or beast." Two months later, or in the seventh month of 607 B.C., they forsook the land, fleeing in disregard of Jeremiah's instruction down into Egypt and taking the prophet with them. Thus the land of the typical kingdom became an astonishing desolation, uninhabited, shunned by men.—2 Kings 25:8-26.

Such was in execution of God's warning to covenant-breakers as given through the inspired prophet Moses, at Leviticus 26:31-39. The prophet Jeremiah warned against this divine punishment. He began sounding warning forty years before Jerusalem's fall. (Jeremiah 25:1-3, 8-13) As respects the carrying out of this prophecy upon the covenant-breaking Israelites the chronicler writes this about Jerusalem's destruction by Nebuchadnezzar: "And them that had escaped from the sword carried he away to Babylon; where they were servants to him and his sons until the reign of the kingdom of Persia: to fulfil the word of the LORD by the mouth of Jeremiah, until the land had enjoyed her sabbaths: for as long as she lay desolate she kept sabbath, to fulfil threescore and ten years"; that is to say, seventy years. —2 Chronicles 36:20, 21.

But why enforce seventy year-long sabbaths upon the land? Because the land was Jehovah's and he had commanded it to be let enjoy regular sabbath years by his covenant people. (Leviticus 25:1-23) According to God's covenant with Israel, within every fifty years the God-given land was to enjoy eight sabbath years: one sabbath year every seventh year and a sabbath on the fiftieth or jubilee year. If we calculate the time based on the measurement given us at 1 Kings 6:1, then from the time the Israelites entered the Land of Promise and were obliged to begin counting, down till Jerusalem was destroyed and the land was desolated, in 607 B.C., 867 years passed. Within that period of time 17 jubilee sabbaths could have been kept on the land, and also 121 seventh-year sabbaths, or a total of 138 sabbath years of rest to the land.

No doubt exists that, during the times that the Israelites were faithful to their covenant, they observed these land sabbaths as they fell due. How many all together is not disclosed. But the number seventy represents completeness, it being a multiple of 10×7; 10 symbolizing earthly completeness, and 7 symbolizing spiritual completeness. Hence Jehovah God let the number 70 stand as a figure to represent comprehensively all the sabbath-year rests of the land they had failed to observe. Then he let 70 years of enforced desolation of the land offset or make up for all those unkept sabbath-years. His word and righteous law were vindicated!

During those years of desolation the royal line of David, of kings sitting upon a material throne in an earthly capital, was interrupted. Never afterward during the further history did that line sit enthroned at Zion or Jerusalem. This did not mean that Jehovah's covenant with David had failed and would never be fulfilled in completion. No; but to King Zedekiah Jehovah sent this message by his prophet Ezekiel: "Because ye have made your iniquity to be remembered, in that your transgressions are discovered, so that in all your doings your sins do appear; because, I say, that ye are come to remembrance, ye shall be taken with the hand. And thou, profane wicked prince of Israel, whose day is come, when iniquity shall have an end, Thus saith the Lord GOD; Remove the diadem, and take off the crown: this shall not be the same: exalt him that is low, and abase him that is high. I will overturn, overturn, overturn, it: and it shall be no more, until he come whose right it is; and I will give it him."—Ezekiel 21: 24-27.

The interruption to the reigning of David's royal line was directly from Almighty God, but was only temporary. It must continue only until the coming of David's worthy Heir, the Seed of God's "woman". Then Jehovah would crown the Kingdom covenant with glory by giving the Government unto him "whose right it is" to rule. Jehovah's covenant will never fail.—Jeremiah 33: 15-22, 25, 26.

IMPORTANT: In the book ''The Truth Shall Make You Free'', published in 1943, the chronology on pages 150, 151 concerning the kings of Jerusalem, from Solomon's successor to Zedekiah, is based on the book of 2 Chronicles, chapters 12 to 36. This appears to show the reigns of those kings as successive, end to end. Actually, however, this was not so, as is plainly shown in the books of 1 and 2 Kings, which books give us a countercheck on the successors of Solomon by a comparison of these kings of Judah with the neighbor kings of the ten-tribe kingdom of Israel. The chronological TABLE OF CONTEMPORARY KINGS AND PROPHETS AND RELATED EVENTS, on the next four pages, shows how the books of 1 and 2 Kings give a more accurate check on the reigns of the kings of Judah than does 2 Chronicles.

Measured by 2 Chronicles, the period of kings from Saul to Zedekiah was 513 years. Measured by the more precise and detailed books of Kings, the period was actually 511 years, or 2 years less. This fact affects the chronology as a whole and pulls man's creation 2 years closer to A.D. 1 and gives it the date 4026 B.C., not 4028 B.C.

The following chronology shows the date of Jerusalem's destruction as in the year 607 before Christ. This recognizes the fact that the ancient reckoning of the vulgar year began in the fall. In other words, the vulgar year 606 B.C. really began in the fall of 607 B.C. As stated on page 239 (¶1) of ''The Truth Shall Make You Free'': ''Inasmuch as the count of the Gentile 'seven times' began its first year at the fall of 607 B.C., it is simple to calculate when they end. From the fall of 607 B.C. to the fall of B.C. 1 is exactly 606 years. . . . Hence from the fall of B.C. 1 to the fall of A.D. 1914 is 1,914 years.''

TABLE of CONTEMPORARY KINGS and PROPHETS and RELATED EVENTS
(With Scripture Proof-Texts)

KINGS of JUDAH	PROPHETS	B.C.	KINGS of ISRAEL	PROPHETS
[SAUL] (40 years) Acts 13:21	SAMUEL 1 Sam. 10:1; Acts 13:20	1117	[SAUL made king in spring] 1 Sam. 11:15; 12:1, 2, 17	
DAVID (40) 1 Chron. 29:27; 1 Ki. 2:11	GAD 1 Sam. 22:5; 1 Chron. 21:9 NATHAN 1 Chron. 17:1; 2 Sam. 12:1-15	1077		
SOLOMON (40) 2 Chron. 9:30; 1 Ki. 11:42	NATHAN 1 Ki. 1:34; 2 Chron. 9:29	1037		
REHOBOAM (17) 1 Ki. 14:21; 2 Chron. 12:13	SHEMAIAH 1 Ki. 12:22, 23; 2 Chron. 11:2, 3	997	JEROBOAM (22) 1 Ki. 14:20; 2 Chron. 10:12-19	AHIJAH 1 Ki. 11:29-31; 1 Ki. 14:1-6 MAN OF GOD 1 Ki. 13:1, 2
ABIJAM (ABIJAH) (3) 1 Ki. 15:1, 2; 2 Chron. 13:1, 2	IDDO 2 Chron. 12:15; 2 Chron. 13:22	980		
ASA (41) [1 year with Abijam] 1 Ki. 15:1, 2, 9, 10; 2 Chron. 14:1; 16:13	AZARIAH 2 Chron. 15:1, 2	978		
	HANANI 2 Chron. 16:7	977	NADAB (2) 1 Ki. 15:25	
		976	BAASHA (24) 1 Ki. 15:33	JEHU, son of Hanani 1 Ki. 16:1, 7, 12, 13
		953	ELAH (2) 1 Ki. 16:8	
		952	ZIMRI (7 days) 1 Ki. 16:15	
		952	TIBNI and OMRI (4) 1 Ki. 16:21	
		948	OMRI alone (8) 1 Ki. 16:23	
		941	AHAB (22) 1 Ki. 16:29; 2 Chron. 18:1, 2	ELIJAH 1 Ki. 17:1 MICAIAH 1 Ki. 22:8, 14; 2 Chron. 18:7-28
JEHOSHAPHAT (25) [1 year with Asa] 1 Ki. 22:41, 42 2 Chron. 20:31	JEHU, son of Hanani 2 Chron. 19:2 JAHAZIEL 2 Chron. 20:14-18 ELIEZER 2 Chron. 20:35-37	938		
		922	AHAZIAH (2) 1 Ki. 22:51, 52	ELIJAH 2 Ki. 1:2, 3, 17
		921	JEHORAM (12) 2 Ki. 3:1	ELISHA 2 Ki. 3:1, 11-14

Kings of Judah	Prophets (Judah)	Date	Kings of Israel	Prophets (Israel)
JEHORAM (8) [4 years with Jehoshaphat] 2 Ki. 8:16, 17; 1 Ki. 22:42; 2 Chron. 21:5, 20	ELIJAH 2 Chron. 21:12 JOEL (?)	917		ELISHA 2 Ki. 9:1-4
AHAZIAH (1) [1 year with Jehoram] 2 Ki. 8:25, 26; 9:29; 2 Chron. 22:2	JOEL (?)	910		
[QUEEN ATHALIAH] (6) 2 Ki. 11:1-3; 2 Chron. 22:10-12	JOEL (?)	909	JEHU (28) 2 Ki. 9:24, 27; 2 Ki. 10:36	
JEHOASH (JOASH) (40) 2 Ki. 12:1; 2 Chron. 24:1	ZECHARIAH 2 Chron. 24:19-22	903		
		881	JEHOAHAZ (17) 2 Ki. 13:1	ELISHA 2 Ki. 13:14
		867	JEHOASH (JOASH) (16) 2 Ki. 13:10	
AMAZIAH (29) [3 years with Joash] 2 Ki. 14:1, 2; 2 Chron. 25:1	MAN OF GOD 2 Chron. 25:7-9, 15	866		
		852	JEROBOAM II (41) 2 Ki. 14:23	JONAH (?) 2 Ki. 14:23-25; Jonah 1:1
INTERREGNUM (11) 2 Ki. 14:1, 2; 15:1		837		
UZZIAH (AZARIAH) (52) 2 Ki. 15:1, 2; 2 Chron. 26:3	AMOS Amos 1:1; HOSEA Hos. 1:1 ISAIAH Isa. 1:1	826		HOSEA Hos. 1:1 AMOS Amos 1:1
		811	INTERREGNUM (22) 2 Ki. 14:23; 15:8	
		789	ZACHARIAH (6 months) 2 Ki. 15:8	
		788	SHALLUM (1 month) 2 Ki. 15:13	
		788	MENAHEM (10) 2 Ki. 15:17	
		778	INTERREGNUM (1) 2 Ki. 15:17, 23	
JOTHAM (16) 2 Ki. 15:32, 33; 2 Chron. 27:1	HOSEA Hos. 1:1; ISAIAH Isa. 1:1 MICAH Mic. 1:1	777	PEKAHIAH (2) 2 Ki. 15:23	
		775		
		774	PEKAH (20) 2 Ki. 15:27; 2 Chron. 28:6	

KINGS of JUDAH	PROPHETS	B.C.	KINGS of ISRAEL	PROPHETS
AHAZ (16) [1 year with Jotham] 2 Ki. 16:1, 2; 2 Chron. 28:1	HOSEA Hos. 1:1; ISAIAH Isa. 1:1 MICAH Mic. 1:1	759		ODED 2 Chron. 28:6-9 [Tiglath-pileser king of Assyria accepts pay from Ahaz and captures Damascus and kills Rezin king of Syria] 2 Ki. 16:7-9
		755 753 748	INTERREGNUM (7) 2 Ki. 15:30 [Founding of Rome] HOSEA (9) 2 Ki. 17:1; 18:1, 9, 10	
HEZEKIAH (29) [2 years with Ahaz] 2 Ki. 18:1, 2, 10; 2 Chron. 29:1	HOSEA Hos. 1:1 ISAIAH Isa. 1:1; 2 Chron. 32:20 MICAH Mic. 1:1	745		
		740	[Fall of Samaria] 2 Ki. 17:6, 13, 20, 23	
MANASSEH (55) 2 Ki. 21:1; 2 Chron. 33:1	PROPHETS 2 Ki. 21:10-16 2 Chron. 33:10, 18 NAHUM Nah. 1:1 (?)	716		
			IMPORTANT EVENTS	
	ZEPHANIAH Zeph. 1:1	661		
AMON (2) 2 Ki. 21:19; 2 Chron. 33:21		659		
JOSIAH (31) 2 Ki. 22:1; 2 Chron. 34:1	JEREMIAH Jer. 1:1-3; 25:1-3 HULDAH 2 Chron. 34:1, 8, 22 2 Ki. 22:3, 14, 15	647 642		
JEHOAHAZ (3 months) 2 Ki. 23:31; 2 Chron. 36:2 JEHOIAKIM (ELIAKIM) (11) 2 Ki. 23:36; 2 Chron. 36:5	JEREMIAH Jer. 1:1-3 HABAKKUK (?) Hab. 1:5, 6; 2:20	628 628		
	DANIEL Dan. 1:1-6	625	[Nebuchadnezzar reigns, and defeats the Egyptian army in the battle of Carchemish at the Euphrates river] Jer. 25:1; 46:2; 2 Ki. 24:7	
JEHOIACHIN (3 months 10 days) 2 Ki. 24:6, 8, 12 2 Chron. 36:9, 10, margin		618	[Nebuchadnezzar subdues Jerusalem and carries many thousands of important and essential Israelites captive to Babylon] 2 Ki. 24:8-17	
ZEDEKIAH (MATTANIAH) (11) 2 Ki. 24:17, 18; 2 Chron. 36:11	JEREMIAH Jer. 1:1-3 2 Chron. 36:11, 12 EZEKIEL Ezek. 1:1, 2	617 613		

Event	Date	Note
[Jerusalem destroyed in fifth month (Ab)] 2 Ki. 25:2, 8; Jer. 52:12-14	607	[Land of Judah abandoned and left desolate in seventh month (Ethanim)]. 2 Ki. 25:22-26; Jer. 41:1-3; 43:1-7
OBADIAH Obad. 11-14 (?) JEREMIAH Jer. 43:8; 44:1 DANIEL Dan. 2:1, 19 EZEKIEL Ezek. 29:17	607 to	
	591	[Nebuchadnezzar invades Egypt and defeats Pharaoh-hophra] Jer. 43:8-13; 44:1, 11-14, 24-30
	588	[Babylon falls and Darius rules]
DANIEL Dan. 5:18-31; 11:1	539	[First year of Cyrus] 2 Chron. 36:20-23
[Jerusalem's 70-year desolation ends] 2 Chron. 36:21-23; Ezra 1:1; 3:1	537	[Third year of Cyrus]
DANIEL Dan. 10:1 HAGGAI Hag. 1:1 ZECHARIAH Zech. 1:1; Ezra 5:1	535	[Second year of Darius II]
	520	[Sixth year of Darius II]
[Rebuilding of temple completed] Ezra 6:14, 15	516	
[Jerusalem's walls are rebuilt] Neh. 1:1; 2:1, 11; 6:15	454	[Twentieth year of Artaxerxes III]
MALACHI Mal. 3:10 (?)	332	[Greek rule over Judea]
[Greek Septuagint (LXX) Bible translation begun]	About 280	
ANNA, prophetess Luke 2:36-38	63	[Roman rule over Judea]
JESUS IS BORN (about October 1) Luke 2:1-17	2	[John the Baptist is born, six months before Jesus] Luke 1:26, 36, 57-63
	A.D.	
	14	[August 19, Caesar Augustus dies; Tiberius succeeds him] [Fifteenth year of Emperor Tiberius Caesar of Rome] Luke 3:1
JOHN THE BAPTIST Matt. 11:9-11	29	
JESUS IS BAPTIZED and anointed. Matt. 3:13-17; Luke 3:21-23	29	[70th week begins] Dan. 9:24-27
JESUS ANNOUNCES the Kingdom at hand. Matt. 4:12-17	30	[John the Baptist imprisoned] Mark 1:14, 15; Luke 3:19, 20
JESUS DIES on tree (on 14th of Nisan). Matt. 27:37-50	33	[Midst of the 70th week] Dan. 9:24-27
JESUS RAISED from dead (on 16th of Nisan). Matt. 28:1-10	33	
Holy spirit poured out at Pentecost. Acts 2:1-4	33	
Cornelius the Gentile receives the spirit. Acts 10:1-46	36	[End of the 70th week] Dan. 9:24-27
JESUS ENTHRONED as Theocratic King. Rev. 12:1-5	1914	["Seven times," or "the times of the Gentiles", end about October] Dan. 4:16, 23, 25, 32; Luke 21:24
THE KING comes to the temple (spring). Mal. 3:1	1918	[World War I used as means to stop the witness to the Kingdom]

CHAPTER XII

RISE AND FALL
OF SATAN'S KINGDOM

T THE destruction of Jerusalem in 607 B.C., bringing interruption to the reign of its kings of David's royal house, the times of complete Gentile domination of the entire earth began. Jerusalem was trodden down of the Gentiles. This was to continue, by divine decree, until those "times of the Gentiles" should be fulfilled. Jehovah's carrying out of his covenant with David regarding the kingdom could mean nothing less than an end to those times of Gentile domination under Satan the Devil. This must bring a great crisis upon Satan's organization. It must portend the early destruction of that wicked organization of demons and men. At the overthrow of the typical Theocracy with its capital at Jerusalem Satan became, in the largest sense, "the god of this world." Without the kingdom of the house of David to stand any longer in the way of his complete rule of the earth, Satan's rule would continue uninterrupted until Jehovah's kingdom covenant should again be put in active operation by the enthroning of the One "whose right it is" to reign in active power.

From the days of its first king, Nimrod, and the confusion of humankind's language at the tower of Babel, the city of Babel or Babylon stayed in the background. There it lingered until the days of the prophet Isaiah, who prophesied of its world domination and then of its doom. (Isaiah, chapters 13, 14, 21, 39, 47, 48; 2 Kings 17: 24, 30; 20: 12-19) At the coming of mighty Nebuchadnezzar to power at Babylon in the visible part of Satan's organization, the third head of Satan's dragon organization became the foremost head under its demon "prince of Babylon". Its earthly counterpart, the empire of Babylon, became the third world power. The second world power, Assyria, was subjugated, and even "the king of the south", or Egypt, was subdued. Babylon, as now representing "the king of the north", became the head of the kingdoms of this world. That mighty empire became a symbol of Satan's organization as a whole in heaven and in earth. Therefore Satan's world organization is symbolized in the Bible as a proud, wicked queen, a "woman" named "Babylon".

In the eighth year of Nebuchadnezzar the rebellion of King Jehoiakim caused him to come against Jerusalem. At that time the king's son and successor, Jehoiachin, surrendered to Nebuchadnezzar without a fight, and was carried captive to Babylon. Among those of noble lineage whom Nebuchadnezzar carried off with him was the young man Daniel. At Babylon Daniel and three of his companions were selected to receive special court training for three years, and thereafter they were introduced to Nebuchadnezzar. They were found to be the wisest men in all his empire. In the nineteenth year of his rule Nebuchadnezzar was used as God's executioner to destroy the unfaithful city of Jerusalem and to interrupt the rule of the kings of David's line. Then Nebuchadnezzar began reigning in a unique way, as the first of the world rulers of the Gentile times. In the second year of his reign *in this special capacity,* when the power of Babylon's empire seemed firmly fixed, Jehovah God served notice upon him of the coming doom of all Satan's organization. The notice was by means of an inspired dream and its inspired interpretation, as recorded in Daniel's prophecy, chapter two.

"And in the second year of the reign of Nebuchadnezzar Nebuchadnezzar dreamed dreams, wherewith his spirit was troubled, and his sleep brake from him." On awaking the king could not recall the dream. He called upon all his religious counselors and learned men to bring back the dream to him and to explain its meaning. When they confessed the inability of their demon gods to help them to do this, the king ordered their execution. This order was so broad that it included also Daniel and his three Hebrew companions. Daniel sent the request for the king to stay the execution, because he would come with the dream's interpretation. Then at the instance of united prayer by Daniel and his companions, Jehovah revealed to Daniel the secret and Daniel was brought in before Nebuchadnezzar. There Daniel disclaimed any credit, and ascribed all wisdom for solving the problem to Jehovah God. He was thereby a faithful witness for Jehovah. This is the dream that he told:

"Thou, O king, sawest, and behold a great image. This great image, whose brightness was excellent, stood before thee; and the form thereof was terrible. This image's head was of fine gold, his breast and his arms of silver, his belly and his thighs of brass, his legs of iron, his feet part of iron and part of clay. Thou sawest till that a stone was cut out without hands, which smote the image upon his feet that were of iron and clay, and brake them to pieces. Then was the iron, the clay, the brass, the silver, and the gold, broken to pieces together, and became like the chaff of the summer threshingfloors; and the wind carried them away, that no place was found for them: and the stone that smote the image became a great mountain, and filled the whole earth."—Daniel 2: 31-35.

Religious clergymen have attempted an interpretation of this dream, making it refer to the rise and fall of the four successive world powers, Babylon, Medo-Persia, Greece, and the Roman empire. The smiting of the image they explain to mean the introduction of Christianity, followed up by the interference of the Roman Catholic Hierarchy and other religious denominations in the political systems of the whole earth. The mountain's filling the entire earth the religionists interpret to mean the adoption of the name "Christian nation" by all the countries of so-called "Christendom", but without changing their political governments. It is further claimed that "all the other empires, kingdoms, and states on the face of the earth may become Christian, *and preserve their characteristic forms of political government*". (*Clarke*)

Viewed in the increasing light shining upon God's Holy Word, such religious interpretation becomes more and more untenable and manifest as wrong. It is an interpretation of demon origin to hide the truth on the primary doctrine of the Bible, the kingdom of Jehovah God by his Son Jesus Christ. Through his prophet Daniel the great Revealer of secrets furnished a general interpretation of the dream.

In these latter years the same God of revelation provides the Scriptural interpretation of the prophetic dream by means of the unlocking of the Scriptures and by physical facts in fulfillment of the dream.

Daniel proceeded: "This is the dream; and we will tell the interpretation thereof before the king. Thou, O king, art a king of kings: for the God of heaven hath given thee a kingdom, power, and strength, and glory. And wheresoever the children of men dwell, the

beasts of the field
and the fowls of
the heaven hath
he given into thine
hand, and hath made thee ruler over them all.
Thou art this head of gold. And after thee shall
arise another kingdom inferior to thee, and another third kingdom of brass, which shall bear
rule over all the earth. And the fourth kingdom

 shall be strong as iron: for-
asmuch as iron breaketh in
pieces and subdueth all
things: and as iron that
breaketh all these, shall it
break in pieces and bruise.
And whereas thou sawest
the feet and toes, part of
potters' clay, and part of
iron, the kingdom shall be divided; but there
shall be in it of the strength of the iron, forasmuch as thou sawest the iron mixed with miry
clay. And as the toes of the feet were part of
iron, and part of clay, so the kingdom shall be

partly strong,
and partly bro-
ken. And where-
as thou sawest
iron mixed with
miry clay, they
shall mingle
themselves with
the seed of men:
but they shall

not cleave one to another, even as iron is not mixed with clay.

"And in the days of these kings shall the God of heaven set up a kingdom, which shall never be destroyed: and the kingdom shall not be left to other people, but it shall break in pieces and consume all these kingdoms, and it shall stand for ever. Forasmuch as thou sawest that the stone was cut out of the mountain without hands, and that it brake in pieces the iron, the brass, the clay, the silver, and the gold; the great God hath made known to the king what shall come to pass hereafter: and the dream is certain, and the interpretation thereof sure." —Daniel 2: 36-45.

In view of the further visions given to the prophet and recorded by him at Daniel chapters 7, 8, 11 and 12, it is manifest that Jehovah God is not forecasting at chapter 2 what should be repeated several times over later on. As the first of a series of prophecies this one is fundamental and stands distinct. It does not apply simply to certain earthly parts of Satan's organization. The image of the dream represents Satan's organization as a whole, invisible and visible, and including "the god of this world" himself. It pictures Satan's entire *world* or *kosmos,* composed of both the heavens and the earth which he organized since the flood, "the heavens and the earth, which are now." (2 Peter 3: 7) It is all one organization from head to foot. Its destruction means the world's end.

Satan the Devil is the golden head of the image, pretending to be divine, and aiming to "be like the Most High". That he was pictured or represented by the demon-worshiping Nebuchadnezzar, king of Babylon, is manifest from Isaiah's prophecy, chapter 14, where Babylon's king is spoken of as the bright-shining one, Heylel, or Lucifer. At the time of man's creation in Eden, Lucifer was given an organization of holy angels and was appointed as "the covering cherub" respecting mankind and their interests. The perfect man under Lucifer was mandated to have dominion over all the beasts, birds, and fishes and to subdue all the earth and fill it with a righteous human race. This is what is meant by Daniel's statement to the king (picturing Satan) that Jehovah had given to him a "kingdom, power, and strength, and glory", and had made him ruler over all living creatures on earth. Lucifer's station being from divine source, he was as a "head of gold".

When Lucifer rebelled and took humankind along with him in the rebellion, God did not destroy him or remove him from being invisible overlord to humankind. God permitted this rebellious cherub to continue to be "the prince of the power of the air, the spirit that now worketh in the children of disobedience". (Ephesians 2:2) And in 607 B.C., when God by means of Nebuchadnezzar overturned His typical Theocracy, he allowed Satan the Devil the widest latitude in his exercise of his world domination. Later on, by a second dream to Nebuchadnezzar

(Daniel, chapter 4),* it was disclosed that thereafter Satan should have a *world* (*aion*) or an uninterrupted rule of "seven times", which times the Scriptures show to mean 2,520 years from and after 607 B.C. Thus King Nebuchadnezzar as ruler of the then dominant political power on earth, and during whose rule the Gentile "seven times" began, was a fit symbol of his god, Satan.

After Lucifer stepped out from under Jehovah's universal domination and turned humankind away from submitting to the great Theocrat, he applied himself to the organization of angels under him, to make them his organization. That he largely succeeded in his aim is Scripturally shown in that he is called "the prince of the devils", or "the prince of the demons"; and legions of these unclean spirits are actively serving Satan's ambitions against Jehovah's universal sovereignty. (Matthew 12: 24-27, *Am. Stan. Ver.;* Luke 11: 15) Satan's spirit organization was broken up at the end of "the world of the ungodly" in the flood, but thereafter he reorganized his unclean spirits, the demons. Those who showed the greatest capabilities and aggressiveness Satan selected to form a superior or princely section of his invisible organization. These are symbolically pictured in God's exposure of this hidden organization as the seven heads of a fiery dragon in heaven. Of this it is written: "There appeared another wonder in heaven; and behold a great red drag-

* See the book *"The Truth Shall Make You Free"*, chapter XVIII.

on, having seven heads and ten horns, and seven crowns upon his heads. And his tail drew the third part of the stars of heaven, and did cast them to the earth."—Revelation 12: 3, 4.

These demon princelings Satan appointed to be the invisible princes over the dominant political powers or empires that should arise in their historic order on the earth. Among such demon princes the Bible names "the prince of Persia" or "prince of the kingdom of Persia", and "the prince of Grecia", as opposed to God's mighty spirit Son, Michael, the prince over Jehovah's people. The formation of this demon-prince organization under and subject to Satan after the flood is what is meant by the statement: "And after thee shall arise another kingdom inferior to thee." But the "head of gold" remains on top, as chief, and the demon princelings under him form the 'breast and the arms of silver'.

The legions of other spirit demons Satan the Devil formed into a subsidiary organization under the demon princes. He appointed them to have immediate or closest touch with humankind upon the earth. They would be intermediate between man and the spirit princes. The assigning of this position to such demons or unclean spirits may be what is pictured in the Revelation as the dragon's drawing a third part of the stars of heaven with his tail and casting them down to the earth. These keep in touch with religious humankind by means of spirit mediums, astrologers, magicians, and other religious racketeers, and spread their "doctrines

of demons" by means of religious clergymen.
(1 Timothy 4:1; Deuteronomy 18:10-12; Isaiah
47:1, 12, 13) The religious clergy are the direct
visible link between mankind and the invisible
demons. The organization of this lower order of
spirit demons next under the spirit princes is
what the prophecy means in saying: "And after
thee shall arise . . . another third kingdom of
brass, which shall bear rule over all the earth."
They correspond, therefore, with the 'belly and
thighs of copper' in the terrible image, and are
under the gold head.

Brass (or copper), and silver, and gold, are
superior metals, and hence are well used in symbolizing the unseen spiritual parts of Satan's
totalitarian organization. It is with these super-
human spirits that the Christians, Jehovah's
witnesses, have a conflict, rather than with men;
as it is written: "We wrestle not against flesh
and blood, but against principalities, against
powers, against the rulers of the darkness of
this world, against wicked spirits in heavenly
places."—Ephesians 6:12, marginal reading.

It was many years after the flood, and first
in the days of Noah's great-grandchildren, that
Satan the Devil succeeded in getting a new visible, earthly organization under way. This was
through the establishment of the first kingdom
on earth, that of Nimrod at Babel, or Babylon.
(Genesis 10:1, 6-12) This was in the north, in
the bridge of land between Asia and Europe.
Other descendants of Noah, notably Nimrod's
brothers, went southward into Africa and

shortly the kingdom of Egypt appeared on the stage of action. It early took the place as the first dominant political power of earth. However, in course of time there developed a dominant northern power in conflict with the dominant southern power. These two spheres of political influence and power are spoken of in Daniel, chapter 11, as "the king of the north" and "the king of the south".

Those two "kings" are both of them parts of the one visible organization of Satan the Devil, the "head of gold". It is most likely that the image of Nebuchadnezzar's dream faced the east, in opposition to the "kings of the east" who in due time destroy Satan's organization. The Babylonians also were sun-worshipers and faced eastward in worship to the rising sun. Thus the two iron legs of the image would be planted, one to the north and one to the south, and symbolized the divided political powers of men. The power of the place of "the king of the north" passed successively from the political organization of Assyria to Babylon, then to Medo-Persia, westward to Greece, and onward to Rome. The place of "the king of the south" was duly taken over by the democratic allies of Egypt, particularly by the British Empire and America jointly. These visible, iron-like powers are the means the golden, silvery and coppery parts of the image have used to "break in pieces and bruise" humankind. Thus "the fourth kingdom shall be strong as iron".

The feet and toes of the image of the king's dream were seen to be of iron mixed with clay, picturing divided power and organization. Hardened clay looks like stone, but is not strong like real stone. Hence it is the weakest part of the terrible image. The miry clay, therefore, pictures religion and its clergy, which religion pretends to be Christianity and which clergy palm themselves off as representatives of God's kingdom. The clergy of clay have mingled themselves with the iron-like politicians and meddled in politics and made themselves a part of this world by spiritual fornication. But the politicians have failed to draw any real strength from this union of religion and the political state; their reliance upon religion is as placed on brittle dry clay. It is an unnatural mix, and they will not cleave together. When the great crisis of Satan's world is reached in the near future, the political *iron* will sharply divide off from the religious *clay*. The ten toes of the image picture the complete number or all of the religious-political governments of men at the time of such climax.

The "mountain" out of which the stone of destruction is cut without human hands pictures the mountain of God. Out of it the traitor Lucifer was cast, namely, Jehovah's universal organization of holy spirit creatures. That organization is his "woman" out of whom he 'cuts' or brings forth the Seed which is destined to bruise the head of the great Serpent and destroy all his nest of reptiles.

It must be, then, that the cut-out stone pictures the Seed in whom Jehovah's covenant for the Kingdom is fulfilled, namely, Jesus Christ the King. The Stone's being cut out points to Christ Jesus at being enthroned and invested with power to act at the end of "the times of the Gentiles", when Satan's uninterruptedness of rule runs out. As regards this Daniel's prophecy says: "And in the days of these kings shall the God of heaven set up a kingdom, which shall never be destroyed." The expression "these kings" does not refer simply to the present political and religious rulers represented by the besmeared toes of the image. The gold, the silver, the brass, and the iron of the image are all used to represent *kingdoms,* and hence "these kings" must refer to the invisible principalities, powers, rulers of this world's darkness, and wicked spirits in high places, as well as to the visible kings or rulers on earth. It is not merely the toes and the feet of the image that are doomed to destruction, but the entire organization, the demon parts and the human part together, all now existent as one image.

In the days when the complete organization of God's adversary is in power and actively ruling and bruising and breaking in pieces all humankind, it is then that the God of heaven cuts out his "Stone" and sets up the kingdom of the Seed of his "woman". This kingdom takes the place over mankind that was vacated by Lucifer when he quit Jehovah's organization at Eden. The kingdom will have no successor, for it will be eternal. When Jehovah fulfills the covenant for the Kingdom in completion, then the Son of David, who takes over the Kingdom, will have no successor. Why? Because he has the power of eternal life, immortality. He continues King forever, 'a priest *forever* after the order of Melchizedek.'—Hebrews 7:17, 23-25.

Then the issue of Jehovah's universal domination will be settled once and for all time. His kingdom of his Son, The Stone, and the symbolic image of Satan's organization cannot exist alongside each other forever. The "image" is opposed to the Kingdom, because The Stone represents Jehovah's universal domination and upholds and enforces it against all opposers. Therefore the "stone" takes the initiative against the "image".

Already the Stone is in motion against that terrible "image". In the "battle of that great day of God Almighty", now near, it will strike the image with irresistible momentum, hitting first the visible iron-clay part of Satan's organization. Then after the demons have witnessed the crushing of their earthly organization, Jehovah's Stone will invade the invisible part of Satan's organization and even crush the head of the great Serpent himself. God's active force like a powerful wind will remove every trace of Satan's organization from the universe. Jehovah's kingdom in his Son's hands will remain, standing forever like a mountain filling all the earth. Its power to bless "men of good-will" will reach to every part of the earth.

CHAPTER XIII

A REMNANT RETURNS

ANIEL the prophet was greatly interested in the prophecy of a fellow witness of Jehovah, namely, Jeremiah, as to the seventy-years' desolation of Jerusalem. He longed for that desolation to end. He knew that its end would mean that a remnant of Jehovah's covenant people would be repatriated and that the holy city and her temple would be rebuilt upon their old sites again. Therefore he humbled himself before Jehovah and prayed for the return of divine favor to his covenant people at the appointed time. The Lord, by his angel Gabriel, gave a comforting answer to Daniel and assured him that Jerusalem would be rebuilt and, furthermore, that at a definite time, namely, 69 weeks of years after Jerusalem's walls were ordered rebuilt, Messiah the King would come. (Daniel 9:1-27) At the test of disregarding a mischievously framed law of the imperial government of Medo-Persia and being cast into a den of lions for so doing, Daniel kept up praying to God with his chamber windows opened toward Jerusalem. He was delivered from the lions, because Daniel was right, and the man-made law was wrong, being contrary to God's law.—Daniel 6:1-28.

In Babylon a faithful Jewish remnant like Daniel remembered King Solomon's words when dedicating the temple at Jerusalem: "Yet if they shall bethink themselves in the land whither they were carried captives, and repent, and make supplication unto thee in the land of them that carried them captives, saying, We have sinned, and have done perversely, we have committed wickedness; and so return unto thee with all their heart, and with all their soul, in the land of their enemies, which led them away captive, and pray unto thee toward their land, which thou gavest unto their fathers, the city which thou hast chosen, and the house which I have built for thy name: then hear thou their prayer and their supplication in heaven thy dwelling place, and maintain their cause, and forgive thy people that have sinned against thee, and all their transgressions wherein they have transgressed against thee, and give them compassion before them who carried them captive, that they may have compassion on them: for they be thy people." (1 Kings 8:46-53) This prayer of Solomon was not offered in vain, nor recorded in vain in the Bible record, but was preserved for the comfort and guidance of Jehovah's people when found in this sore difficulty.

The faithful God was prepared to answer this prayer of deliverance of his devoted remnant, if it took the toppling over of the mighty empire of Babylon to do so. And Almighty God did so, exactly at his appointed time, even though it was to restore to freedom a small faithful remnant. More than a remnant of Israelites or Jews was involved. The issue was that of universal domination, and of who is supreme and almighty, and of whose word and name shall be vindicated. God had inspired his prophet Isaiah to declare: "The remnant shall return, even the remnant of Jacob, unto the mighty God. For though thy people Israel be as the sand of the sea, yet a remnant of them shall return: the consumption decreed shall overflow with righteousness." (Isaiah 10: 21, 22) That Babylon should have compassion upon the Jewish captives was not to be expected, for it was said prophetically of Babylon's king, who acted for Satan the Devil, that he "opened not the house of his prisoners". (Isaiah 14: 4, 17) Therefore Babylon's days were numbered. She was "weighed in the balances" and "found wanting". Jehovah brought down her oppressive power by dividing her kingdom among the conquering Medes and Persians.—Daniel 5: 24-31.

Foretelling the very name of Babylon's conqueror and that the conquest would be in fulfillment of Jehovah's judgment upon the oppressor, Isaiah prophesied: "Thus saith the LORD to his anointed, to Cyrus, whose right hand I have holden, to subdue nations before him; and I will loose the loins of kings, to open before him the two leaved gates [of Babylon over the Euphrates river]; and the gates shall not be shut. I have raised him up in righteousness, and I will direct all his ways: he shall build

my city, and he shall let go my captives, not
for price nor reward, saith the LORD of hosts.
. . . Israel shall be saved in the LORD with an
everlasting salvation: ye shall not be ashamed
nor confounded world without end." (Isaiah
45: 1, 13, 17) Though this prophecy pointed forward to a much grander, final fulfillment by a
King Greater than Cyrus, yet the prophecy
must have an initial or typical fulfillment upon
the typical people of Jehovah.—1 Corinthians
10: 6, 11.

The captive city, Jerusalem, must rise again,
and messengers upon the heights must joyfully
announce her rebuilding as an evidence that
Jehovah reigns as The Theocrat. The prophet
Isaiah so predicted two hundred years in advance: "Awake, awake; put on thy strength, O
Zion; put on thy beautiful garments, O Jerusalem, the holy city: . . . Shake thyself from the
dust; arise, and sit down, O Jerusalem: loose
thyself from the bands of thy neck, O captive
daughter of Zion. How beautiful upon the
mountains are the feet of him that bringeth
good tidings, that publisheth peace; that bringeth good tidings of good, that publisheth salvation; that saith unto Zion, THY GOD REIGNETH!
Thy watchmen shall lift up the voice; with the
voice together shall they sing: for they shall see
eye to eye, when the LORD [Jehovah] shall bring
again Zion." (Isaiah 52:1, 2, 7, 8) The fulfillment of this prophecy upon the typical Jerusalem is a guarantee of its complete fulfillment

in a grander manner upon a faithful remnant in our day, in proof that Jehovah reigns.

According to the most accurate histories, Darius the Mede and Cyrus the Persian, his nephew, jointly took the capital of the Babylonian empire in 539 B.C. After Darius' brief rule there, Cyrus came to power, in 537 B.C. That year marked the end of the seventy years' desolation of Jerusalem, and that very year Jehovah God stirred up the heart of Cyrus to let his captives go free. For his own name's sake Jehovah did this: "I had pity [upon them] for mine holy name, which the house of Israel had profaned among the heathen, whither they went. Therefore say unto the house of Israel, Thus saith the Lord GOD; I do not this for your sakes, O house of Israel, but for mine holy name's sake, which ye have profaned among the heathen, whither ye went. And I will sanctify my great name, . . . For I will take you from among the heathen, and gather you out of all countries, and will bring you into your own land. . . . And they shall say, This land that was desolate is become like the garden of Eden; and the waste and desolate and ruined cities are become fenced, and are inhabited. Then the heathen that are left round about you shall know that I the LORD build the ruined places, and plant that that was desolate: I the LORD [Jehovah] have spoken it, and I will do it." —Ezekiel 36: 21-24, 32, 35, 36.

What was the chief purpose in releasing the Jewish captives to return to their homeland and to the desolate site of Jerusalem, or Zion, the captive city? Was it for the sake of their "political independence", so called? No; but for the restoration of worship to the true and living God and for the freedom to worship him in accord with his Theocratic law. To this end the decree in the opening year of the king's reign read: "Thus saith Cyrus king of Persia, All the kingdoms of the earth hath Jehovah, the God of heaven, given me; and he hath charged me to build him a house in Jerusalem, which is in Judah. Whosoever there is among you of all his people, his God be with him, and let him go up to Jerusalem, which is in Judah, and build the house of Jehovah, the God of Israel (he is God), which is in Jerusalem." (Ezra 1: 1-3, *Am. Stan. Ver.;* 2 Chronicles 36: 22, 23) King Cyrus also restored to the Jewish remnant that departed from Babylon "the vessels of the house of the LORD, which Nebuchadnezzar had brought forth out of Jerusalem, and had put them in the house of his gods". The vessel-bearers were ordered and required to be clean from defilement with Babylon's religion. Sheshbazzar was official treasurer.—Isaiah 52: 11; Ezra 1: 7-11.

A congregation of 42,360, together with 7,337 servants and maids, and 200 special singers, or, all together, a company of 49,897 devoted men and women, undertook the perilous journey and returned to their desolated homeland. By the miraculous safeguarding of Almighty God the land had lain uninhabited for the seventy years of sabbath-keeping. A lineal descendant of

King David was made the governor of the restored remnant, to supervise the rebuilding of the temple, namely, Zerubbabel, the son of Shealtiel, of the tribe of Judah. This is the Zerubbabel that appears in both of the lines of the ancestry leading down to Jesus, and it is in Zerubbabel that both of the lines of descent from King David, the one line through Solomon and the other line through Solomon's brother, Nathan, meet. According to 1 Chronicles 3: 17-19, Zerubbabel was evidently the grandson of Salathiel (Shealtiel) and the son of Pedaiah. But, however the fact, Zerubbabel was a descendant of Jehoiachin (Jeconiah), the second-last king of Jerusalem.

Prominently associated with Governor Zerubbabel in the temple work was the high priest Joshua (or Jeshua). (Ezra 2: 1, 2, 64-70; 3: 1-4) The return of the remnant to their homeland was so timed that in the very month of the year in which the complete desolation of the land went into effect a new altar was erected at the temple site in Jerusalem and the remnant were able to celebrate the feast of tabernacles. That was the feast of the seventh month.

Because of their leading connection with the raising up again of Jehovah's temple, both the high priest Joshua and also Zerubbabel the prince of Judah are used as types. Types of whom? Of the Builder of the true temple, namely, Christ Jesus. Zechariah, addressing both men as prefiguring Christ Jesus the High Priest and Headstone of God's house, wrote:

"Hear now, O Joshua the high priest, thou, and thy fellows that sit before thee: for they are men wondered at [men of wonder, or sign]: for, behold, I will bring forth my servant The BRANCH. For behold the stone that I have laid before Joshua; upon one stone shall be seven eyes: behold, I will engrave the graving thereof, saith the LORD of hosts. . . .

"This is the word of the LORD unto Zerubbabel, saying, Not by might, nor by power, but by my spirit, saith the LORD of hosts. Who art thou, O great mountain? before Zerubbabel thou shalt become a plain: and he shall bring forth the headstone thereof with shoutings, crying, Grace, grace unto it." "The hands of Zerubbabel have laid the foundation of this house; his hands shall also finish it; and thou shalt know that the LORD of hosts hath sent me unto you." (Zechariah 3:8, 9; 4:6, 7, 9) And the prophet Haggai writes: "Speak to Zerubbabel, governor of Judah, saying, I will shake the heavens and the earth; and I will overthrow the throne of the kingdoms, and I will destroy the strength of kingdoms of the heathen; and I will overthrow the chariots, and those that ride in them; and the horses and their riders shall come down, every one by the sword of his brother. In that day, saith the LORD of hosts, will I take thee, O Zerubbabel, my servant, the son of Shealtiel, saith the LORD, and will make thee as a signet: for I have chosen thee, saith the LORD of hosts."—Haggai 2:20-23.

Opposition to rebuilding the temple broke out among the Gentile nations in Palestine. They carried on an official persecution of the temple builders and tried to hold up their work all the days of King Cyrus. Then they joined in sending a letter to Cyrus' successor, King Artaxerxes, and accused the temple builders of seditious aims against the political state. King Artaxerxes believed the accusation. Contrary to the law of the Medes and Persians, he countermanded the temple decree of Cyrus, and had the temple work stopped. "So it ceased unto the second year of the reign of Darius king of Persia." But God's purpose was not to be frustrated. The typical fulfillment of his prophecies must be carried out for his name's sake. After about sixteen years of interruption to reconstructing the temple Jehovah God raised up his prophets Haggai and Zechariah. These prophets he used to stir up Zerubbabel and high priest Joshua to renew the temple work in spite of the decree of the political state. The work went on!

The enemies appealed to King Darius to punish these seeming violators of the law of the state. Courageously the temple builders contended that their God-given work was not against the interests of the state but was perfectly legal according to the original decree of King Cyrus. Thereupon King Darius turned to basic law and had search made in the state archives. The decree of King Cyrus was uncovered. It must stand and be enforced according to the rule of the law of the Medes and Persians, which changes not.

Then the state's approval of the temple work was reaffirmed, and Zerubbabel and Joshua finished building the temple. The enemies looked on with chagrin. Worse still, they were ordered by the king to furnish aid to the temple work. In the twelfth month, which is the month Adar, and in the sixth year of King Darius, the rebuilt temple was dedicated with great joy by the remnant, and Jehovah's word and name were vindicated.—Ezra, chapters 4 to 6.

Later, in the seventh year of the reign of Artaxerxes III, there came from Babylon to Jerusalem the Levite priest named Ezra, "a ready scribe in the law of Moses." He was accompanied by another band of Jewish repatriates. He brought a letter from the king providing for the support of the temple and its services. The royal letter also decreed that those ministering at the temple should be exempt from state taxation. It read: "Also we certify you, that touching any of the priests and Levites, singers, porters, Nethinims, or ministers of this house of God, it shall not be lawful to impose toll, tribute, or custom, upon them." (Ezra, chapter 7) It is understood that from the time of scribe Ezra forward there was an increased copying of the Hebrew books of the Bible, and the circulation of Holy Writ was spread by the remnant.

Meantime the walls of Jerusalem continued in a state of disrepair. This fact came to the

notice of the Jew Nehemiah, the cupbearer of
Artaxerxes III at Shushan in Elam. It greatly
grieved him to learn that "the remnant that are
left of the captivity there in the province are in
great affliction and reproach: the wall of Jerusalem also is broken down, and the gates thereof are burned with fire". In the twentieth year
of Artaxerxes III, in the first Jewish month of
the sacred year, or Nisan, sorrowful Nehemiah
made this known to the king. At Nehemiah's
request, the king gave forth "the commandment
to restore and to build Jerusalem", as foretold
at Daniel 9:25. Hence the twentieth year of
Artaxerxes III marked the beginning of the

seventy weeks of years, or 490 years, that the angel Gabriel told Daniel would be climaxed with the appearance of the Messiah. That year corresponds with the year 454 B.C., which vulgar year actually began about October of 455 B.C. Thus, at the due time, Nehemiah was authorized to oversee the rebuilding of Jerusalem's walls. Promptly he set out on the four-months-long journey to the city, as Ezra had done years before.—Ezra 7:8, 9.

First, Nehemiah viewed the walls and made his estimates. Then about the third day of the fifth month of the year he set the faithful remnant to the work of surrounding Jerusalem with suitable walls. Nehemiah soon began to experience the fulfillment of the prophecy, at Daniel 9:25, concerning Jerusalem, that "the street shall be built again, and the wall, even in troublous times", or, "in the distress of the times." —Young's translation.

Once again the demonized enemies tried to interfere with the progress of the work of the remnant. The enemy leaders, Sanballat the Moabite, Tobiah the Ammonite, and Geshem the Arabian, conspired together to halt the wall repairs. But in Nehemiah they met no pacifist. He arose to the defense of the interests of the Lord's work against the unwarranted illegal assaults of the foe. He armed the wall-builders and put them on guard day and night on every section of the wall. His command was: "Be not ye afraid of them: remember the Lord [Jehovah], which is great and terrible, and FIGHT FOR

YOUR BRETHREN, your sons, and your daughters, your wives, and your houses." (Nehemiah, chapter 4) Foiled, the enemies schemed to draw Nehemiah away from the work to kill him, but Nehemiah refused to abandon the work to waste time talking with enemies. These then raised the charge that the wall-building remnant had seditious designs against the state. They spread the propaganda that Nehemiah had hired men to say of him at Jerusalem, "There is a king in Judah," and that this treason would be reported to Artaxerxes. However, all efforts to weaken the working hands of the remnant and to lure Nehemiah to his death failed. Under Jehovah's blessing and protection Nehemiah finished his commissioned work. "So the wall was finished in the twenty and fifth day of the month Elul [the sixth month], in fifty and two days."—Nehemiah, chapters 4-6.

When the seventh month arrived all the Israelite remnant were quite comfortably and safely lodged in all their cities. Then the scribe Ezra and Governor Nehemiah instructed the people from the law of their covenant with God that this is the month for the celebration of the feast of tabernacles. They encouraged the remnant to turn now from their grief at sin to rejoicing in the Lord Jehovah, saying: "The joy of the Lord is your strength." Joyfully, on the proper days, the remnant then celebrated the feast. (Nehemiah, chapter 8) Thereafter steps were taken to provide a steady support by the remnant to the temple, to "charge ourselves yearly with the third part of a shekel for the service of the house of our God". Sincere efforts were also made to cleanse the remnant from any improper connections with religionists, to guard them against being entrapped into religion.—Nehemiah, chapters 10-13.

The "times of the Gentiles" still had more than two thousand years to run. Hence Nehemiah, when praying before the people inside the rewalled Jerusalem, said: "Behold, we are servants this day, and for the land that thou gavest unto our fathers to eat the fruit thereof and the good thereof, behold, we are servants in it: and it yieldeth much increase unto the kings whom thou hast set over us because of our sins: also they have dominion over our bodies, and over our cattle, at their pleasure, and we are in great distress. And because of all this we make a sure covenant, and write it; and our princes, Levites, and priests, seal unto it." (Nehemiah 9: 33-38; Ezra 9: 7, 8) And Hosea prophesied: "The children of Israel shall abide many days without a king, and without a prince, and without a sacrifice, . . . Afterward shall the children of Israel return, and seek the LORD their God, and David their king; and shall fear the LORD and his goodness in the latter days." —Hosea 3: 4, 5.

In process of time the dominion over the restored remnant passed from the hands of the Medo-Persians into those of the Greeks, and thereafter, in 63 B.C., into the hands of imperial Rome.

CHAPTER XIV

THE KING AT HAND!

FTER Nehemiah and Ezra, and down till the beginning of the A.D. or *Anno Domini* period, only one prophet of Jehovah God appeared among the restored remnant of His people. That was Malachi, or Malachiah, whose name means "messenger (or angel) of Jehovah". His prophecy closed the canon (or collection of inspired books) of the Hebrew Scriptures, from the first five books of Moses forward. Malachi's was a temple prophecy, urging for a clean Levitic priesthood and for the pure worship of Jehovah God with worthy sacrifices to Him. And why? Because Jehovah, by his great Messenger of the covenant with Abraham concerning the royal Seed of blessing, is coming to the temple for judgment. "Behold, I will send my messenger, and he shall prepare the way before me: and the Lord, whom ye seek, shall suddenly come to his temple, even the MESSENGER OF THE COVENANT, whom ye delight in: behold, he shall come, saith the LORD of hosts. But who may abide the day of his coming? and who shall stand when he appeareth? for he is like a refiner's fire, and like fullers' sope; and he shall sit as a refiner and purifier of silver: and he shall purify the sons of Levi, and purge them as gold and silver, that they may offer unto the LORD an offering in righteousness." This betokened that the coming of the Messiah, Christ the King, was drawing near.

Besides the above, Malachi also foretold of the coming of a fiery day of destruction. That day would be preceded by the sending of a prophet, a prophet like that Elijah who caused Queen Jezebel's 450 priests of Baal religion to be slain after a test by fire at Mount Carmel. "For, behold, the day cometh, it burneth as a furnace; and all the proud, and all that work wickedness, shall be stubble; and the day that cometh shall burn them up, saith Jehovah of hosts, that it shall leave them neither root nor branch. But unto you that fear my name shall the sun of righteousness arise with healing in its wings; . . . Behold, I will send you Elijah the prophet before the great and terrible day of Jehovah come. And he shall turn the heart of the fathers to the children, and the heart of the children to their fathers; lest I come and smite the earth with a curse."—Malachi 3:1-3; 4:1, 2, 5, 6, *Am. Stan. Ver.*

These prophecies about the forerunner who should precede the Messenger of Jehovah's covenant and the troublous day of Jehovah had a measure of application to John the Baptist. The angel Gabriel and also Christ Jesus so applied them. As in other cases, however, the fulfillment of such prophecies in a partial way at the first coming of Jehovah's Messenger points to a far grander and final fulfillment at the coming of the Kingdom in power. In keeping with the miniature fulfillment of the prophecies, John was born six months before Jesus.—Luke 1: 13-17, 36; Matthew 11: 7-10; 17: 10-13.

Jehovah God always vindicates his word, proving it true and always bringing to pass what it says. David, with whom the Kingdom covenant was made, was born at Bethlehem in the tribe of Judah, for which cause Bethlehem was called "the city of David". In view of a future like event, the prophet Micah was inspired to say concerning Jehovah's beloved King of whom David was a type or prophetic figure: "But thou, Bethlehem Ephratah, though thou be little among the thousands of Judah, yet out of thee shall he come forth unto me that is to be ruler in Israel; whose goings forth have been from of old, from everlasting." (Micah 5: 2) The promised One was due to be born in the flesh at David's native city in the fall of the year 2 B.C., because the last of the "seventy weeks" as foretold to the prophet Daniel must begin in the fall of A.D. 29. The birth at Bethlehem was to mark, not the coming of the Messiah or Christ, but merely the bringing forth of the One destined to be the Messiah or Christ the Lord. He could not appear as Christ until anointed.

Months preceding this miraculous event the beloved and only begotten Son of God, "The Word," disappeared from among the holy angels of heaven. He had divested or emptied himself of all his celestial glory and power and

had submitted to his heavenly Father's purpose
to transfer his life from the heavenly organism
to the womb of a faithful Jewish virgin. Under
Jehovah's holy power and protection the child
thus conceived was developed to the point of
birth. Then the heavenly Father notified the
angels of heaven and delegated them to bear
witness to the birth to such men as were chosen
to be worthy witnesses of that fact. The Record
reads:

"And Joseph also went up from Galilee, out
of the city of Nazareth, into Judæa, unto the
city of David, which is called Bethlehem; (because he was of the house and lineage of David:)
to be taxed with Mary his espoused wife, being
great with child. And so it was, that, while they
were there, the days were accomplished that
she should be delivered. And she brought forth
her firstborn son, and wrapped him in swaddling clothes, and laid him in a manger; because there was no room for them in the inn.
And there were in the same country shepherds
abiding in the field, keeping watch over their
flock by night. And, lo, the angel of the Lord
came upon them, and the glory of the Lord
shone round about them: and they were sore
afraid. And the angel said unto them, Fear not:
for, behold, I bring you good tidings of great
joy, which shall be to all people. For unto you
is born this day in the city of David a Saviour,
which is Christ the Lord. And this shall be a
sign unto you; Ye shall find the babe wrapped
in swaddling clothes, lying in a manger. And

suddenly there was with the angel a multitude
of the heavenly host praising God, and saying,
Glory to God in the highest, and on earth peace,
good will toward men [and on earth peace to
men of good will]."—Luke 2:4-14; and *Douay
Version*.

A so-called "star in the east" was not the
"sign" given to the shepherds. They did not
have to depend upon a magical, astrological cal-
culation to discover that the future King had
been born. They did not look to a star to guide
them through that autumn night and to stand
over the place where the child lay within the
manger. They had the angel's announcement,
and they knew the sign by which to identify the
future Messiah or Christ. This was given to
them that they might go and see for themselves,
and become witnesses to the truth of the birth.
After seeing, they bore witness to others of
what things had come to pass. "And when they
had seen it, they made known abroad the saying which was told them concerning this child.
And all they that heard it wondered at those
things which were told them by the shepherds.
. . . And the shepherds returned, glorifying
and praising God for all the things that they
had heard and seen, as it was told unto them."
—Luke 2:15-20.

How wise it was of Jehovah to make this
birth known to God-fearing shepherds of Bethlehem, such as David once was, rather than to
the high priests and lawyers and other prominent religious leaders at Jerusalem, six miles

northward! Those religious dignitaries were willing to play right into the hand of Satan the Devil. They used the prophecy of Micah to tip off murder-inclined King Herod that the child for whom the Eastern magi or stargazers were searching was born at Bethlehem. No "sign" could they give by which to identify him. They did not even get stirred up by the astrological calculations of the magi as regards the birth and did not interest themselves to go and see for themselves and to hail the future Messiah. Those religious leaders remained indifferently at Jerusalem. While it was proper that they did not believe the demon-inspired conclusions of the oriental magi, yet their unconcern as to making their own investigation shows that they would not have believed the true report by the eyewitnesses, the lowly shepherds of Bethlehem. Little that mattered, however. Satan the Serpent was not interested in exciting those sanctimonious religionists by the illusion of the traveling "star", so called, to go and see and believe. He was interested in exciting King Herod to fear for his kingdom and to send his soldiers to slaughter the babe at Bethlehem, if possible.—Matthew 2: 1-18.

At Jerusalem only two persons were privileged, by revelation from the Lord, to become witnesses of Jesus' birth. They were the faithful Simeon and the prophetess Anna. They were favored with beholding the child. That was when he was brought to the temple for presentation to the Lord at the end of Mary's purification of forty days, according to God's law by Moses.—Luke 2: 21-39; Leviticus 12: 1-8.

Moses foretold that God would raise up a prophet like unto himself. Satan the Devil once sought to destroy Moses as a babe, but Moses grew up and later left Egypt. Likewise the Devil tried to destroy the babe Jesus. Under God's direction the parents fled with the child into Egypt and brought him out again after Herod's death. This was in harmony with the prophecy of Hosea 11: 1: "Out of Egypt have I called my son." Because Herod's son Archelaus then reigned in Judea, Jesus' parents took him north into the separate province of Galilee, to the city of Nazareth, from which they had gone to Bethlehem. This was that "it might be fulfilled which was spoken by the prophets, He shall be called a Nazarene". This fact later caused doubt to arise as to his being the Messiah, the son of David. It was said respecting him: "Search, and look: for out of Galilee ariseth no prophet." (Matthew 2: 13-23; John 7: 50-52) Because of Nazareth's low reputation due to the presence of so many Gentiles there, this was cause of offense against Jesus. Pointing to him, the question was raised: "Can there any good thing come out of Nazareth?" (John 1: 46) Eventually his association with Nazareth of Galilee brought Jesus into the presence of King Herod Antipas. (Luke 23: 5-15) However, at such a discredited place it was, by God's will, that "Jesus increased in wisdom and stature, and in favour with God and man". There he was known as "the carpenter" or "the carpenter's son".—Luke 2: 51, 52; Matthew 13: 55.

For many years after Jerusalem's destruction no one of David's line was anointed king over Israel. When Jesus' ancestor David attained to thirty years, he was anointed by a Levite priest to be ruler of Judah at Hebron, and thus became the *anointed* king of Jehovah's typical Theocracy. According to Gabriel's word to Daniel, the time was to be 62 weeks and 7 weeks, or a sum of 69 weeks, from the order to rebuild Jerusalem's walls "unto the Messiah the Prince". (Daniel 9 : 25) *Messiah* or *Christ* means *Anointed One*. The end of the 69th week of years, in A.D. 29, found Jesus a mature man of thirty years of age. He must then become Messiah, according to God's appointed time. Because he was to be anointed unto the "kingdom of heaven" he must be anointed by One higher than man and with something of greater virtue than oil. He therefore came to John the Baptist, a Levite and son of a priest, not to be anointed, but to be immersed in water.

Jesus' baptism in water symbolized his consecration of himself to do God's will, which will he had been born as a man to do. As early as a child of twelve years of age he realized he had a mission in harmony with his heavenly Father's will. This he showed at the temple where he had been asking questions, when he said to his parents: "How is it that ye sought me? wist ye not that I must be about my Father's business?" After that Jesus, though he was heir of the Kingdom covenant, returned to Nazareth and was subject to Joseph and Mary, because "the heir, as long as he is a child, differeth nothing from a servant, though he be lord of all; but is under tutors and governors until the time appointed of the father". (Luke 2:41-52; Galatians 4:1, 2) At his majority and no longer a child, Jesus came to do his Father's business. To that end he consecrated himself. "Lo, I come (in the volume of the book it is written of me,) to do thy will, O God." (Hebrews 10:5-9) The revealing of that will must certainly come after his anointing to be King.

The anointing immediately followed Jesus' baptism. It was an anointing with his Father's spirit or active force, which is invisible and holy. It was accompanied with dynamic power. Regarding this the apostle Peter said: "The word which God sent unto the children of Israel, preaching peace by Jesus Christ: (he is Lord of all:) that word, I say, ye know, which was published throughout all Judæa, and began from Galilee, after the baptism which John preached; how God anointed Jesus of Nazareth with the holy [spirit] and with power: who went about doing good, and healing all that were oppressed of the devil; for God was with him." (Acts 10:36-38) By this anointing Jesus became Messiah or Christ, and *Messiah the Prince* was now come. His Father Jehovah anointed him as such. There the Anointed One came, "whose right it is," and Jehovah God gave to him the right to the "kingdom of heaven" and fully brought him into the covenant for the everlasting Kingdom.—Ezekiel 21:27.

A mere man, such as Jesus had been born to be from Mary's womb, could not be King in the "kingdom of heaven". The Scripture rule forbids it, saying: "Flesh and blood cannot inherit the kingdom of God." (1 Corinthians 15:50) It was not as a human creature that Jesus was anointed to the Kingdom. Though he was yet in the flesh, it was as a "new creature" that Jesus was anointed. He had not taken human nature to stay a man for ever, but in order to make proof of his integrity toward God down here and then to sacrifice that humanity for ever for man's benefit. Hence he came bringing to God no animal sacrifices to make atonement for mankind's sin. He came offering *himself* as a sacrifice, to lay aside his perfect human nature and its life-rights. Said he: "Sacrifice and offering thou wouldest not, but a body hast thou prepared me." And according to the will of God his followers are "sanctified through the offering of the body of Jesus Christ once for all." (Hebrews 10:5-10) By this Jesus became a sacrificing priest at his baptism, as foreshadowed or typified by the sacrificial high priest Aaron.

It becomes clear, therefore, that at Jesus' baptism he was begotten of God's spirit, that same spirit which had come upon Mary when he was conceived in her womb. Thus the baptized Jesus was begotten or brought forth to be a "new creature" with spiritual or heavenly hopes. This fact is attested to or proved by

God's voice from heaven as heard by John the Baptist: "This is my beloved Son, in whom I am well pleased." At that event God's "woman", or heavenly universal organization, brought forth the Seed whom Satan hates.

It was this newly begotten Son, this "new creature", that was anointed with God's spirit. It was this anointed new creature that, after the complete sacrifice of his circumcised flesh, would enter into the heavenly realm of the kingdom. "For in Christ Jesus neither circumcision availeth any thing, nor uncircumcision, but a new creature." (Luke 2:21; Galatians 6:15) As pertaining to this begetting of Jesus to be a new creature it is written: "And no man taketh this honour unto himself, but he that is called of God, as was Aaron. So also Christ glorified not himself to be made an high priest; but he that said unto him, Thou art my Son, to day have I begotten thee." (Hebrews 5:4, 5) He was spoken of to God the Father as "thy holy child Jesus, whom thou hast anointed".—Acts 4:27.

Was Jesus anointed to begin immediately to reign as King? Was such the will of the great Theocrat who anointed him? That became the selfish desire of the common people in whose behalf Jesus performed so many miracles by means of that power which attended his anointing, but Jesus knew it was not God's will. "When Jesus therefore perceived that they would come and take him by force, to make him a king, he departed again into a mountain himself alone." This temptation to begin reigning

before God's time met no more success than did
the temptation in the mountain when Satan the
Devil displayed to him all the kingdoms of this
world and their glory and offered such to Jesus
to buy Jesus' worship. (John 6:15; Matthew
4:8-10) How, then, could anyone claiming to be
a follower of Jesus and inferior to him accept
an earthly kingdom at anyone's hands? Jesus
well knew that the Kingdom was not an earthly
government and that certain work must be done
before its establishment.

During the forty days spent in the wilderness
after his anointing, Jesus, with the heavens or
heavenly things opened up to his eyes of understanding, determined what he must do on earth.
What he must do he showed when he bore witness to the Jewish ruler Nicodemus concerning
the kingdom of God. (John 3:1-24) His mission he also showed at the well in Samaria,
when the Samaritan woman said to him: "I
know that Messias cometh, which is called
Christ: when he is come, he will tell us all
things"; and Jesus said to her: "I that speak
unto thee am he." And the Samaritans, on hearing him, said: "We have heard him ourselves,
and know that this is indeed the Christ, the
Saviour of the world." (John 4:1-30, 39-43)
Then came the imprisonment of Jesus' forerunner, John the Baptist, who had cried out:
"Repent ye: for the kingdom of heaven is at
hand." Having passed through Samaria and
come again into Galilee, Jesus increased his
Kingdom proclamation. "Now after that John

was put in prison, Jesus came into Galilee, preaching the gospel of the kingdom of God, and saying, The time is fulfilled, and the kingdom of God is at hand: repent ye, and believe the gospel." "From that time Jesus began to preach, and to say, Repent: for the kingdom of heaven is at hand."—Mark 1:14, 15; Matthew 4:17; Luke 4:14, 15.

That Jesus was faithfully doing then what he was anointed or commissioned to do, he expressly made known during this preaching tour in Galilee. There he disclosed that his primary work on earth was to be a witness for the kingdom of Jehovah God and by it to vindicate Jehovah's name and word. "And he came to Nazareth, where he had been brought up: and, as his custom was, he went into the synagogue on the sabbath day, and stood up for to read. And there was delivered unto him the book of the prophet Esaias. And when he had opened the book, he found the place where it was written, *The spirit of the Lord [Jehovah] is upon me, because he hath anointed me to preach the gospel to the poor; he hath sent me to heal the brokenhearted, to preach deliverance to the captives, and recovering of sight to the blind, to set at liberty them that are bruised, to preach the acceptable year of the Lord.*" The words which Jesus here quoted are found at Isaiah 61:1, 2. (*Esaias* is the Greek way of saying *Isaiah*.) Whether Jesus read the Greek translation of the Bible or read the Hebrew original is not certain, but the evidence is that Jesus, of

Galilee of the nations, could speak both Greek and Hebrew. "And he closed the book, and he gave it again to the minister, and sat down. And the eyes of all them that were in the synagogue were fastened on him. And he began to say unto them, This day is this scripture fulfilled in your ears." (Luke 4:16-21) He meant that this prophecy of the anointing was fulfilled in him and he was and is the Christ or Messiah.

When his audience countered this announcement with the words of doubt, "Is not this Joseph's son?" Jesus warned them that "no prophet is accepted in his own country". He then illustrated that by reference to the cases of the prophets Elijah and Elisha. Feeling condemned by his words, his fellow countrymen then sought to do the will of Satan the Serpent and to bruise the heel of the Seed of God's "woman" by stoning him to death. "But he passing through the midst of them went his way," and kept on preaching.

Meanwhile, those disciples who had left John the Baptist and who had gone with Jesus turned aside for at least part of the time to their aforetime earthly occupations. Jesus, on the other hand, knew that "the time is fulfilled, and the kingdom of God is at hand", and that therefore it was the time to increase the Kingdom proclamation and to bring in more proclaimers into the work as his helpers. "And it came to pass, that, as the people pressed upon him to hear the word of God, he stood by the lake of Gennesaret [the sea of Tiberias or Galilee], and saw two ships standing by the lake: but the fishermen were gone out of them, and were washing their nets. And he entered into one of the ships, which was Simon's, and prayed him that he would thrust out a little from the land. And he sat down, and taught the people out of the ship. Now when he had left speaking, he said unto Simon, Launch out into the deep, and let down your nets for a draught. And Simon answering said unto him, Master, we have toiled all the night, and have taken nothing: nevertheless at thy word I will let down the net.

"And when they had this done, they inclosed a great multitude of fishes: and their net brake. And they beckoned unto their partners, which were in the other ship, that they should come and help them. And they came, and filled both the ships, so that they began to sink. When Simon Peter saw it, he fell down at Jesus' knees, saying, Depart from me; for I am a sinful man, O Lord. For he was astonished, and all that were with him, at the draught of the fishes which they had taken: and so was also James, and John, the sons of Zebedee, which were partners with Simon.

"And Jesus said unto Simon, Fear not; from henceforth thou shalt catch men. And when they had brought their ships to land, they forsook all, and followed him." (Luke 5:1-11) The four that here left the fishing business, the brothers Simon Peter and Andrew, and the brothers James and John, followed Jesus thenceforth to the end of his preaching ministry, to become "fishers of men". (Matthew 4:18-22; Mark 1:16-20) Afterward in the progress of his work Jesus called other men to follow him exclusively all their time. In due course, while still in Galilee, he organized them for the witness work. "And he goeth up into a mountain, and calleth unto him whom he would: and they came unto him. And he ordained twelve, that they should be with him, and that he might send them forth to preach, and to have power to heal sicknesses, and to cast out devils: and Simon he surnamed Peter; and James the son of Zebedee, and John the brother of James; and he surnamed them Boanerges [Hebrew: *B'nei Rogez*], which is, The sons of thunder: and Andrew, and Philip, and Bartholomew, and Matthew, and Thomas, and James the son of Alphæus, and Thaddæus, and Simon the Canaanite, and Judas Iscariot, which also betrayed him."—Mark 3:13-19; Luke 6:12-16.

Jesus' discourse to the people gathered at the mountain followed this. Therein he made it plain that others were to be joined with him in the "kingdom of heaven", and he set forth the requirements for gaining that privilege. He stated many blessednesses, such as "Blessed are the poor in spirit: for theirs is the kingdom of heaven. . . . Blessed are they which are persecuted for righteousness' sake: for theirs is the kingdom of heaven. Blessed are ye, when men shall revile you, and persecute you, and shall say all manner of evil against you falsely, for my sake. Rejoice, and be exceeding glad:

for great is your reward in heaven: for so persecuted they the prophets which were before you."—Matthew 5:1-12.

Then he told them that the foremost thing in all their prayers should be the vindication of Jehovah's name by the establishment of the "kingdom of heaven". He taught them: "After this manner therefore pray ye: Our Father which art in heaven, Hallowed be thy name. Thy kingdom come. Thy will be done in earth, as it is in heaven. Give us this day our daily bread. And forgive us our debts, as we forgive our debtors. And lead us not into temptation, but deliver us from evil." In harmony with such prayer they should make the service of that kingdom the first concern of their lives. They need not worry about or seek after the passing material things. Such God will supply for his faithful servants without fail. "But seek ye first the kingdom of God, and his righteousness; and all these things shall be added unto you."

Jesus then said that a lot of religionists would address him as "Lord" and that they would do many seemingly charitable works to which they would presumptuously attach the name of "Christ" or of "Jesus", but that they would be hypocritical and would not gain the Kingdom. "Not every one that saith unto me, Lord, Lord, shall enter into the kingdom of heaven; but he that doeth the will of my Father which is in heaven. Many will say to me in that day, Lord, Lord, have we not prophesied in thy name? and in thy name have cast out devils?

and in thy name done many wonderful works?
And then will I profess unto them, I never knew
you: depart from me, ye that work iniquity."
The wise ones are those who heed Jesus' words
and do them. The foolish are those who hear but
who do not, and who will therefore suffer disaster.—Matthew, chapters 5 to 7.

Thereafter, to impress more deeply the importance of the Kingdom as well as to with-
hold its truths from the foolish and selfish, Jesus gave many parables or Kingdom illustrations based upon true life. Asked why he did so,
he made it clear that his purpose was not to
convert the world before the setting up of the
Kingdom. Said he to his obedient disciples: "Because it is given unto you to know the mysteries
of the kingdom of heaven, but to them it is not
given. . . . Therefore speak I to them in parables: because they seeing see not; and hearing
they hear not, neither do they understand. And
in them is fulfilled the prophecy of Esaias, . . .
But blessed are your eyes, for they see: and
your ears, for they hear. For verily I say unto
you, That many prophets and righteous men
have desired to see those things which ye see,
and have not seen them; and to hear those
things which ye hear, and have not heard them."
(Matthew 13: 3, 10-17) By that he indicated that
such prophets and righteous men would not be
members in the "kingdom of heaven", but would
be favored otherwise with everlasting life on
earth under the Kingdom. Hence those in the
Kingdom must be higher and greater than such

favored ones on earth. This is the sense of Jesus' words relative to John the Baptist: "Verily I say unto you, Among them that are born of women there hath not risen a greater than John the Baptist: notwithstanding he that is least in the kingdom of heaven is greater than he. And from the days of John the Baptist until now the kingdom of heaven suffereth violence, and the violent take it by force. For all the prophets and the law prophesied until John."—Matthew 11:11-13.

PIONEERING FROM HOUSE TO HOUSE

Jesus was Jehovah's leading witness for the Kingdom and was the most faithful and exemplary preacher of it. To educate the people freely concerning the Kingdom, Jesus pioneered directly to the people with the message. No building of a temple or costly cathedral, no ringing of bells to have people turn out to hear him preach, nothing of such for him! The record of his ministry reads: "He went throughout every city and village, preaching and shewing the glad tidings of the kingdom of God: and the twelve were with him." (Luke 8:1) Besides going to the public synagogues when the people met there, he went to the homes of the people. He built up interest in the Kingdom message in their homes. He made revisits or back-calls upon the families. In the four accounts of his life by Matthew, Mark, Luke and John, making up 89 chapters all together, the words *house* and *home* occur more than 130 times; and in the vast majority of these cases they refer to the abodes of the common people that Jesus visited in order to preach and give Kingdom instruction. Look up all these words in a Bible concordance.

Jesus told his disciples to follow his example as to the manner of preaching. On one occasion he said to them: "The harvest truly is plenteous, but the labourers are few; pray ye therefore the Lord [Jehovah] of the harvest, that he will send forth labourers into his harvest." Then Jesus sent forth his own close disciples, the twelve apostles, from village to village and from house to house. Jesus did not himself go to the pagan heathen in order to convert the world, neither did he send his disciples to such. He sent them to the covenant people of God. Said he: "Go not into the way of the Gen-tiles, and into any city of the Samaritans enter ye not: but go rather to the lost sheep of the house of Israel. And as ye go, preach, saying, The kingdom of heaven is at hand. . . . And into whatsoever city or town ye shall enter, inquire who in it is worthy; and there abide till ye go thence. And when ye come into an *house,* salute it. And if the *house* be worthy, let your peace

come upon it: but if it be not worthy, let your peace return to you. And whosoever shall not receive you, nor hear your words, when ye depart out of that *house* or city, shake off the dust of your feet.... What I tell you in darkness, that speak ye in light: and what ye hear in the ear, that preach ye upon the *house*tops."

Immediately after sending forth the twelve apostles on such pioneer preaching activity, he himself "departed thence to teach and to preach in their cities".—Matthew 10:1-42; 11:1.

Still later Jesus broadened and speeded up the house-to-house witness work by still more Kingdom publishers. "After these things the Lord appointed other seventy also, and sent them two and two before his face into every city and place, whither he himself would come. Therefore said he unto them, . . . And into whatsoever *house* ye enter, first say, Peace be to this *house*. And if the son of peace be there, your peace shall rest upon it: if not, it shall turn to you again. And in the same *house* remain, eating and drinking such things as they give: for the labourer is worthy of his hire. Go not from *house* to *house* [to eat and drink material things]. And into whatsoever city ye enter, and they receive you, eat such things as are set before you: and heal the sick that are therein, and say unto them, The kingdom of God is come nigh unto you. But into whatsoever city ye enter, and they receive you not, go your ways out into the streets of the same, and say, Even the very dust of your city, which cleaveth on us, we do wipe off against you: notwithstanding be ye sure of this, that the kingdom of God is come nigh unto you." Then Jesus said: "He that heareth you heareth me; and he that despiseth you despiseth me; and he that despiseth me despiseth him that sent me."—Luke 10:1-16.

Some will ask: Were not the publishers mistaken in preaching "The kingdom of heaven is at hand", since Jesus did not then and there establish the kingdom and begin reigning? No; they were quite right. On what basis? On this: *Kingdom* means not merely a monarchy or a government in action, the head of which is a king. It may also mean the one having the rank, quality, attributes and authority of a king. And if such one has others associated with him of royal rank, these would be included within the term *kingdom*. The government of the Kingdom did not need to be set in active operation in Jesus' day for the Kingdom to be at hand or to have approached. Jesus himself, the one "whose right it is" to rule according to the Kingdom covenant and the one who was anointed of God to be King, was present. By reason of this fact the kingdom of God or the kingdom of heaven was at hand; indeed, it was present. Moreover, when the sent-ones or legates of the Lord Jesus went forth preaching the Kingdom as being at hand, they went forth as his representatives, by his authority and with his message, and they themselves were in line to be members of the Kingdom with him. Whoever rejected their message rejected the King that sent him.

From this viewpoint are to be understood Jesus' words to his enemies, the religious Pharisees, to whom Jesus once said: "Ye are of your father the devil." "And when he was demanded of the Pharisees, when the kingdom of God should come, he answered them and said, The kingdom of God cometh not with observation; neither shall they say, Lo here! or, lo there! for, behold, the kingdom of God is within you." (Luke 17: 20, 21) Another authoritative translation of Jesus' words reads: "The kingdom of God cometh not with narrow watching; neither shall they say—Lo here! or There. For lo! the

kingdom of, God is among you." (Rotherham's
The Emphasised Bible) Still another authoritative translation reads: "The kingdom of God
comes not with outward show; nor shall they
say, 'Behold here! or there!' for, behold, God's
royal majesty is among you." (*The Emphatic
Diaglott*) The King whom God anointed was
to be recognized and identified, not by a lot of
gawdy trappings and other observable outward
show, but by his words and works. Neither was
he kept in secret in the temple or elsewhere out
of fear of the Gentile political powers, as Joash
was during the reign of bloody Queen Athaliah
at Jerusalem. To the contrary, here He was in
person, openly among them his enemies and
boldly preaching "The kingdom of heaven is at
hand", without regard for Governor Pontius
Pilate, or King Herod Antipas, or Emperor
Tiberius Caesar.

The days would come, however, when the
King was not to be in their midst on earth.
"And he said unto the disciples, The days will
come, when ye shall desire to see one of the
days of the Son of man, and ye shall not see it.
And they shall say to you, See here; or, see
there: go not after them, nor follow them. For
as the lightning, that lighteneth out of the one
part under heaven, shineth unto the other part
under heaven; so shall also the Son of man be
in his day. But first must he suffer many things,
and be rejected of this generation." (Luke
17: 22-25) In that interval of absence the mes-

sage, "The kingdom of heaven is at hand," would be silent.

Once, when Jesus healed a boy that was blind, dumb, and possessed of a demon or unclean spirit, the people said, "Is not this the son of David?" Hearing this, the religious leaders tried to blind the people to the fact that the King, the rightful heir of David, was in their midst. "When the Pharisees heard it, they said, This fellow doth not cast out devils, but by Beelzebub the prince of the devils. And Jesus knew their thoughts, and said unto them, Every kingdom divided against itself is brought to desolation; and every city or house divided against itself shall not stand. And if Satan cast out Satan, he is divided against himself; how shall then his kingdom stand? And if I by Beelzebub cast out devils, by whom do your children cast them out? therefore they shall be your judges. But if I cast out devils by the spirit of God, then the kingdom of God is come unto you. . . . The queen of the south shall rise up in the judgment with this generation, and shall condemn it: for she came from the uttermost parts of the earth to hear the wisdom of [King] Solomon; and, behold, a greater than Solomon is here."—Matthew 12: 22-42; Luke 11: 14-31.

Verily, the King was at hand! Messiah the Prince had come, but not in the way that religion desired it. His presence was distinguished by the preaching of the good news of the Kingdom by himself and his disciples, from city to city and from house to house.

CHAPTER XV

BRUISING THE KING'S HEEL

HE seed of the Serpent continually trailed the steps of God's anointed King, Christ Jesus, the foretold Seed of the "woman". At Eden Jehovah God had said that the Serpent should bruise the heel of the woman's Seed. So the Serpent and his seed hissed out enmity against him. They bared their fangs ready to squirt the venom of death through them and into their victim. Their phosphorescent eyes gleamed with maliciousness ready to do him mortal injury even for an innocent word. The Devil's dragon organization in the heavens poised its sixth crowned "head", namely, the demon "prince of Rome", ready with sharpened horn of power to pierce to the death any challenger of Satan's power. The demons that obsessed men and women cried out at Jesus: "Let us alone; what have we to do with thee, thou Jesus of Nazareth? art thou come to destroy us? I know thee who thou art; the Holy One of God." And, on being cast out of their victims, their enmity toward Jesus was not at all lessened.—Luke 4: 33-36; 8: 2, 27-33; Matthew 8: 28-32.

The religious leaders opposed the Kingdom message, and Jesus said to them: "Woe unto you, scribes and Pharisees, hypocrites! for ye shut up the kingdom of heaven against men: for ye neither go in yourselves, neither suffer ye them that are entering to go in. . . . Ye serpents, ye generation of vipers, how can ye escape the damnation of hell?" (Matthew 23:13, 33) Even among the twelve disciples the great Serpent planted one of his seed and entered into his heart. Meaning that one, Jesus said to his apostles: "Have not I chosen you twelve, and one of you is a devil?" "He spake of Judas Iscariot the son of Simon: for he it was that should betray him, being one of the twelve." —John 6:70, 71; 13:2, 27; Luke 22:3.

The time came that Jesus began to tell his apostles privately that he would suffer death at the instance of Satan and his seed. This was after these apostles had come to the firm conviction that Jesus is "the Christ, the Son of the living God". Naturally, then, they were expecting the Kingdom to be set up shortly and all the opposition to be put down. (Luke 19:11) "And he began to teach them, that the Son of man must suffer many things, and be rejected of the elders, and of the chief priests, and scribes, and be killed, and after three days rise again. And he spake that saying openly. And Peter took him, and began to rebuke him [saying, Be it far from thee, Lord: this shall not be unto thee]. But when he had turned about and looked on his disciples, he rebuked Peter, saying, Get thee behind me, Satan: for thou savourest not the things that be of God, but the things that be of

men. And when he had called the people unto
him with his disciples also, he said unto them,
Whosoever will come after me, let him deny
himself, and take up his [stake, *stauros*
(Greek)], and follow me. For whosoever will
save his life shall lose it; but whosoever shall
lose his life for my sake and the gospel's, the
same shall save it." (Mark 8: 31-37; Matthew
16: 21-26) Those desiring to share with him in
the covenant for the Kingdom must, like their
King of kings, die a sacrificial death for his
sake and in the service of the gospel of the
Kingdom.

One's failure to preach the good news of the
Kingdom and of Christ its King deserves one's
rejection for any place with Him in The Theocratic Government. As to this, Jesus said:
"Whosoever therefore shall be ashamed of me
and of my words in this adulterous and sinful
generation, of him also shall the Son of man
be ashamed, when he cometh in the glory of his
Father with the holy angels." Following this,
Jesus said: "There be some of them that stand
here, which shall not taste of death, till they
have seen the kingdom of God come with power"; "till they see the Son of man coming in his
kingdom."–Mark 8:38; 9:1; Matthew 16:27,28.

A week later this prophecy had a symbolic
fulfillment, pointing ahead nineteen centuries
to an actual fulfillment upon a small faithful
remnant. "About an eight days after these
sayings, he took Peter and John and James,
and went up into a mountain to pray. And as he

prayed, the fashion of his countenance was altered, and his raiment was white and glistering. And, behold, there talked with him two men, which were Moses and Elias: who appeared in glory, and spake of his decease which he should accomplish at Jerusalem. But Peter and they that were with him were heavy with sleep: and when they were awake, they saw his glory, and the two men that stood with him. And it came to pass, as they departed from him, Peter said unto Jesus, Master, it is good for us to be here: and let us make three tabernacles; one for thee, and one for Moses, and one for Elias: not knowing what he said. While he thus spake, there came a cloud, and overshadowed them: and they feared as they entered into the cloud. And there came a voice out of the cloud, saying, This is my beloved Son: hear him. And when the voice was past, Jesus was found alone."—Luke 9: 28-36; 2 Peter 1: 16-18.

The Moses and Elijah that the three disciples saw were only visionary. They were not flesh-and-blood men resurrected from the dead, neither were they Moses and Elijah come down from heaven. Moses and Elijah were dead. Jesus said that neither of them was greater than John the Baptist, and that even the least in the kingdom of heaven was greater than John and hence was also greater than Moses and Elijah. After Jesus himself ascended to heaven, the apostle Peter, who was one of those that saw the vision of Jesus' transfiguration, said of King David: "David is not ascended into the heavens," but "he is both dead and buried". Hence Moses and Elijah were in the same condition as David was. Furthermore, as Jesus and those three disciples "came down from the mountain, Jesus charged them, saying, Tell the VISION to no man, until the Son of man be risen again from the dead". He went on to say that the Elijah whom Malachi prophesied to come was not the Elijah in the vision, but was John the Baptist, in a first or miniature fulfillment of Malachi's prophecy.—Matthew 17: 9-13; Acts 2: 29, 34; 12: 9.

Why, then, did those prophets appear in the *vision?* To portray that Christ Jesus in Kingdom glory is the Prophet like unto Moses whom Jehovah said He would raise up to his covenant people, and whom these disciples must hear and obey or else be destroyed. (Peter himself confessed to that fact, at Acts 3: 20-23.) It was to portray also that Jesus at his coming in his kingdom would do a work destructive of religion as Elijah had done in Queen Jezebel's day. Such work the King Christ Jesus accomplishes through his followers then on earth. It was foreshadowed by Elijah's work but is greater than his and greater than what John the Baptist did as a first fulfilment of Elijah.—Acts 7: 37; Malachi 4: 5, 6; Matthew 17: 12.

After this, on his last journey up to Jerusalem, Jesus told the Pharisees that God's kingdom, as represented in Jesus, was among them. As Jesus drew nearer to Jerusalem, Zebedee's wife came with her two sons, James and John, and asked him: "Grant that these my two sons may sit, the one on thy right hand, and the other on the left, in thy kingdom." To this Jesus said: "Ye know not what ye ask: can ye drink of the cup that I drink of? and be baptized with the baptism that I am baptized with?" They said: "We can." Jesus said to them: "Ye shall indeed drink of the cup that I drink of; and with the baptism that I am baptized withal shall ye be baptized: but to sit on my right hand and on my left hand is not mine to give; but it shall be given to them for whom it is prepared"; that is, "prepared of my Father." (Mark 10:35-40; Matthew 20:20-23) This shows that it is presumptuous for any "religious pontiff" in Italy to claim to canonize dead persons to be saints and to put them in the kingdom of heaven. Jehovah God is the Author of the covenant for the Kingdom, and he controls its fulfillment and determines the positions in the Kingdom. As it is written, at 1 Corinthians 12:18: "But now hath God set the members every one of them in the body, as it hath pleased him."

The spring equinox of A.D. 33 passed, and the moon was in its crescent stage when Jesus reached the town of Bethany on the Mount of Olives, east of Jerusalem. The people's expectations concerning him were then running high. Another miniature fulfillment of prophecy must now take place. It appears the day was the tenth of Nisan, the day upon which the Jews in Egypt were under instructions to take the passover lamb into their dwellings to be reserved for the passover supper on Nisan 14. This day Jesus sent disciples ahead to procure the colt of an ass for him to ride upon.

"All this was done, that it might be fulfilled which was spoken by the prophet [Zechariah 9:9], saying, Tell ye the daughter of Sion, Behold, thy King cometh unto thee, meek, and sitting upon an ass, and a colt the foal of an ass. And the disciples went, and did as Jesus commanded them, and brought the ass, and the colt, and put on them their clothes, and they set him thereon." A great multitude of persons of goodwill collected to accompany his ride. "And when he was come nigh, even now at the descent of the mount of Olives, the whole multitude of the disciples began to rejoice and praise God with a loud voice for all the mighty works that they had seen; saying, Blessed be the King that cometh in the name of the Lord: peace in heaven, and glory in the highest." Others that went before and that followed shouted: "Hosanna to the son of David: Blessed is he that cometh in the name of the Lord; Hosanna in the highest." —Matthew 21:1-9; Luke 19:29-38; Psalm 118: 25, 26.

By such conduct these people of good-will were receiving, in a figure, into their homes "the Lamb of God, which taketh away the sin of the world". They "took branches of palm trees, and went forth to meet him, and cried, Hosanna: Blessed is the King of Israel that cometh in the name of the Lord". The religious leaders, however, were sore displeased. "The Pharisees therefore said among themselves, Perceive ye how ye prevail nothing? behold, the world is gone after him." (John 12: 12-19) Jesus went into the court of the temple, where it was customary in days of the typical kingdom for the high priest to anoint the royal heir to be king, at a pillar or tribunal there. (2 Kings 11: 14) Did the religious rulers think to do such a thing to Jesus? Let the Record speak: "And the blind and the lame came to him in the temple; and he healed them. And when the chief priests and scribes saw the wonderful things that he did, and the children crying in the temple, and saying, Hosanna to the son of David; they were sore displeased, and said unto him, Hearest thou what these say?" And some of the Pharisees said: "Master, rebuke thy disciples." Jesus let these coronation shouts continue, because it fulfilled prophecy and was also prophetic of events in our day. He said: "Yea; have ye never read, Out of the mouth of babes and sucklings thou hast perfected praise?" Then he added: "I tell you that, if these should hold their peace, the stones would immediately cry out."—Matthew 21: 14-16; Luke 19: 39, 40.

Being rejected, like a headstone discarded by temple builders, Jesus went back to Bethany. Next day he returned to Jerusalem. He "went into the temple, and began to cast out them that sold and bought in the temple, and overthrew the tables of the money-changers, and the seats of them that sold doves; and would not suffer that any man should carry any vessel through the temple. And he taught, saying unto them, Is it not written, My house shall be called of all nations the house of prayer? but ye have made it a den of thieves. And the scribes and chief priests heard it, and sought how they might destroy him: for they feared him, because all the people was astonished at his doctrine." (Mark 11:11-18) Jesus' action here was a partial fulfillment of Malachi's prophecy that Jehovah's "messenger of the covenant" should come to the temple to cleanse it. What Jesus did also illustrated how Malachi 3:1-4 would be finally fulfilled in completion in our generation.

All faithful Jews contributed a tax to the support of the temple. (Matthew 17:24-27; Nehemiah 10:32) As a taxpayer Jesus used the temple courts in which to teach. Incensed at his educational activities, the chief priests and elders challenged his work.

"By what authority doest thou these things? and who gave thee this authority?" Jesus did not receive it of men; no more than did John the Baptist. If Jesus were to say he had authority from heaven, the religionists would not believe him and stop interfering. They thought themselves to be children of the kingdom, that is, in line for and sure of a place in it; but Jesus took down their pride, saying: "The publicans and the harlots go into the kingdom of God before you," because of repentance and belief. Then he exposed their murderous antichrist intentions by giving the parable of the vineyard, the laborers of which slew the owner's son and heir but were in turn themselves destroyed, permitting the vineyard to be let out to others. Jesus at once made the parable fit, saying: "Did ye never read in the scriptures [Psalm 118: 22, 23], *The stone which the builders rejected, the same is become the head of the corner: this is the Lord's doing, and it is marvellous in our eyes?* Therefore say I unto you, The kingdom of God shall be taken from you, and given to a nation bringing forth the fruits thereof. And whosoever shall fall on this stone shall be broken: but on whomsoever it shall fall, it will grind him to powder." Only their fear of the men of good-will toward Jesus kept the chief priests and Pharisees from assaulting him.—Matthew 21: 23-44.

Along came those hyphenated political Jews, the Herodians. Their sly efforts to bring Jesus into conflict with the Roman state on the tax question were balked by Jesus' comment on a Roman *denarius* or penny: "Render therefore unto Cæsar the things which are Cæsar's; and unto God the things that are God's." (Matthew 22: 16-21) That is to say, all laws of Caesar or laws of the political state are to be obeyed by Christ's followers, except where they take away from or encroach upon the obedience to the Most High God. Then the disciples of Christ must render obedience and service to God rather than to Caesar or any other men.—Acts 5: 29; 4: 19, 20.

Jerusalem's judgment was on! The evidence showed that she, as standing for the whole Jewish people under their religious heads, had failed to discern and know that this was the time of God's visitation to her by means of his beloved Son. Therefore she and her temple or house bearing God's name were doomed. Before a large audience Jesus said: "O Jerusalem, Jerusalem, thou that killest the prophets, and stonest them which are sent unto thee, how often would I have gathered thy children together, even as a hen gathereth her chickens under her wings, and ye would not! Behold, your house is left unto you desolate. For I say unto you, Ye shall not see me henceforth, till ye shall say, Blessed is he that cometh in the name of the Lord." (Matthew 23: 37-39; Luke 19: 44) Henceforth no Jew could expect to discern Jesus as Messiah unless he accepted and hailed him as the One sent with authority from Jehovah God.

Shortly thereafter Jesus predicted that such literal house or temple would suffer the same fate of destruction as the temple built by Solomon, due to its defilement by religion. Certain of his disciples privately asked him: "Tell us, when shall these things be? and what shall be the sign of thy coming, and of the end of the world?" Jesus gave a long-range prophecy that reaches to our very day. He pointed ahead to that which was foreshadowed by the reducing of Jerusalem's temple to a rubble heap. What? God's destruction in our day of the world-wide religious organization. Having related all the visible signs that would appear to our sight, Jesus said, really for our benefit now: "So ye in like manner, when ye shall see these things come to pass, know that it is nigh, even at the doors." "So likewise ye, when ye see these things come to pass, know ye that the kingdom of God is nigh at hand." Then to the generation witnessing these Kingdom signs he issued the warning against becoming weighted down and preoccupied by the things of this world, saying: "This generation shall not pass away, till all be fulfilled. Heaven and earth shall pass away: but my words shall not pass away."—Matthew 24; Mark 13; Luke 21.

THE SERPENT STRIKES

Meantime, in the religious camp, under guidance of the wily Serpent, the conspiracy is developing to bring about Jesus' death while at Jerusalem. Who comes there? He answers to the name of Judas Iscariot. He identifies himself as one of Jesus' own disciples. He has lifted up his heel against his Master. He has come to the religionists for a deal, to betray Jesus into their hands when the people could not interfere. They strike a bargain with Judas for thirty pieces of silver, the price usually offered to buy an adult slave. They do not look up Zechariah 11:12, 13, to notice that their infamous deal was foreseen and foretold by the Lord God. Their foul opportunity comes, too, as foretold, two days later, on passover night, Nisan 14, the time when the passover lamb must be slain in Jerusalem and eaten in the houses.

Nisan 14 began at sundown, and extended over to the following sunset. The moon was at its full that night when Jesus met with his disciples in an upper room in Jerusalem to celebrate the passover as commanded by Jehovah's law through Moses. Therefore the death of the lamb they ate preceded by but some hours on the same day the death of the antitypical Lamb. He is "Christ our passover". (1 Corinthians 5: 7) While the passover meal was in progress, Jesus let Judas know that *he* knew that one's plans to betray him. Then he dismissed Judas from their midst. With Judas gone, Jesus now closed the passover meal and began a new observance for his disciples. By it he disclosed these facts to them, namely: Jehovah God had arranged for him to have a body of followers who should pour out their lives in sacrificial death as Jesus was doing. In such manner they would be joined with him in his death. Furthermore, his own death in perfect integrity toward God not only would vindicate Jehovah's name, but would also provide a sacrifice for the sins of his many future believers. It would be the basis for the making of a new and better covenant between Jehovah God and his body members. Thereby Jesus acted as the Mediator greater than Moses in effecting this new covenant. The Scripture Record of this reads:

"And as they were eating, Jesus took bread, and blessed, and brake it; and he gave to the disciples, and said, Take, eat; this is my body. And he took a cup, and gave thanks, and gave to them, saying, Drink ye all of it; for this is my blood of the covenant, which is poured out for many unto remission of sins. But I say unto you, I shall not drink henceforth of this fruit of the vine, until that day when I drink it new with you in my Father's kingdom." (Matthew 26: 26-29, *Am. Stan. Ver.*) Here was the assurance that, having faithfully participated in his death, they would participate with him in the kingdom of God.—2 Timothy 2: 11, 12.

The covenant for the Kingdom then came under discussion on this wise: "There was also a contention among them, which of them should be thought the greatest. And he said to them, 'The kings of the nations exercise dominion over them; and those having authority over them are styled Benefactors. But you must not be so; but let the greatest among you become as the least, and the governor as he who serves. For who is greater, he who reclines, or he who serves? Is not he who reclines? but I am among you as he who serves. And you are they who have continued with me in my trials. And I covenant for you, even as my Father has covenanted for me, a kingdom, that you may eat and drink at my table in my kingdom, and sit on thrones, judging the twelve tribes of Israel." (Luke 22: 24-30, *The Emphatic Diaglott*) This saying could tie up in the disciples' minds with his earlier words: "But rather seek ye the kingdom of God; and all these things shall be added unto you. Fear not, little flock; for it is your Father's good pleasure to give you the kingdom." (Luke 12: 31, 32) It was clear-cut assurance that Jesus was not to be alone in the covenant for the Kingdom nor alone in the "kingdom of heaven". The faithful members of his "body" or "little flock" of followers must also be brought into the covenant for the Kingdom and finally perfected in the Kingdom itself.

In harmony with the foregoing, Jesus closed his words of comfort to his disciples with prayer to Jehovah God. In the prayer he said: "And the glory which thou gavest me I have given them; that they may be one, even as we are one: I in them, and thou in me, that they may be made perfect in one; and that the world may know that thou hast sent me, and hast loved them, as thou hast loved me. Father, I will that they also, whom thou hast given me, be with me where I am; that they may behold my glory, which thou hast given me: for thou lovedst me before the foundation of the world." (John 17: 22-24) After now singing a song, Jesus and his eleven faithful apostles went forth through the moonlit night to the garden of Gethsemane. A season of agonizing prayer there, and then came his arrest by an armed band whom Judas Iscariot led thither.

The enemies' hour had arrived. Amid the darkness the head of the Serpent was reared to strike the King in the heel. "Then Jesus said unto the chief priests, and captains of the temple, and the elders, which were come to him, Be ye come out, as against a thief, with swords and staves? When I was daily with you in the tem-

ple, ye stretched forth no hands against me: but
this is your hour, and the power of darkness."
—Luke 22:52, 53.

Jesus was not permitting any man to take his
life from him; he was laying it down of himself
voluntarily. He could have called to his rescue
"more than twelve legions of angels", but he
chose to drink the cup of suffering, reproach
and death which his Father had poured for
him. He asked that his disciples be let go un-
molested; and these, in a spasm of fear, fled
from him, as prophecy had foretold. (Matthew
26:51-56) Forsaken by all on earth, he was determined to hold fast his integrity toward the
Universal Sovereign, Jehovah God, by faultless
obedience and submission to the divine will.
—John 16:32; 10:17, 18.

Satan the Serpent and his chief earthly seed,
the religionists, were engineering a speedy violent death to the Seed of God's *woman*. That
becomes manifest from the first court before
which Jesus was brought and tried, a religious
court, the Jewish Sanhedrin. Out of respect to
the father-in-law of the high priest, the gang of
religious puppets led Jesus first to Annas for a
preliminary hearing and smiting. Then they
put him on the stand before the high priest,
Caiaphas, presiding over an illegal meeting of
the Sanhedrin by night. They failed to get Jesus to testify against himself, and had to rely
upon their own hired false witnesses. "And the
high priest answered and said unto him, I ad-
jure thee by the living God, that thou tell us

whether thou be the Christ, the Son of God."
Fearless, and with no effort to shield himself
from any misconstruing of his words by the
presiding judge and court, Jesus let them have
the truth: "I am: and ye shall see the Son of
man sitting on the right hand of power, and
coming in the clouds of heaven." For the effect's
sake, "then the high priest rent his clothes, saying, He hath spoken blasphemy; what further
need have we of witnesses? behold, now ye have
heard his blasphemy. What think ye?" "They
answered and said, He is guilty of death. Then
did they spit in his face, and buffeted him; and
others smote him with the palms of their hands,
saying, Prophesy unto us, thou Christ, Who is
he that smote thee?" Coupled with this mock
trial, Peter outside in the palace courtyard denied three times this One undergoing trial.
—Mark 14:53-72; John 18:13-24; Matthew
26:57-75.

It was piously thought well to camouflage
over that Jesus was being done to death out of
a religious grudge and religious intolerance;
hence a political color must be given to the
reasons for demanding the death of the "Lamb
of God". Accordingly, having ratified their sentence of death against him at another meeting
at daybreak, the religious authorities haled Jesus before the political ruler of Judea, Governor Pontius Pilate. The closely watching and
inwardly upset Judas Iscariot, seeing in actuality to what his perfidy had led, flung back his
thirty pieces of silver to those that hired him,

declaring that the man he betrayed was not an impostor and blasphemer. Then this "son of perdition" hanged himself, like his early prototype, David's unfaithful counselor Ahithophel. When the rope broke, he dashed onto the rocks below. (Matthew 27:3-10; Acts 1:16-19) "When the morning was come, all the chief priests and elders of the people took counsel against Jesus to put him to death: and when they had bound him, they led him away, and delivered him to Pontius Pilate the governor."—Matthew 27:1, 2; Mark 15:1; Luke 22:66-71.

Fearing to sustain religious defilement, Jesus' captors would not go into the judgment hall of the Gentile governor, and Pilate came out to them. "What accusation bring ye against this man?" he asked. The religionists, feeling too holy to make a mistake and to sin, answered: "If he were not a malefactor, we would not have delivered him up unto thee." Judging the case not to be within his jurisdiction, Pilate replied: "Take ye him, and judge him according to your law." The religionists had their answer: "It is not lawful for us to put any man to death"; "that the saying of Jesus might be fulfilled, which he spake, signifying what death he should die." Not long thereafter they did not let such an excuse keep them from stoning Stephen to death, under the supervision of Saul of Tarsus. (Acts 7:57-60) They were hypocritical, intent on framing Jesus as a political offender, all because of the kingdom of God. They accused Jesus, saying: "We found this fellow perverting

the nation, and forbidding to give tribute to
Cæsar, saying that he himself is Christ a King."
—John 18: 28-32; Luke 23: 1, 2.

Now, for his faithfulness, there came to Jesus
the opportunity to reach the climax of his witness to the universal sovereignty of Jehovah
God before the highest authority of the land,
the representative of Tiberius Caesar, emperor
of Rome. Pilate called Jesus into the judgment
hall for private questioning and asked: "Art
thou the King of the Jews?" Jesus asked whether this was a mere legal question or whether
Pilate was asking out of sincere interest for
personal guidance: "Sayest thou this thing of
thyself, or did others tell it thee of me?" Pilate
was no Jew looking for a Messiah, and said:
"Am I a Jew? Thine own nation and the chief
priests have delivered thee unto me: what hast
thou done?" Jesus then testified: "My kingdom
is not of this world [*kosmos*]: if my kingdom
were of this world, then would my servants
fight, that I should not be delivered to the Jews:
but now is my kingdom not from hence." Pilate
asked: "Art thou a king then?" Jesus, now
pointing to his chief and primary mission in
coming down from heaven to earth, said: "Thou
sayest that I am a king. To this end was I born,
and for this cause came I into the world, that I
should bear witness unto the truth. Every one
that is of the truth heareth my voice." Was it
sarcasm when Pilate commented: "What is
truth?" But even what he had heard from Jesus'

own lips did not convince him that Jesus was
seditious against the political state.

Trying to shift the responsibility, Pilate sent
Jesus, because a Galilean, over to King Herod,
down on a visit from Galilee. Jesus not satisfy-
ing the king's curiosity, Herod mocked Jesus'
royal claims and sent him back to the governor.
Pilate was minded to give Jesus the benefit of
his usual custom to release a prisoner at the
Jews' passover time, but the Jews cried out a
preference for the release of the notorious rob-
ber Barabbas. Pilate's soldiers then scourged
Jesus and made sport of his kingship. In a purple robe and with a crown of thorns Jesus was
exhibited to the people by Pilate as being found

guiltless, and Pilate said: "Behold the man!" But howls of "Stake him, stake him!"* came from the chief priests and officers. Pilate told them to do it themselves, for he found no guilt in Jesus. When the Jews retorted that even according to their own law Jesus ought to die "because he made himself the Son of God", Pilate was more afraid. Again he privately questioned Jesus: "Whence art thou?" Getting no answer, Pilate said: "Speakest thou not unto me? knowest thou not that I have power to [stake] thee, and have power to release thee?" Thereupon Jesus opened his mouth in support of the universal sovereignty and supreme power of the great Theocrat Jehovah, saying: "Thou couldest have no power at all against me, except it were given thee from above: therefore he that delivered me unto thee hath the greater sin."—John 19: 1-12.

The political state did not want to punish Jesus, but the religionists would not lift their pressure off the state. At Pilate's efforts to release the victim of religious intolerance the Jews cried out, saying, "If thou let this man go, thou art not Cæsar's friend: whosoever maketh himself a king, speaketh against Cæsar." It was going on toward high noon, the sixth hour of daylight, when Pilate made an appeal to their sense of patriotism, saying of Jesus: "Behold your King!" Up went yells: "Away with him, away with him, [stake] him." Pilate cried back:

* The Greek word here is *staúrooson*, meaning, *Put on a stake.*

"Shall I [stake] your King?" It is almost unbelievable that the chief priests, supposed to be serving Jehovah God, should be the ones to answer Pilate: "We have no king but Cæsar." The chief priests themselves had spoken. That was final. A riot was about to break forth, inflamed by the religious leaders. Pilate, under unyielding pressure, surrendered up Jesus to their demands. Shortly, Jesus, bearing a stake, was being led out of Jerusalem to a place, not a "green hill", but a location called "the place of a skull", *Golgotha* in Hebrew and *Calvary* in Latin. There they nailed Jesus to the stake between criminals.

The charge which Pilate caused to be posted in writing up above Jesus on the stake should have reminded the religionists that they were rejecting their King. It read: "This is the King of the Jews." Hardened in their course, the chief priests objected to the manner of stating the charge, but Pilate let it remain, saying: "What I have written I have written."—John 19:13-22; Luke 23:38.

Not knowing that "thus it behoved Christ to suffer, and to rise from the dead the third day", one of the malefactors impaled alongside Jesus cried out: "If thou be Christ, save thyself and us." He was imitating the near-by chief priests, scribes and elders, who said: "He saved others; himself he cannot save. If he be the King of Israel, let him now come down from the [stake], and we will believe him. He trusted in God; let him deliver him now, if he will have him: for he said, I am the Son of God." But Jesus had entered into a covenant of sacrifice with his God. He was called to be a great High Priest and he refused to break his covenant and withdraw the priestly sacrifice. He maintained his integrity in office.

An honest man now spoke up as the second malefactor answered the first: "Dost not thou fear God, seeing thou art in the same condemnation? And we indeed justly; for we receive the due reward of our deeds: but this man hath done nothing amiss." Then to Jesus he said: "Lord, remember me when thou comest into thy kingdom." This malefactor must have expected Jesus to come into his kingdom only by a resurrection of the dead, because all Jews of goodwill, Jesus' apostles included, expected the kingdom to be set up on earth in the land of Israel. (Acts 1: 1-6) The malefactor was not asking to be taken to heaven, but was asking for a resurrection from the dead when Messiah Christ should reign over the earth.

"And he said unto him—Verily I say unto thee this day: With me shalt thou be in Paradise." (Rotherham's *The Emphasized Bible*) The misplacing of a comma by translators to after the word *thee* and before the word *Today* or *This day* has caused the religious clergy to argue that Jesus went to heaven that day and took the unbaptized, unregenerated malefactor with him to heaven. But in the historian Luke's original record in Greek, and in the early copies of his record, there were no punctuation marks such as commas, periods, etc. These were inserted by later printers and translators according to the general religious understanding, as in the *King James Version* and *Douay Version* renderings of the Bible. Jesus did not go to Paradise that day of his death. Paradise is yet to be restored to this earth under the established kingdom of God.

Jesus went to "hell" (the grave or *Hades*), and the malefactor went to "hell" with Jesus. Jesus did not expect to get out of hell until the third day. The malefactor is yet in hell awaiting to be remembered by Jesus in His kingdom and to be awakened from the dead when the Kingdom shall have restored Paradise to this earth. Then the question will have to be decided by the awakened malefactor in Paradise, Will you continue with or on the side of Jesus? If he does then remain *with* Jesus as Rightful King, it will mean everlasting life on earth for such erstwhile malefactor, through the sacrifice of the One alongside of whom he died.–Luke 23: 39-43.

Unnatural darkness settled over the land from noontide on. At about 3 p.m. Jesus, on the stake, commended all to his Father Jehovah and died, having finished his earthly work with integrity. A mighty earthquake, and a rending in twain of the temple's inner veil, signalized that The King was dead. The Serpent had bruised him as at the heel. Messiah the Prince was "cut off" from earthly life, although without having forfeited his right to earthly life. Long previous to this the angel Gabriel told Daniel of the seven weeks followed by sixty-two weeks "unto the anointed one, the prince", and that "after the threescore and two weeks shall the anointed one be cut off, and shall have nothing". (Daniel 9: 25, 26, *Am. Stan. Ver.*) The seventieth week of years was now half past, it having begun in the autumn of A.D. 29, when Jesus was immersed and anointed; and the time was now the spring of A.D. 33.

By his own sacrifice of perfect humanity Christ Jesus provided the true redeeming sacrifice and oblation for sin of humankind, thus making the typical sacrifice of animals by the Jews no longer fitting nor of effect with God. This occurring in the midst of the seventieth week of years, this was what Gabriel foretold, saying of Messiah the Prince, God's Messenger of the covenant: "And he shall make a firm covenant with many for one week: and in the midst of the week he shall cause the sacrifice and the oblation to cease." (Daniel 9: 27, *Am. Stan. Ver.*; Hebrews 10: 1-9) This was not what Satan the Serpent intended by bruising the heel of the royal Seed of God's "woman". That the merit of his ransom sacrifice might be presented to God in heaven in behalf of humankind, and also that the Seed might bruise the Serpent's head at the end of this world, the heel wound must be and was healed.

CHAPTER XVI

KEYS OF THE KINGDOM

AT THE time foreordained in Jehovah's irresistible purpose his King died, "faithful unto death" and not having compromised with the Devil or his seed or with religion. The day was the passover day, Nisan 14. Now Jehovah's law through Moses must be carried out, that if a man "be put to death, and thou hang him on a tree: his body shall not remain all night upon the tree, but thou shalt in any wise bury him that day; (for he that is hanged is accursed of God;) that thy land be not defiled, which the LORD thy God giveth thee for an inheritance". (Deuteronomy 21: 22, 23) That same day, therefore, "they took him down from the tree, and laid him in a sepulchre." (Acts 13: 29) Why, though, was Jesus hanged upon a tree and thereby made a curse? In order to pay the ransom for humankind, only the death of a perfect man, the equal of Adam in Eden, was required (Deuteronomy 19: 21); and why, then, was Jesus put to such a painful, reproachful death like a common slave? The apostle Paul answers: "Christ hath redeemed us from the curse of the law, being made a curse for us: for it is written, Cursed is every one that hangeth on a tree." —Galatians 3: 13.

The law covenant was made with the nation of Israel. It was added to the Abrahamic covenant which promised the Seed of blessing, and which Abrahamic covenant was a covenant pertaining to the Kingdom. The Israelites, by coming into the law covenant with God Jehovah, became a Theocratic nation and came into line for the Kingdom with Christ Jesus, who is the Seed of Abraham. (Galatians 3: 15-19) Thereby the nation of Israel came under a special responsibility before Jehovah God, one not shared by any of the Gentile nations. The Gentile peoples, by reason of inheriting sin and death, were indeed under condemnation before God. The Jews, however, by failing to confirm and do all the words of the law covenant and by thus failing as a Theocratic nation and rejecting the rightful King, came under Jehovah's curse. (Deuteronomy 27: 26) It therefore became needful for Christ the Redeemer to be made a curse for them in order to lift that disabling curse from all those Jews that should accept him as their Savior. Such curse did not stand in the way of believing Gentiles.—Galatians 3: 10.

Nisan 15, the day after the passover, was a twofold sabbath, it being both the weekly or seventh-day sabbath and also the sabbath day that was ordained to follow on the next day after passover. That sabbath day Jesus was resting in *hell* or the grave. (Isaiah 53: 9) As to this state of God's Holy One, Psalm 16: 10, 11 foretold: "For thou wilt not leave my soul in hell; neither wilt thou suffer thine Holy One to see corruption. Thou wilt shew me the path of life." Nisan 16, the day following the sabbath after the passover, was the time that God's law covenant appointed for the Levite priest to offer at the temple the firstfruits of their grain harvest. This day, the third day from Jesus' death and burial, was the due time for Psalm 16:10, 11 to be fulfilled toward him; and it was. God then healed the wound inflicted by the Serpent upon the heel of the Seed of his "woman" by raising Jesus from the dead.

Peter saw Jesus after His resurrection from the dead and said: "Whom God hath raised up, having loosed the pains of death: because it was not possible that he should be holden of it. For David speaketh concerning him, *I foresaw the Lord always before my face, . . . thou wilt not leave my soul in hell, neither wilt thou suffer thine Holy One to see corruption. . . .* Men and brethren, let me freely speak unto you of the patriarch David, that he is both dead and buried, and his sepulchre is with us unto this day. Therefore being a prophet, and knowing that God had sworn with an oath to him, that of the fruit of his loins, according to the flesh, he would raise up Christ to sit on his throne; he seeing this before spake of the resurrection of Christ, that his soul was not left in hell, neither his flesh did see corruption. This Jesus hath God raised up, whereof we all are witnesses. . . . For David is not ascended into the heavens."—Acts 2:23-34.

Also the apostle Paul testifies: "Christ died for our sins according to the scriptures; and that he was buried, and that he rose again the third day according to the scriptures; . . . now is Christ risen from the dead, and become the firstfruits of them that slept." (1 Corinthians 15:3, 4, 20) "And he is the head of the body, the church: who is the beginning, the firstborn from the dead; that in all things he might have the pre-eminence." (Colossians 1:18) Christ Jesus was therefore the first one in universal history to be raised from the dead to life everlasting. His reviving was the beginning of "the first resurrection", in which all his faithful body of followers must share.—Revelation 1:5; 20:6.

At Jordan river, after immersion, Jesus was begotten of God's spirit to be a "new creature", with a heavenly inheritance. At death he laid aside the human organism in which he ministered as a new creature for three and a half years; and in his resurrection he was no more human. He was raised as a spirit creature, one such both in organism and in right to spirit life in heaven. Peter, who saw His manifestations after being resurrected, testifies: "Christ also suffered for sins once, the righteous for the unrighteous, that he might bring us to God; being PUT TO DEATH IN THE FLESH, BUT MADE ALIVE IN THE SPIRIT." (1 Peter 3:18, *Am. Stan. Ver.*) The "body" of his faithful followers are destined to take part in the "first resurrection", or "his resurrection"; and as to the resurrection of such church-body it is written: "It is sown a

natural body; it is raised a spiritual body."
(1 Corinthians 15:44) Jesus was raised to immortality, beyond the power of death to touch
him again, and never can die for sins again.
—Romans 6:9, 10.

Therefore the bodies in which Jesus manifested himself to his disciples after his return
to life were not the body in which he was nailed
to the tree. They were merely materialized for
the occasion, resembling on one or two occasions the body in which he died, but on the majority of occasions being unrecognizable by his
most intimate disciples. The body which was
put in the sepulcher was disposed of without
corruption according to God's prophecy and by
his almighty power. Years after, when the
resurrected Jesus appeared to Saul of Tarsus
without a body of flesh to veil his heavenly
glory, that future apostle Paul was smitten
blind. His sight was restored three days later
by a miracle.—Acts 9:3-18.

When Jehovah raised his beloved Son from
death to life immortal, then in the completest
sense He begot him by His spirit by means of
which spirit he resurrected him. Says the apostle Paul: "We declare unto you glad tidings,
how that the promise which was made unto the
fathers, God hath fulfilled the same unto us
their children, in that he hath raised up Jesus
again; as it is also written in the second psalm,
Thou art my Son, this day have I begotten thee.
And as concerning that he raised him up from
the dead, now no more to return to corruption,

he said on this wise, *I will give you the sure mercies of David*."—Acts 13:32-34; Isaiah 55:3.

By virtue of Jesus' immortal life thenceforth, his resurrection was a raising of him to the priesthood after Melchizedek's order in a lasting way. This was due to the "oath by him that saith of him, *The Lord* [*Jehovah*] *sware and will not repent himself, Thou art a priest for ever*); by so much also hath Jesus become the surety of a better covenant. . . . he, because he abideth for ever, hath his priesthood unchangeable. Wherefore also he is able to save to the uttermost them that draw near unto God through him, seeing he ever liveth to make intercession for them. For such a high priest became us, holy, guileless, undefiled, separated from sinners, and made higher than the heavens; . . . a Son, perfected for evermore." (Hebrews 7:21-28, *Am. Stan. Ver.*) Like Melchizedek, but only greater than him, Jesus is a "priest upon his throne", and he says: "I am he that liveth, and was dead; and, behold, I am alive for evermore, Amen; and have the keys of hell and of death."—Zechariah 6:12, 13; Revelation 1:13-18.

On his resurrection day Jesus did not ascend to heaven, nor for forty days therefrom. (John 20:17) "God raised him from the dead: and he was seen many days of them which came up with him from Galilee to Jerusalem, who are his witnesses unto the people." "Until the day in which he was taken up, after that he through the holy [spirit] had given commandments unto the apostles whom he had chosen: to whom also he shewed himself alive after his passion by many infallible proofs, being seen of them forty days, and speaking of the things pertaining to the kingdom of God." (Acts 13:30, 31; 1:2, 3) Once, on his resurrection day, he breathed upon his disciples and said to them, "Receive ye the holy [spirit]." But that was merely a preliminary notice of what they were to receive in due time, for he told them beforehand: "It is expedient for you that I go away: for if I go not away, the Comforter will not come unto you; but if I depart, I will send him unto you." (John 20:22; 16:7) He, "being assembled together with them, commanded them that they should not depart from Jerusalem, but wait for the promise of the Father, which, saith he, ye have heard of me. For John truly baptized with water; but ye shall be baptized with the holy [spirit] not many days hence." —Acts 1:4, 5.

The disciples still did not understand, not having received the baptism of the holy spirit. They thought that the Kingdom was now to be re-established in the earthly nation of Israel. "When they therefore were come together, they asked of him, saying, Lord, wilt thou at this time restore again the kingdom to Israel? And he said unto them, It is not for you to know the times or the seasons, which the Father hath put in his own power. But ye shall receive power, after that the holy [spirit] is come upon you: and ye shall be witnesses unto me both in Jerusalem, and in all Judæa, and in Samaria, and unto the uttermost part of the earth." This was a plain statement that a world-wide witness work was to follow, under the power of God's holy spirit or active force. "And when he had spoken these things, while they beheld, he was taken up; and a cloud received him out of their sight. And while they looked stedfastly toward heaven as he went up, behold, two men stood by them in white apparel; which also said, Ye men of Galilee, why stand ye gazing up into heaven? this same Jesus, which is taken up from you into heaven, shall so come in like manner as ye have seen him go into heaven." (Acts 1:6-11) He would come again, not in a fleshly body such as he had before disappearing from their sight behind a cloud, but "in like *manner*", quietly and unobserved by the world, and discerned at first only by his disciples.—John 14:19.

When the resurrected King finally ascended to heaven into the presence of God to present the merit or redemptive value of his human sacrifice, did he then set up the Kingdom and begin its active operation? No; it was not Jehovah's due time. The glorified Jesus must wait until the end of the "times of the Gentiles", in A.D. 1914. King David of old acknowledged the coming Seed of God's "woman" as *My Lord,* and said prophetically: "Jehovah saith unto my Lord, Sit thou at my right hand, until I make thine enemies thy footstool. Jehovah hath sworn, and will not repent: Thou art a priest for ever after the order of Melchizedek." (Psalm

110: 1, 4, *Am. Stan. Ver.*) Under inspiration the apostle Paul applies this Psalm 110 to Jesus and says: "But he, having offered one enduring sacrifice on behalf of sins, sat down at the right hand of God; henceforth WAITING till his enemies may be placed underneath his feet." (Hebrews 10:12, 13, *The Emphatic Diaglott*) Religious clergymen have denied these words and have said, and continue to say, that Jesus did establish his kingdom nineteen centuries ago. They say it was a so-called "kingdom of grace" and that his kingdom is his "rule in the hearts of men", and they misinterpret Romans 14:17 and 1 Corinthians 4:20. Never was the falsity of such a religious interpretation more visible than in the conditions and events of this twentieth century, even within so-called "Christendom".

In A.D. 33, Nisan 16 was the day on which the Jewish high priest offered the firstfruits of the grain harvest at the temple and also the day when Jesus was raised to "become the firstfruits of them that slept". It was the day when fifty days must begin counting to the feast of weeks or Pentecost, the name *Pentecost* meaning *fiftieth day*. On Pentecost the Jewish high priest at the temple offered a second firstfruits, two wave loaves of leavened wheat bread from the first-ripe wheat of the harvest. (Exodus 34:22) What, like unto such, did the glorified High Priest in heaven, Christ Jesus, do on that same Pentecostal day? It should be something that was typified or foreshadowed by the offer-

ing of those two leavened wave loaves to the
Lord God. Note the Record on what happened:

"And when the day of Pentecost was fully
come, they were all with one accord in one
place. And suddenly there came a sound from
heaven as of a rushing mighty wind, and it
filled all the house where they were sitting. And
there appeared unto them cloven tongues like
as of fire, and it sat upon each of them. And.
they were all filled with the holy [spirit], and
began to speak with other tongues, as the spirit
gave them utterance."—Acts 2:1-5.

This was no baptism of fire. The baptism of
fiery destruction was reserved for the enemies
of Jehovah God that rejected his Messianic
King. This was a baptism of the holy spirit.
When Jesus was thus baptized, this invisible
active force of Jehovah God was manifested under the emblem of an innocent dove, but it was
no baptism with a dove. On the day of Pentecost
the invisible active force of Jehovah God was
manifested as fiery tongues upon the head of
those baptized with the spirit. In Jesus' case,
the spirit's descent upon him was evidence that
his consecration to God was accepted, that he
was taken into a covenant of sacrifice as the
ransom for sinful humankind, and that he was
anointed or commissioned to the service of the
"kingdom of heaven". The spirit's outpouring
at Pentecost was evidence that Jesus had appeared in the presence of God in behalf of his
faithful disciples, about 120 of whom were gathered with one accord at one place in Jerusalem.

(Acts 1:15) It was evidence that the merit of his sacrifice had been offered and was accepted by God and applied in their behalf; and that they were taken into the covenant for the Kingdom as spiritual children of God and were anointed unto Kingdom service.—Hebrews 9:24-26.

This was foreshadowed in the Pentecostal type of the two loaves of wheat firstfruits: "And the priest shall wave [the sacrifices] with the bread of the firstfruits for a wave offering before the LORD, with the two lambs: they shall be holy to the LORD for the priest." (Leviticus 23:20) Both wave loaves of the firstfruits of the wheat harvest were holy to Jehovah God, and neither one of the loaves was rejected or thrown away. Those two loaves pictured the disciples of Jesus as being waved or presented by the High Priest Christ Jesus before Jehovah God as holy unto Him. The fact that both wheat loaves were leavened pictured that these disciples were naturally, by birth inheritance, sinful creatures; but the merit of Jesus Christ which was presented in their behalf justified them in the sight of God and thus they were "holy" unto Him.

The loaves were two in number. This showed that, unlike the barley firstfruits offered on Nisan 16, which pictured Christ Jesus alone, the wave loaves pictured more than one person and that this second firstfruits was made up of many, those who should become the members of Christ's "body". It further showed that there should be two classes in this "firstfruits" company, namely, (1) a remnant of Christian believers from among the natural Jews; and (2) the remainder of body members that are taken from among the non-Jews or "Gentiles". Not all the ones composing this "firstfruits" class were offered up or waved before the Lord on the day of Pentecost, but the beginning of the offering of them up was then made. The representative or foundation members thereof, namely, the apostles of Jesus Christ, were presented at Pentecost. Those thus offered up are not waved or presented as human creatures, but as spirit-begotten children of God. To this effect it is written: "Of his own will begat he us with the word of truth, that we should be a kind of FIRSTFRUITS of his creatures." (James 1:18) "These were redeemed from among men, being the firstfruits unto God and to the Lamb [the High Priest Christ Jesus]."—Revelation 14:4.

On that very day of Pentecost Jehovah God interpreted this event as an opening or miniature fulfillment of the prophecy of Joel 2:28-32. Jehovah had his inspired mouthpiece rise and say: "This is that which was spoken by the prophet Joel: *And it shall come to pass in the last days, saith God, I will pour out of my spirit upon all flesh: and your sons and your daughters shall prophesy, and your young men shall see visions, and your old men shall dream dreams: and on my servants and on my handmaidens I will pour out, in those days, of my spirit; and they shall prophesy: and I will shew wonders in heaven above, and signs in the earth beneath; blood, and fire, and vapour of smoke: the sun shall be turned into darkness, and the moon into blood, before that great and notable day of the Lord come: and it shall come to pass, that whosoever shall call on the name of the Lord [Jehovah] shall be saved."* (Acts 2: 16-21) Not all human flesh was baptized with the holy spirit that day of Pentecost nor has *all flesh* received the outpouring of the spirit during the nineteen centuries since. Only Jehovah God's "servants" and "handmaidens" have had the spirit poured out upon them, to show that *all flesh* means all faithful, consecrated spirit-begotten ones in the flesh. The fact, also, that the other spectacular things named in the prophecy, such as blood, smoke, darkness, did not come to pass at that Pentecost proves that the manifestation back there was merely a partial or miniature fulfillment of the prophecy, and that the complete and grand-scale fulfillment must come to pass in these "last days", as Peter said.

Many Jews from inside and outside of the Roman Empire were in Jerusalem at that time for the celebration of the "feast of weeks" or Pentecost, and they heard about this outpouring of God's spirit. "And there were dwelling at Jerusalem Jews, devout men, out of every nation under heaven. Now when this was noised abroad, the multitude came together, and were confounded, because that every man heard them speak in his own language. And they were all

amazed and marvelled, saying one to another,
Behold, are not all these which speak Gali-
læans? and how hear we every man in our own
tongue, wherein we were born? Parthians, and
Medes, and Elamites, and the dwellers in Mesopotamia, and in Judæa, and Cappadocia, in Pon-
tus, and Asia, Phrygia, and Pamphylia, in
Egypt, and in the parts of Libya about Cyrene,
and strangers of Rome, Jews and proselytes,
Cretes and Arabians, we do hear them speak in
our tongues the wonderful works of God. And
they were all amazed, and were in doubt, saying
one to another, What meaneth this?"—Acts
2:5-12.

At this critical moment, who of those anointed
with the spirit was to be favored with the privilege of explaining what all this meant? Who
would thus unlock to the understanding of these
"Jews and proselytes" the opportunities of calling upon the name of Jehovah and being taken
into the covenant for the Kingdom? This privilege was not conferred upon the religious
scribes and Pharisees and doctors of Jewish
law; for to them Jesus said: "Woe unto you,
scribes and Pharisees, hypocrites! for ye shut
up the kingdom of heaven against men: for ye
neither go in yourselves, neither suffer ye them
that are entering to go in." "Woe unto you,
lawyers! for ye have taken away the key of
knowledge: ye entered not in yourselves, and
them that were entering in ye hindered." (Matthew 23:13; Luke 11:52) Instead of those
clergymen, the one now favored from heaven to

use the key of knowledge to unlock the understanding of the inquiring Jews was the one to whom Jesus had said: "And I say also unto thee, That thou art Peter [*Petros*], and upon this rock [*petra*] I will build my church; and the gates of hell shall not prevail against it. And I will give unto thee the keys of the kingdom of heaven: and whatsoever thou shalt bind on earth shall be bound in heaven: and whatsoever thou shalt loose on earth shall be loosed in heaven."—Matthew 16: 18, 19.

This did not mean that Simon Peter was made a *pope,* so called, or that he was given the *primacy* in the Christian church or that he was to have successors in the use of the "keys of the kingdom of heaven". Christ Jesus is the Builder of His church, and he builds it upon the great *petra,* or "rock", which is Himself. To the unbelieving Jews Jesus was "for a stone of stumbling and for a *rock* of offence to both the houses of Israel"; but to the believing Jews he was for a Rock or *petra* on whom to be built as a sure foundation of the church of God. (Isaiah 8: 14; 28: 16; Romans 9: 31-33; 1 Peter 2: 3-8; Acts 4: 8-12) When Jesus himself was with his disciples, "then opened he their understanding, that they might understand the scriptures." (Luke 24: 27, 45) But foreseeing the bringing in of both a Jewish remnant and Gentiles into the church from and after Pentecost, Jesus designated Peter to be the one to use the keys of knowledge on the proper occasion; and heaven would confirm him in the use of those keys.

Keys, being in the plural number, indicates at least two keys, and heaven-guided events proved that there were just two. Up till Pentecost Peter was *bound* from using the keys, because he himself did not have the proper understanding, the holy spirit not having been poured out from heaven until that day. On Pentecost heaven loosed Peter to use the first of the keys to unlock the way to the Jews. In what manner?

"But Peter, standing up with the eleven, lifted up his voice, and said unto them, Ye men of Judæa, and all ye that dwell at Jerusalem, be this known unto you, and hearken to my words." Then Peter explained to those Jews the fulfillment of Joel's prophecy, and that Psalms 16 and 110, written by King David, were fulfilled upon Jesus Christ, the Heir of David as King. "This Jesus hath God raised up, whereof we all are witnesses. Therefore being by the right hand of God exalted, and having received of the Father the promise of the holy [spirit], he hath shed forth this, which ye now see and hear. For David is not ascended into the heavens: but he saith himself, *The Lord* [*Jehovah*] *said unto my Lord, Sit thou on my right hand, until I make thy foes thy footstool.* Therefore let all the house of Israel know assuredly, that God hath made that same Jesus, whom ye have [staked], both Lord and Christ [Messiah]."

The conscience-stricken Jews asked Peter and the rest of the apostles, "What shall we do?" Peter said to them: "Repent, and be baptized

every one of you in the name of Jesus Christ
for the remission of sins, and ye shall receive
the gift of the holy [spirit]. For the promise is
unto you, and to your children, and to all that
are afar off, even as many as the Lord our God
shall call. . . . Save yourselves from this un-
toward generation."—Acts 2: 14-40.

No one could possibly become Peter's successor to use that first key, because the work with
it was finished and the door of opportunity was
shown to be open to the natural Jews. As a result about three thousand souls were added to
the church of Jesus Christ that day. These were
baptized in water in Jesus' name to symbolize
their full consecration of themselves to Jehovah God through Jesus. When these received
the "gift of the holy spirit", there was no manifestation of fiery tongues or a rushing wind respecting them. Such a spectacle was no more
necessary. It was once used only to betoken the
beginning of the outpouring of the spirit upon
the natural Jews that were consecrated to Jehovah God by Christ Jesus.

When Jesus was anointed with the spirit of
God, he began to preach and give a witness to
the kingdom of God. How was the Pentecostal
outpouring of the holy spirit upon all consecrated flesh marked? By renewing the public
preaching that had been silenced by reason of
arresting and killing Jesus and scattering the
disciples. House-to-house witnessing to carry
the spiritual bread to the people at their homes
was also renewed. Concerning the three thou-

sand converts of Pentecost and later believers the Record says: "And they, continuing daily with one accord in the temple, and breaking bread from house to house, did eat their meat with gladness and singleness of heart, praising God, and having favour with all the people." (Acts 2: 41-47) It is markworthy, however, that then and during the rest of the apostolic days they did not preach "The kingdom of heaven is at hand". They preached about the kingdom, but not that it was at hand and had approached. Why not? Because the King Christ Jesus had ascended to heaven and was absent, and the signs he foretold had not yet appeared to denote his coming and the end of this world.—Acts 8: 12; 14: 22; 19: 8; 20: 25; 28: 23, 31.

Several years next passed. The angel Gabriel's prophecy to Daniel concerning the seventy weeks stated as to the last or the seventieth week: "Shall Messiah be cut off, but not for himself: . . . And he shall confirm the covenant with many for one week: and in the midst of the week he shall cause the sacrifice and the oblation to cease." In this seventieth week, by the anointing of Jesus and by the offering of his sacrifice to justify sinners from sin and from the curse, and by the later events during that seven-year week, Jehovah God accomplished to "finish the transgression, and to make an end of sins, and to make reconciliation for iniquity, and to bring in everlasting righteousness, and to seal up the vision and prophecy [as being true], and to anoint the most Holy". (Daniel

9:24-27) The midst of the week, when Messiah was cut off in death, was in the spring of A.D. 33. Hence the remainder of the week had three and a half years to go, namely, till the autumn of A.D. 36. This is the *one week* during which Messiah the Prince confirmed the Abrahamic covenant with many Jews, the believers.

During the first half of that week Jesus confined his preaching and that of his disciples solely to the Jews, saying: "I am not sent but unto the lost sheep of the house of Israel." "Go not into the way of the Gentiles, and into any city of the Samaritans enter ye not: but go rather to the lost sheep of the house of Israel." (Matthew 15:24; 10:5, 6) For the rest of that week of seven years Jesus, by his apostles, continued to confirm the covenant with the natural Jews. During the "week" he did not loose Peter from proclaiming the privileges of the Kingdom covenant to any but the Jews and the related Samaritans. From heaven Jesus bound Peter from carrying the Kingdom message to the non-Jews or Gentiles.

Thus during the seventieth week down till A.D. 36 Jehovah God was showing respect to the natural Jews out of consideration of their forefathers, Abraham, Isaac, and Jacob. If a sufficient number of them had answered to the opportunity to make up the full membership of the royal family or "body" of Christ, those consecrated Jews would have exclusively become to Jehovah "a kingdom of priests, and an holy nation". However, only a remnant of "Israel after the flesh" appreciated God's special favor and responded to the opportunity to become the "elect" of God. The apostle Paul, who came in during that seventieth week, writes: "Even so then at this present time also there is a remnant according to the election of grace. . . . Israel hath not obtained that which he seeketh for; but the election hath obtained it, and the rest were blinded." (Exodus 19:6; Romans 11:5, 7) When the seventieth week closed, in autumn, A.D. 36, God discontinued to show exclusive respect to the fleshly Israelites, and opened the Kingdom doors to the non-Jews or Gentiles. The remainder of the "body of Christ" must be made up largely from among those of the Gentiles that should now believe. Heaven must loose Peter to use the second Kingdom key. How?

Peter was then at Joppa, on the seaside, about thirty miles southwest of Caesarea. At Caesarea lived an Italian centurion named Cornelius, not an outright heathen or pagan, but a Gentile who feared the God of the Jews and devoutly prayed to Jehovah God. God sent his angel to Cornelius, notified him that his prayers and alms were remembered by God, and instructed him to send to Joppa for Simon Peter. At the time of the arrival of Cornelius' messengers, Peter was on a rooftop. Up there, while at prayer, he had been given a symbolic vision in which it was three times said to him: "What God hath cleansed, that call not thou common." While Peter pondered over the vision, God by his spirit said: "Behold, three men seek thee. Arise therefore, and get thee down, and go with them, doubting nothing: for I have sent them." Two days later Peter arrived at the house of Cornelius, whose home Peter till now would have thought it common or unclean for a natural Jew to enter.

When Cornelius fell down at Peter's feet, Peter refused to accept such obeisance, and lifted him up, saying: "Stand up; I myself also am a man." He explained that it had been unlawful for a Jew to keep company with or to come to one of Gentile extraction; "but God hath shewed me that I should not call any man common or unclean." Cornelius related the angel's visit to him, and then for the first time Peter said: "Of a truth I perceive that God is no respecter of persons: but in every nation he that feareth him, and worketh righteousness, is accepted with him." Thereupon Peter proceeded to use the second 'key of the kingdom of heaven'. This he did by giving Cornelius and the assembly in his house a witness about the anointed Jesus, whom the Jews "slew and hanged on a tree", but whom God resurrected to be the Judge of the living and the dead.

Peter's use of the *keys* was here finished; and he needed no successor to further handle them. Then heaven confirmed Peter's use of the *key*. "While Peter yet spake these words, the holy [spirit] fell on all them which heard the word." The circumcised Jews that came with Peter were astonished, "because that on the Gentiles also was poured out the gift of the holy [spirit].

For they heard them speak with tongues, and magnify God." This was no second Pentecost, it being now autumn, but was an extension of that which began three and a half years before at Pentecost. Now the outpouring of the holy spirit had reached the Gentiles, and these were brought into the covenant for the Kingdom and into Christ's "body".

"Then answered Peter, Can any man forbid water, that these should not be baptized, which have received the holy [spirit] as well as we? And he commanded them to be baptized in the name of the Lord." (Acts 10: 1-48) That was not the baptism which John the Baptist once preached. His baptism was strictly for Jews on account of their sins against the law covenant. Some time after Cornelius' immersion, other Gentiles were baptized in water by Apollos, an adherent to John's baptism. These did not receive the holy spirit. The apostle Paul said to them: "Unto what then were ye baptized?" They said: "Unto John's baptism." Then Paul explained. When these Gentiles heard this, "they were baptized in the name of the Lord Jesus. And when Paul had laid his hands upon them, the holy [spirit] came on them; and they spake with tongues, and prophesied." (Acts 18:24-28; 19:1-6) It is seen, therefore, that with Cornelius' hearing of the Kingdom gospel the instructions of the resurrected Jesus began taking in their full sweep, namely: "All power is given unto me in heaven and in earth. Go ye therefore, and teach ALL NATIONS, baptizing them in the name of the Father, and of the Son, and of the holy [spirit]: teaching them to observe all things whatsoever I have commanded you: and, lo, I am with you alway, even unto the end of the world. Amen."—Matthew 28:18-20.

From the time of Simon Peter's mission to Cornelius onward, the people for the name of Jehovah God were no longer taken exclusively from among the Jews. Later Peter said to a special meeting of apostles and elders in Jerusalem: "God made choice among us, that the Gentiles by my mouth should hear the word of the gospel, and believe. And God, which knoweth the hearts, bare them witness, giving them the holy [spirit], even as he did unto us." What this event signified James then disclosed, saying to the assembly: "Simeon hath declared how God at the first did visit the Gentiles, to take out of them a people for his name. And to this agree the words of the prophets; as it is written." —Acts 15: 6-18.

Thus the further pouring out of God's holy spirit upon consecrated flesh was made to reach even to the Gentiles. The believing consecrated Gentiles, being adopted of God by the begetting of his spirit and, as sons, being then anointed with his spirit, were made a part of his spiritual Israel. (Romans 2: 28, 29) Thereby they became members of God's called and chosen or elect company. This resulted in an increase of the people for Jehovah's name. These were publishers of the gospel, and the witness work spread out to all the habitable earth then accessible to Jehovah's anointed witnesses. In testimony of this accomplishment one of these witnesses, the apostle Paul, writes: "The gospel which ye heard, which was preached in all creation under heaven; whereof I Paul was made a minister."—Colossians 1: 23, *Am. Stan. Ver.*

CHAPTER XVII

THE ROYAL FAMILY

URING the thousands of years since God's prophecy in Eden, mystery shrouded the answer to the question, namely, Who will be the Seed of God's "woman" to bruise the Serpent's head? Coupled in with this was the question: Who will be the Seed of Abraham in whom all families and nations of the earth are to be blessed?

At the anointing of Jesus to be King, and then his resurrection and ascension to God's right hand, the major part of the mystery was solved. First after the spirit was poured out at Pentecost upon consecrated Jews and thereafter upon consecrated Gentiles the mystery was solved fully. It then became known that there would be a royal family that would be glorified with Christ in the "kingdom of heaven". A modern translator has well rendered the words of the apostle Paul to the Colossians regarding this sacred mystery, thus: "That secret, hidden from the ages and generations, but now disclosed to those who are consecrated to him, to whom God has chosen to make known among the heathen how glorious this mystery of Christ in you, the promise of glorification, really is." (Colossians 1: 26, 27, *Goodspeed*) The same apostle writes further: "The mystery, which was kept secret since the world began, but now is made manifest, and by the scriptures of the prophets, according to the commandment of the everlasting God, made known to all nations for the obedience of faith."—Romans 16: 25, 26.

It is thus unveiled that the mystery or sacred secret is fulfilled, not in Christ Jesus only, but also in the entire royal family of God, Jesus being "the King of kings" in that family and his faithful followers being his associate kings. "He is Lord of lords, and King of kings: and they that are with him are called, and chosen, and faithful." (Revelation 1: 5; 17: 14) The number of those making up the royal family is limited, and hence only a few from creatures here on earth will go to heaven. The perfect human body, such as "the man Christ Jesus" possessed, has a perfect but limited number of members. The royal family of heaven is likened to a perfect human organism, of which Jesus is the head member and all his followers are the body members. To the "saints" or consecrated ones at Rome Paul wrote: "For as we have many members in one body, and all members have not the same office: so we, being many, are one body in Christ, and every one members one of another." (Romans 12: 4, 5) To the church of consecrated ones at Corinth the apostle wrote: "For as the body is one, and hath many members, and all the members of that one body, being many, are one body: so also is Christ. For by one spirit are we all baptized into one body,

whether we be Jews or Gentiles, whether we be
bond or free; and have been all made to drink
into one spirit. For the body is not one member,
but many. . . . God set the members every one
of them in the body, as it hath pleased him. . . .
Now ye are the body of Christ, and members in
particular."—1 Corinthians 12:12-27.

The perfect human body is a marvelous organization of God's creation. So, too, the royal
family of the "kingdom of heaven", being made
up of Jesus the Head and the members of the
"body of Christ", is God's special organization.
Because the Most High God has assigned Christ
Jesus to the highest place in the universe next
to Himself, and because the "body of Christ" is
united with Christ Jesus there, Jehovah God
makes the royal family the chief or capital organization of his universe. To be sure, the royal
family is a part of God's universal organization
of holy creatures. Yet, by reason of its position
and special office, the royal family occupies a
separate place of distinction and it is the capital
of Jehovah's universal organization. Ephesians
1:19-23 testifies that this is according to God's
mighty power, "which he wrought in Christ,
when he raised him from the dead, and set him
at his own right hand in the heavenly places, far
above all principality, and power, and might,
and dominion, and every name that is named,
not only in this world, but also in that which is
to come: and hath put all things under his feet,
and gave him to be the head over all things to
the church, which is his body, the fulness of him

that filleth all in all." Christ Jesus is "gone into heaven, and is on the right hand of God; angels and authorities and powers being made subject unto him". (1 Peter 3:22) For such reason the royal family, as God's capital organization, was foreshadowed by Jerusalem, or Zion, the capital city or royal city of David, king of Israel.

Jehovah God promised the nation of Israel that if they faithfully kept his covenant of the law with them he would make them a "kingdom of priests". The twelve tribes of fleshly Israel failed to supply sufficient members to make up that new "holy nation" of kings and priests. Jehovah's hand was not shortened thereby, but he drew on the Gentile believers to fill out the membership of this "holy nation" of spiritual Israel.—Romans 11:25, 26; Galatians 6:15, 16.

Since the number twelve distinguished natural Israel, it is to be expected that *twelve* would mark the new nation of Israel after the spirit. God has unlocked the mystery to show that under Jesus the fixed number of his royal, capital family will be, all together, a multiple of twelve, increased a thousandfold, namely, $12 \times 12 \times 1000$, or 144,000 members. The apostle John writes: "I heard the number of them which were sealed: and there were sealed an hundred and forty and four thousand of all the tribes of the children of Israel." Then he enumerates 12,000 from each of the twelve tribes of spiritual Israel. (Revelation 7:4-8) Showing the capital position these occupy with Christ Jesus, John writes: "And I looked, and, lo, a

Lamb stood on the mount Sion, and with him an hundred forty and four thousand, having his Father's name written in their foreheads. . . . And they sung as it were a new song before the throne, and before the four beasts, and the elders: and no man could learn that song but the hundred and forty and four thousand, which were redeemed from the earth. These are they which were not defiled with women; for they are virgins. These are they which follow the Lamb whithersoever he goeth." (Revelation 14:1-4) Once their number was unknown, like the stars innumerable.—Genesis 15:5.

From the Scriptures it dawns upon us that the requirements for becoming a member of Jehovah's capital organization Zion must be Theocratic and must be far higher than the standards of men and religionists. Since "strait is the gate, and narrow is the way, which leadeth unto life, and few there be that find it", then the way into the "kingdom of heaven" must indeed be narrow. It was never God's purpose to convert the whole world and take all these billions into the "kingdom of heaven". (Matthew 7:13, 14) What, then, are the steps a creature on earth must take to enter the kingdom?

Christ Jesus laid down a fundamental requirement, which in itself makes it certain that John the Baptist, and all the other faithful men ahead of him clear back to Abel, all of whom died before Pentecost, can not and will not be in the heavenly kingdom. In a night conference with Nicodemus Jesus said to this Jewish ruler:

"Verily, verily, I say unto thee, Except a man be born *again,* he cannot see the kingdom of God." The *Emphatic Diaglott* translation of John 3:3 reads: "Indeed I assure thee, if any one be not born *from above,* he cannot see the kingdom of God." Then Jesus showed Nicodemus that this did not mean that a person would enter a second time into his human mother's womb and be born again from human source, from beneath. "Jesus answered, Verily, verily, I say unto thee, Except a man be born of water and of the spirit, he cannot enter into the kingdom of God. That which is born of the flesh is flesh; and that which is born of the spirit is spirit." (John 3:5, 6) This settles it that the kingdom of God is not any visible human kingdom on this earth and that it has no earthly phase. Those who stay humans will be no part of that heavenly kingdom.

Who, then, are the ones favored by God to be born again or born from above? Certainly not unconsecrated sinners. Since we are all sinners by inheritance from rebellious Adam, how could any from among men attain to the Kingdom? It is all by the grace or undeserved favor of Jehovah God through his Son Jesus Christ. Jesus said: "No man can come to me, except the Father which hath sent me draw him: and I will raise him up at the last day. It is written in the prophets, *And they shall be all taught of God.* Every man therefore that hath heard, and hath learned of the Father, cometh unto me. Not that any man hath seen the Father, save he which is of God, he hath seen the Father. Verily, verily, I say unto you, He that believeth on me hath everlasting life."—John 6:44-47.

Since we cannot see God, how then can we be taught of God and be drawn to Jesus? Jehovah God has provided his written Word, the Bible, as the Textbook for teaching us now, and it is by the study of His inspired Word that we are "taught of God". If we are taught by religious clergymen contrary to the Bible, we are not taught of God. God's Word tells us about Jesus Christ, the Seed of God's "woman", and it is thus by learning from God through his Word that we are drawn to Jesus. If we are honest, we come to him as the Anointed One of God through whom alone God's blessings flow. If we have faith in Jehovah God and hence in his Word, we will please him and he will draw us to his King Christ Jesus. (Hebrew 11:6) The drawing, however, is not a call to the heavenly Kingdom.

Through Jehovah's Word of truth we see the need of coming to Jesus, because we are revealed to be sinners and because Christ Jesus died for our sins and provided the ransom for faithful believers in him. At Romans 6:23 God teaches us: "The wages of sin is death; but the gift of God is eternal life through Jesus Christ our Lord." To get the benefits of Jesus' human sacrifice, the one who at last attains the heavenly kingdom must believe in him, not alone as Redeemer but also as the true Example to follow toward gaining the Kingdom. Believing him means more than just accepting with the mind certain truths as to Jesus' redemptive power. It means also obeying him and following his example.—1 Peter 2: 21.

Jesus himself, in order to gain the Kingdom, did not stay at Nazareth and keep on carpentering, living blamelessly as a perfect human among God's covenant people of Israel. Being maturely perfect at thirty years of age, he then consecrated himself totally to God's service and left behind his carpentry. Such consecration he symbolized openly by being baptized in water. He had no sins for the remission of which he must be baptized in water by John. Then the work which the Father revealed to him as being due to be done by his Son, the consecrated Jesus did. He thus carried out his consecration faithfully to the finish of the work. Of him it was prophetically written: "Then said I, Lo, I come: in the volume of the book it is written of me, I delight to do thy will, O my God: yea, thy law is within my heart. I have preached."—Psalm 40: 7-9.

Jesus said furthermore: "If any man would come after me, let him deny himself, and take up his [stake, *stauros*] daily, and follow me." (Luke 9: 23) The obedient believer denies himself when he consecrates himself to God through Christ Jesus and trusts in the redemptive merit of Jesus' sacrifice to offset his sins and make him acceptable with God. Out of regard for this act of faith and obedience Jehovah justifies such consecrating one by the application to him of the merit of the Redeemer. Then God accepts the consecration.

The interplay of God's grace, Jesus' blood and the consecrating one's faith is set forth in the following scriptures: "Even the righteousness of God which is by faith of Jesus Christ unto all and upon all them that believe: for there is no difference: for all have sinned, and come short of the glory of God; being justified freely by his *grace* through the redemption that is in Christ Jesus: whom God hath set forth to be a propitiation through *faith* in his *blood*." "Who was delivered for our offences, and was raised again for our justification. Therefore being justified by *faith*, we have peace with God through our Lord Jesus Christ: much more then, being now justified by his *blood*, we shall be saved from wrath through him." (Romans 3:22-25; 4:25; 5:1,9; Titus 3:7) Jesus' blood was human, and therefore covers or washes away the inherited sin of the flesh and also the sins accruing therefrom. Hence the justification one receives is as a human creature. One is then from God's standpoint in the state or position of Jesus the perfect man when he presented himself at Jordan river in consecration. The justified one is credited with the right to human life.

It was not God's will that the consecrated Jesus continue to live in the flesh. Neither is eternal life in the flesh His will for the justified follower of Jesus. Hence the right to life on earth of the justified one is sacrificed through

the High Priest Jesus. Now Jehovah begets the
consecrated creature by His spirit or life-
giving force. This begettal is unto spirit life,
unto life in the heavens. While still remaining
in the body of flesh, he has a conditional right to
heavenly life. His right to life determines what
kind of creature he really is before God, and
hence he is a "new creature". (Galatians 6:15,
16) He must now live as such, in hope of eternal
life in the heavens when God's kingdom is set up.

The creature's begettal is not according to
any man's will or power, not even his own, but
is according to God's will. It is through the
truth of God that he has been led and helped to
this relationship with God, and also by the life-
giving power of God's spirit. God's will or de-
termination is that the consecrated creature
should live as a "new creature" with hope of life
above. It is by the power of the truth, like clean
water, that he is enabled to get cleansed of religion and the course of this world. It is by the
power of God's spirit or active force toward
him that he is enabled to live anew, as a "new
creature". (2 Corinthians 5:17) "Not by works
of righteousness which we have done, but according to his mercy he saved us, by the washing of
regeneration, and renewing of the holy [spirit];
which he shed on us abundantly through Jesus
Christ our Saviour; that being justified by his
grace, we should be made heirs according to the
hope of eternal life."—Titus 3:5-7.

It is by that dealing of God that the consecrated, justified one is begotten over again from

above, or "born again" and "born from above".
(In the original Greek text *begotten* and *born*
are one and the same word.) As to those thus
accepting the King and Redeemer Christ Jesus
it is written: "As many as received him, to them
gave he power to become the sons of God, even
to them that believe on his name: which were
born, not of blood, nor of the will of the flesh,
nor of the will of man, but of God." (John
1: 12, 13) "Of his own will begat he us with the
word of truth, that we should be a kind of firstfruits of his creatures." (James 1: 18) This begettal is a being "born of water [picturing the
word of truth] and of the spirit", and it must
precede the consecrated one's seeing and entering into the heavenly kingdom of God.—John
3: 3, 5.

Such begotten son of God, being spiritual, is
taken into God's universal organization, which
is his "woman". In view of man's sin in Eden
and his being dismissed from God's organization, that organization has since been all spiritual, composed of spirit creatures together with
those of God's sons in line for spirit life in the
heavens. Hence that universal organization,
God's "woman", has been *above* as compared
with man who is earthly. God's "woman", in her
state of motherhood to bring forth the royal
Seed that bruises the Serpent's head, is called
Zion or *Jerusalem*. Those who are a part of her
are spoken of as her children. Because of that
fact, the apostle Paul writes to the consecrated,
spirit-begotten ones and says: "But Jerusalem

which is above is free, which is the mother of us all. So then, brethren, we are not children of the bondwoman, but of the free." (Galatians 4:26, 31) Jehovah is the Father of such, and his free "woman" above is their mother.

Since the Government is the "kingdom of heaven", it is these spiritual or spirit-begotten sons that God calls or invites to the Kingdom. It is not a 'calling of sinners to repentance', but of justified sons to the royal Government. (Mark 2:17) Of the heavenly calling it is written: "God is faithful, by whom ye were called unto the fellowship of his Son Jesus Christ our Lord." (1 Corinthians 1:9) While in the flesh, such "called" ones may be Jews or Gentiles, circumcised or uncircumcised, bondservants or free, from the human standpoint, but they are not called as such, but as begotten sons of God. (1 Corinthians 7:18-24) "Walk worthy of the vocation wherewith ye are called, . . . even as ye are called in one hope of your calling." (Ephesians 4:1, 4) "Ye are called in one body." (Colossians 3:15) "Walk worthy of God, who hath called you unto his kingdom and glory." (1 Thessalonians 2:12; 5:24) "He called you by our gospel, to the obtaining of the glory of our Lord Jesus Christ." (2 Thessalonians 2:14) "They which are called might receive the promise of eternal inheritance." (Hebrews 9:15) "The God of all grace, who hath called us unto his eternal glory by Christ Jesus." (1 Peter 5:10; 2 Peter 1:3) Sinners may hear about this calling, but that does not mean it applies to them. Spirit-begetting constitutes the call.

In view of such calling to his kingdom and glory with Christ Jesus, Jehovah God anoints the spirit-begotten son, baptizing him with his spirit of anointing. This is evidence that He has chosen them and that they are his "elect". *Elect* means *chosen out*. To the elect the apostle writes: "Ye have put off the old man with his deeds; and have put on the new man, which is renewed in knowledge after the image of him that created him: where there is neither Greek nor Jew, circumcision nor uncircumcision, Barbarian, Scythian, bond nor free: but Christ is all, and in all. Put on therefore, as the *elect* of God, holy and beloved, bowels of mercies, kindness, humbleness of mind, meekness, longsuffering." (Colossians 3:9-12) Another apostle writes: *"Elect* according to the foreknowledge of God the Father, through sanctification of the spirit, unto obedience and sprinkling of the blood of Jesus Christ." (1 Peter 1:2) At Revelation 17:14 Christ Jesus is mentioned as "King of kings"; and to show who those kings are it is added: "And they that are with him are called, and *elect,* and faithful."—*Douay Version.*

God had foreknowledge of the elect; not meaning that he chose to foreknow the individuals, but that he purposed or predestinated that there should be such an elect company. They were part of or were included in His great "mystery". He did not have to concern himself with the individuals and their names and per-

sonal identities. He simply determined beforehand or predestinated what should be the requirements for membership in this class and
what standards they had to meet and what
qualities they had to display. Hence, without
knowing the individual members in advance,
Almighty God foreknew what kind of company
the elect would be, and their number. He so
deals with the elect that they will be the qualified company he predestinated them to be for
His use and service.

The requirement was predestinated that they
should all be followers of Christ Jesus and conform to his example and course of action; and
this was before Christ Jesus came and laid the
foundation of the New World of righteousness.
"According as he hath chosen [elected] us in
him before the foundation of the world, that we
should be holy and without blame before him in
love: having predestinated us unto the adoption
of children by Jesus Christ to himself, according to the good pleasure of his will. In [Christ]
also we have obtained an inheritance, being predestinated according to the purpose of him who
worketh all things after the counsel of his own
will."—Ephesians 1: 4, 5, 11.

Hence to God's elect the apostle Paul writes:
"We know that to them that love God God works
all things together for good*, even to them that

* According to Vatican Manuscript No. 1209, the Alexan-
drine MS., and some versions; and also the papyrus manuscript P46 of the early third century, much the oldest text
of Paul's epistle to the Romans and discovered in 1935.
See footnote of *The Emphatic Diaglott*, page 532.

are called according to his purpose. For whom he foreknew, he also foreordained to be conformed to the image of his Son, that he might be the firstborn among many brethren: and whom he foreordained, them he also called: and whom he called, them he also justified: and whom he justified, them he also glorified. Who shall lay anything to the charge of God's elect? It is God that justifieth." (Romans 8: 28-30, 33, *Am. Stan. Ver.*, margin) Such "called" ones God the Judge approves or pronounces just and right, and glorifies or honors them with the glorious ministry of the new covenant under Jesus the Mediator.—2 Corinthians 3: 7-18; 4: 1-7.

David of old, when chosen to be king and also when made king, was anointed with oil. However, God's "new creatures", who are the spirit-begotten, called and chosen ones, are anointed with his invisible active force, which is his holy spirit. To these it is said: "Now he which stablisheth us with you in Christ, and hath *anointed* us, is God; who hath also sealed us, and given the earnest [pledge, or earnest-money] of the spirit in our hearts." (2 Corinthians 1: 21, 22) There is no yes and no, or wavering and equivocation about it. God confirms and verifies his called and chosen ones unto Christ Jesus by anointing them with his spirit. He thus puts his seal of approval and acceptance upon them. The fact that they have the spirit of God in their hearts and are bringing forth the fruits of the spirit is a pledge and assurance to them that their hope in Christ is real, to be joined with him at length in the Kingdom as they are now joined with him in proclaiming his kingdom. Ephesians 1: 13, 14 tells them: "After that ye believed, ye were sealed with that holy spirit of promise [or promised holy spirit], which is the earnest [like a first installment] of our inheritance until the redemption of the purchased possession [or until the deliverance of God's purchased church], unto the praise of his glory." Therefore they are warned not to offend against or to go contrary to the spirit of God: "And grieve not the holy spirit of God, whereby ye are sealed unto the day of redemption." —Ephesians 4: 30; 1 Thessalonians 5: 19.

Those anointed with His spirit must be faithful and not fall back into religion. "For it is impossible for those who were once enlightened, and have tasted of the heavenly gift, and were made partakers of the holy [spirit], and have tasted the good word of God, and the powers of the world to come, if they shall fall away, to renew them again unto repentance; seeing they [stake] to themselves the Son of God afresh, and put him to an open shame." "For if we sin wilfully after that we have received the knowledge of the truth, there remaineth no more sacrifice for [willful] sins, but a certain fearful looking for of judgment, and fiery indignation, which shall devour the adversaries."—Hebrews 6: 4, 5; 10: 26, 27.

Some who associate themselves with God's elect on earth may later go out from among them and become antichrists, but those who at last receive the prize of the Kingdom must hold fast the truth and not compromise with this world and its lustful desires. To them the apostle John writes: "And ye have an anointing from the Holy One, and ye know all things. And as for you, the anointing which ye have received of him abideth in you, and ye need not that any one teach you; but as his anointing teacheth you concerning all things, and is true, and is no lie, and even as it taught you, ye abide in him." (1 John 2: 20, 27, *Am. Stan. Ver.*) They know the terms of their commission or what God has anointed them to do. What Jesus quoted from prophecy and applied to himself as their Head applies also to them as members of his body, namely: "The spirit of the Lord GOD is upon me; because the LORD hath anointed me to preach good tidings unto the meek; . . . and the day of vengeance of our God; to comfort all that mourn."—Isaiah 61: 1, 2; Luke 4: 14-21.

To copy their Head, Christ Jesus, his followers should give a public testimony or symbol of their consecration to God by being baptized or immersed *in* water. Christ Jesus was immersed before he received the spirit and was anointed. (Matthew 3: 13-17; 4: 1) Cornelius and his fellow Gentile believers were baptized in water after the holy spirit descended upon them and they were anointed; but that difference from Jesus' case was due to the immediate need of giving open proof that Gentiles were henceforth in line to be taken into Christ's "body". (Acts 10: 44-48) The Samaritan believers, to whom the evangelist Philip preached, were baptized in water, but were not favored with the holy spirit until the coming of the apostles Peter and John. "Who, having gone down, prayed for them that they might receive the holy spirit; for *it* was not yet fallen on any of them; but they had only been immersed into the name of the Lord Jesus. Then they placed their hands on them, and they received the holy spirit."—Acts 8: 15-17, *The Emphatic Diaglott.*

As to the believers at Ephesus, Asia, to whom Paul witnessed, it is stated (Acts 19: 5, 6): "When they heard this, they were baptized in the name of the Lord Jesus. And when Paul had laid his hands upon them, the holy [spirit] came on them; and they spake with tongues, and prophesied." According to Jesus' example and these others, the one consecrating himself to God does not need to wait until there is evidence of being anointed with God's spirit. As early as possible after consecration he should symbolize it by water immersion. No scripture favors that a woman should do the baptizing.

For one who gains life on earth the symbolizing of his consecration to God by water immersion may be the end of it so far as baptism is concerned. However, for those who are taken into the Kingdom there is another baptism, which no human on earth can administer. This is the baptism of the holy spirit, which Christ Jesus administers as Jehovah's Servant. This baptism indicates that the consecrated one has been baptized into the body of Christ. Said Peter at the Pentecostal manifestation of the holy spirit from Christ: "Being by the right hand of God exalted, and having received of the Father the promise of the holy [spirit], he hath shed forth this, which ye now see and hear." (Acts 2:33) It is "one baptism", common to all his body.

To those receiving the gift of the holy spirit and its various manifestations, Paul writes: "But all these things performs the one and the same spirit, distributing to each in particular as *it* will. For just as the body is one, and has many members, but all the members of the body, being many, are one body; so also the Anointed. For, indeed, by one spirit we were all immersed into one body—whether Jews or Greeks, whether slaves or freemen; and were all made to drink one spirit [or, be imbued, saturated, with one spirit]." (1 Corinthians 12:11-13, *The Emphatic Diaglott*) It is the one spirit or active force from God that binds the body and holds it together unto the Head, Christ Jesus, through whom the spirit is poured out.

What does such baptism with God's spirit into the "body of Christ" mean as to the fleshly organism of these "new creatures"? Paul writes in answer: "Know ye not, that so many of us as were baptized into Jesus Christ were baptized into his death? Therefore we are buried with him by baptism into death: that like as Christ was raised up from the dead by the glory of the Father, even so we also should walk in newness of life. For if we have been planted together in the likeness of his death, we shall be also in the likeness of his resurrection: . . . Now if we be dead with Christ, we believe that we shall also live with him: knowing that Christ, being raised from the dead dieth no more; death hath no more dominion over him. For in that he died, he died unto sin once: but in that he liveth, he liveth unto God. Likewise reckon ye also yourselves to be dead indeed unto sin, but alive unto God through Jesus Christ our Lord."—Romans 6: 3-11.

This makes understandable to us Jesus' question to his disciples: "Can ye . . . be baptized with the baptism that I am baptized with?" At expressing themselves willing, he assured them that they would be baptized "with the baptism that I am baptized withal". (Mark 10: 38, 39) This baptism into his death is all over with or finished at the actual death of the human organism. Such baptism brings the consecrated one much distress or difficulty because of the opposing world which tries to force everyone to live and keep alive to its ways and standards. Even Jesus said: "But I have a baptism to be baptized with; and how am I straitened till it be accomplished! Suppose ye that I am come to give peace on earth? I tell you, Nay; but rather division."—Luke 12: 50, 51.

One who becomes a member of the "body of Christ" becomes a part of the Seed of God's "woman". He also becomes a part of the Seed of Abraham in whom all families of the earth are destined to be blessed. By what arrangement? By being adopted as a son of God.

Christ Jesus is primarily the Seed of God and of his "woman": "thy seed, which is Christ." His body members, by adoption as children of God, are counted as one with Jesus, who is the Head and who is fundamentally the Seed. "For ye are all the children of God by faith in Christ Jesus. For as many of you as have been baptized into Christ have put on Christ. There is neither Jew nor Greek, there is neither bond nor free, there is neither male nor female: for ye are all one in Christ Jesus. And if ye be Christ's, then are ye Abraham's seed, and heirs according to the promise. . . . God sent forth his Son, made of a woman, made under the law, to redeem them that were under the law, that we might receive the adoption of sons." (Galatians 3: 16, 26-29; 4: 4, 5) "For ye have not received the spirit of bondage again to fear; but ye have received the spirit of adoption, whereby we cry, Abba, Father. The spirit itself beareth witness with our spirit, that we are the children of God: and if children, then heirs; heirs of God, and joint-heirs with Christ; if so be that we suffer with him, that we may be also glorified together. For I reckon that the sufferings of this present time are not worthy to be compared with the glory that shall be revealed in us." (Romans 8: 15-18) Such joint-heirs are therefore taken into the covenant for the Kingdom with the Greater David, Christ Jesus, "The King of kings." —Luke 22: 28-30, *Diaglott;* Isaiah 55: 3.

God's Word is plain and direct to the ones called to be heirs of God in the Kingdom, that a great test of their integrity toward God will be made by sufferings at the hands of the Serpent and his seed. "For even hereunto were ye called: because Christ also suffered for us, leaving us an example, that ye should follow his steps." (1 Peter 2: 21) Therefore they are exhorted to "continue in the faith, and that we must through much tribulation enter into the kingdom of God". (Acts 14: 22) Paul said of himself: "I suffer trouble, as an evil doer, even unto bonds; but the word of God is not bound. Therefore I endure all things for the elect's sakes, that they may also obtain the salvation which is in Christ Jesus with eternal glory. It is a faithful saying: For if we be dead with him, we shall also live with him: if we suffer, we shall also reign with him."—2 Timothy 2: 9-12.

That his body members may hold fast their integrity and gain the Kingdom, the victorious resurrected Jesus said: "Fear none of those things which thou shalt suffer: behold, the devil shall cast some of you into prison, that ye may be tried; and ye shall have tribulation ten [or all] days: be thou faithful unto death, and I will give thee a crown of life. To him that overcometh will I grant to sit with me in my throne, even as I also overcame, and am set down with my Father in his throne." (Revelation 2: 10; 3: 21) Those that do carry out their consecration to the death and keep their integrity unbreakable have a part with Christ the King in vindicating the Father's name. To them it is said for comfort: "The God of peace shall bruise Satan under your feet shortly."—Romans 16:20.

All this emphasizes the truth repeatedly spoken by Jesus: "He that shall endure unto the end, the same shall be saved." (Matthew 10:22; 24:13) While engaged actively in God's service as proclaimers of his kingdom, and while undergoing the hatred of men and nations for such gospel preaching, the heirs of the Kingdom must practice and do the vital things named by the inspired apostle: "Using all diligence, superadd to your faith fortitude, and to fortitude knowledge, and to knowledge self-control, and to self-control patience, and to patience piety [godliness], and to piety brotherly-kindness, and to brotherly-kindness love. . . . Therefore, brethren, more earnestly endeavor to make your calling and election sure; since by doing these things, you will never fall; for thus richly will be furnished to you the entrance into the [everlasting] kingdom of our Lord and Savior Jesus." (2 Peter 1:5-11, *Diaglott*) Because many do not make their calling sure, "few are chosen."

It is solely by taking the course that "the King of kings" took and sharing in his sufferings and his manner of death that those called to the heavenly kingdom have any hope to have a part in his resurrection. The forward-looking Paul declared this to be his constant endeavor: "That I may know him, and the power of his resurrection, and the fellowship of his sufferings, being made conformable unto his death; if by any means I might attain unto the resur-

rection of the dead. . . . this one thing I do,
forgetting those things which are behind, and
reaching forth unto those things which are before, I press toward the mark for the prize of
the high calling of God in Christ Jesus."
—Philippians 3: 10-14.

The glorious attainment of the royal prize by
those who do no obeisance to any beastly creation of Satan the Devil but who copy Jesus in
being faithful witnesses with Jehovah God's
Word is pictured at Revelation 20: 4-6: "And
I saw thrones, (and they sat on them, and judgment was given them,) and the persons of those
who had been beheaded because of the testimony of Jesus, and because of the word of God,
—even those who did not worship the beast, nor
his image, and did not receive the mark on their
forehead, and on their hand; and they lived
[were restored to life] and reigned with the
Anointed One [Christ] the thousand years. But
the rest of the dead did not live till the thousand
years were ended. This is the first resurrection.
Blessed and holy is he who has a portion in the
first resurrection; over these the second death
has no authority, but they shall be priests of
God and of the Anointed, and shall reign with
him a thousand years."—*Diaglott;* footnote.

Theirs is the "first resurrection", first in time,
because Christ Jesus their Head was the first
ever to be resurrected to eternal life and at his
second coming "the dead in Christ shall rise
first" (1 Thessalonians 4: 16); also first in importance, for it is the resurrection of the royal

family, the heirs of the Kingdom which is Jehovah's capital organization over the universe. The "first resurrection" of Christ Jesus and of the "body of Christ" is described at 1 Corinthians 15: 20, 42-57, as follows:

"But now is Christ risen from the dead, and become the firstfruits of them that slept. So also is the resurrection of the dead. It is sown in corruption; it is raised in incorruption; it is sown in dishonour; it is raised in glory: it is sown in weakness; it is raised in power: it is sown a natural body; it is raised a spiritual body. There is a natural body, and there is a spiritual body. And so it is written, The first man Adam was made a living soul; the last Adam was made a quickening spirit. Howbeit that was not first which is spiritual, but that which is natural; and afterward that which is spiritual. The first man is of the earth, earthy: the second man is the Lord from heaven. As is the earthy, such are they also that are earthy: and as is the heavenly, such are they also that are heavenly. And as we have borne the image of the earthy, we shall also bear the image of the heavenly.

"Now this I say, brethren, that flesh and blood cannot inherit the kingdom of God; neither doth corruption inherit incorruption. Behold, I shew you a mystery; We shall not all sleep, but we shall all be changed, in a moment, in the twinkling of an eye, at the last trump: for the trumpet shall sound, and the dead shall be raised incorruptible, and we shall be changed. For this corruptible must put on incorruption, and this mortal must put on immortality. So when this corruptible [body of Christ] shall have put on incorruption, and this mortal shall have put on immortality, then shall be brought to pass the saying that is written, Death is swallowed up in victory. O death, where is thy sting? O grave [(marginal reading) O hell], where is thy victory? The sting of death is sin; and the strength of sin is the law. But thanks be to God, which giveth us the victory through our Lord Jesus Christ."

For the above-described reasons the resurrection of the members of the "body of Christ" must be invisible to human eyes. Unlike Jesus' case for forty days after his resurrection, there will be no materializations by them in fleshly bodies after their resurrection, to prove to humans on earth that the dead members of the royal family have been restored to life because the Kingdom has been set up. "That which is born of the spirit is spirit," said Jesus. By the resurrection, "the body of Christ" which is at first composed of anointed creatures in the flesh in humiliation undergoes a change. Why? The apostle explains to the Kingdom heirs: "For our citizenship is in heaven; whence also we wait for a Saviour, the Lord Jesus Christ: who shall fashion anew the body of our humiliation, that it may be conformed to the body of his glory, according to the working whereby he is able even to subject all things unto himself." —Philippians 3: 20, 21, *Am. Stan. Ver.*

The royal family must all share heavenly glory. Hence the members of Christ's "body" must be transformed to be a glorious "body", sharing and reflecting the glory of the kingly Head, Christ Jesus. Then from heaven all the royal family will reign as kings and priests for a thousand years over the earth to bless all "men of good-will". (Revelation 5:10; 20:4, 6) Thus to these 144,000 saints, or consecrated ones, who are "called, and chosen, and faithful" with Christ Jesus in spite of the war of opposition carried on against them by Satan's organization, Jehovah God, "the Ancient of days," gives his judgment of approval and to them he assigns an abiding place with his beloved Son in the Kingdom. A vision of this triumphant occasion was given long ago, as it is written: "The Ancient of days came [to his temple by his kingly representative Christ Jesus], and judgment was given to the saints of the most High; and the time came that the saints possessed the kingdom [of the new world]. And the kingdom and dominion, and the greatness of the kingdom under the whole heaven, shall be given to the people of the saints of the most High, whose kingdom is an everlasting kingdom, and all dominions shall serve and obey him."— Daniel 7:22, 27.

CHAPTER XVIII

THEOCRACY'S AMBASSADORS

UE to the fact that John the Baptist and Jesus Christ confined their ministry to the Jews in Palestine, the message "The kingdom of heaven is at hand" was never heralded to the Gentile nations of the world. Jesus' coming as the King Messiah the Prince, nineteen centuries ago, was of such importance that it was preceded by a forerunner, John the Baptist, specially raised up of Almighty God. This prepared a people for the arrival and appearance of the King himself. However, the coming or establishment of the Kingdom itself in power is of the greatest importance in universal history, because the Kingdom is The Theocratic Government and by means of it the Most High God Jehovah will vindicate his great and holy name. "The kingdom of heaven" is, as the foregoing pages unite to agree, the foremost doctrine of God's Word, the Bible.

It is to be expected, then, that the event of greatest importance to God's name and to all His universal organization would be preceded by all deserved advance publicity. Jehovah's own Word has guaranteed that it should be so. The establishment of his Theocratic Government in the hands of his anointed King leads to the most terrible warfare and battle in creation's history, and there is dire need of warning to mankind. Jehovah promised to give full warning before the day on which, by his Kingdom, he fights the battle, saying: "Behold, I will send you Elijah the prophet before the great and terrible day of Jehovah come. And he shall turn the heart of the fathers to the children, and the heart of the children to their fathers; lest I come and smite the earth with a curse."—Malachi 4:5, 6, *Am. Stan. Ver.*

John's proclamation work in A.D. 29-30 was only a miniature fulfillment of that prophecy. The "great and terrible day of Jehovah" did not follow upon John's ministry. His voice was stilled in death by beheading, and King Herod and the other Gentile rulers and the religious rulers continued in power and even brought about the death of Jehovah's anointed King. Forty years later from John, namely, in A.D. 70, when the city of Jerusalem was destroyed by the Gentile Roman armies, Christ Jesus did not then come again. At that destruction of unfaithful Jerusalem he did not personally act as God's executioner, neither did he then gather unto himself all his disciples. They were obliged to flee out of Jerusalem and were widely scattered. (Luke 21:20-24) Jehovah's day must yet come!

Now, once again, after a silence nineteen hundred years long on the subject, the message "The kingdom of heaven is at hand" is going forth in the greatest publicity campaign of human history. All the religionists of "Christendom" challenge the message. How, then, are we to know that the message is true and properly timed? Can it be the forerunner signifying that Jehovah's day of battle is immediately ahead with victory for his kingdom? Where is the Elijah that was foretold to come? What do the modern facts show?

The prophet's name "Elijah" means "My God is Jehovah", *jah* being the abbreviation for *Jehovah*. Elijah of old was a witness for Jehovah as God. After he exposed the priests of religion by his spectacular fire-test on Mount Carmel the people shouted, "Jehovah, he is God; Jehovah, he is God!" Directly after that the priests of religion were executed. Then came Elijah's flight from the murderous Queen Jezebel. At his hiding-place Elijah was instructed by the Lord God to go forth again as Jehovah's servant and to anoint his successor Elisha and also to anoint Jehu to be king. This Jehu is the one who trapped the religionists in the temple of Baal and executed them all and thus wiped out Baal religion from the kingdom of Israel. He also killed their promoter, Queen Jezebel.

Furthermore, before resuming his prophetic work, Elijah was told that Jehovah had a remnant of true worshipers left in the land, "seven thousand in Israel, all the knees which have not bowed unto Baal, and every mouth which hath not kissed him." (1 Kings, chapters 18 and 19; 2 Kings, chapters 9 and 10) After Elijah was taken away in a whirlwind, Elisha carried on as his successor. During Elisha's days King Jehu did his work against religion. The name "Elisha" means "God is Savior" or "God is salvation".

John the Baptist worked "in the spirit and power of Elijah". Like Elijah, he did a destructive work against religion, denouncing the religious Pharisees and Sadducees (which included the priests) as being a "generation of vipers" subject to Jehovah's wrath. He announced the Kingdom as at hand. The unbelieving religionists were greatly relieved at John's death, but then Jesus and his disciples carried on, preaching publicly and from house to house.

The name *Jesus* corresponds very closely with *Elisha* (*Eliseus*) in that it means "Jehovah is salvation". The work of Elijah and Elisha in the days of the typical kingdom of Israel, and the work of John the Baptist and of Jesus and his disciples in the days of the presence of God's anointed King, both foreshadowed a greater work to be done in connection with the establishment of Jehovah's kingdom. Such work which is destructive to religion and which advertises the Kingdom is done under the supervision of the King Christ Jesus. He is the Greater Elijah and the Greater Elisha, and he associates with himself in this work the remnant of faithful members of his "body". These carry on under Him their Head. Hence the Elijah that Jehovah promised to send in due time is not an individual, but is a company of His servants on earth acting under their Head Christ Jesus. It is a most certain and eloquent sign that "the kingdom of heaven is at hand".

As it was foretold concerning Jesus by the prophet Isaiah: "Bind up the testimony, seal the law among my disciples. Behold, I and the children whom Jehovah hath given me are for signs and for wonders in Israel from Jehovah of hosts, who dwelleth in mount Zion."—Isaiah 8: 16, 18, *Am. Stan. Ver.;* Hebrews 2: 13.

In July of A.D. 1879 a small but portentous publication began to appear. It was a magazine called *Zion's Watch Tower and Herald of Christ's Presence.* Its name spoke for it. The Christians back of this publication were consecrated persons that had separated themselves from all religious organizations of "Christendom" and heathendom. They were applying themselves to a direct search of the pure Word of God unmixed with religious traditions of men. Who the individuals were is unimportant; their being consecrated directly to God by Jesus Christ and the message they were used of Him to put forth are the important thing. As early as its issue of June, 1880, the magazine published that the end of the Gentile times of uninterrupted rule would end in 1914. It showed the Bible proof therefor. The same publishers of the magazine issued in 1889 a book entitled "The Time Is at Hand", and in 1891 another book entitled "Thy Kingdom Come". Both books attained a circulation of millions of copies, in many languages, and both showed that God's kingdom would take over the power at the end of the times of the Gentiles in 1914. There were many other Watch Tower publications, and in

1909 the magazine was given a change of title to *The Watch Tower and Herald of Christ's Presence.* Everywhere the religionists, Catholic, Protestant, and Jewish, ridiculed the message and opposed it. Only a remnant were convinced by the message and consecrated themselves to Jehovah God and took part in the publicity work.

A.D. 1914 was a test year. Something, the aftermath of which is still affecting the entire globe, *did* take place that year. With the venomous spirit of the seed of the Serpent, the combined religious forces used the emergency conditions of World War I to put political pressure upon those publishers of God's kingdom. Publications of their Society were banned by governments, distributors of the message were arrested or mobbed and driven out, and in 1918 in the United States of America the highest officials of the Society were falsely charged and railroaded off to imprisonment for an 80-year term each. The work of the only organization on earth proclaiming that Jehovah's heavenly kingdom was at hand was stricken low. It was then remembered with comfort that, when Elijah was taken away in a whirlwind, his successor saw him go. The anointed Elisha took up the prophet's mantle and smote Jordan's waters and crossed over to carry on the work of witnessing to Jehovah as God against all the religionists of the land. Likewise after John the Baptist had his head taken off by King Herod at the instigation of the religious Herodias and her daughter Salome, Jesus and his faithful disciples carried forward the message of the Kingdom into practically every city, village and home of the Jews in Galilee and Judea. Hence the witness work, which was foreshadowed by the two witnesses Elijah and John the Baptist and was killed in 1918, was not destined to remain lying in disgrace in the dust like a corpse. It was due to rise again. It did so, in due time, by Almighty God's power, and as foretold at Ezekiel 37: 1-14 and Revelation 11: 1-13.

In March, 1919, the Society's imprisoned officials were released and later vindicated of all false charges. Then the witness work was revived with courage, as when Governor Zerubbabel and High Priest Joshua resumed the building of the temple in spite of the unjust law the enemies had procured against them contrary to Cyrus' decree. The effect was as at Pentecost of A.D. 33, after the disciples of Jesus had recovered from their scattering at Jesus' death and their inactivity. (Zechariah 12: 10) Back there the spirit came upon the remnant of Jewish believers and moved them to perform a witness throughout their nation and Samaria. It led also to great persecution and opposition from the religious leaders. Three and a half years later the witness work was broadened to go to all nations and peoples when God gave a fresh manifestation of the outpouring of the holy spirit upon the first Gentile believers. Three and a half years from March, 1919, namely, in September, 1922, at the largest international assembly of Kingdom publishers held up till then, the witness to Jehovah's Theocratic Government was infused with greater spirit of power and action than theretofore, under the stirring cry, "Advertise the King and his kingdom!"

A phenomenal witness to Jehovah's name and kingdom followed upon 1922, in more than eighty languages and in all the earth and by every means of publicity. That still-growing witness speaks forth to say that since 1919 the prophecy of Joel 2: 28-32 is undergoing its complete and final fulfillment. It reads: "And it shall come to pass afterward, that I will pour out my spirit upon all flesh; and your sons and your daughters shall prophesy, your old men shall dream dreams, your young men shall see visions: and also upon the servants and upon the handmaids in those days will I pour out my spirit. . . . And it shall come to pass, that whosoever shall call on the name of Jehovah shall be delivered; for in mount Zion and in Jerusalem there shall be those that escape, as Jehovah hath said, and among the remnant those whom Jehovah doth call." (*Am. Stan. Ver.*) The apostle Peter, with utterance by God's spirit, commented upon Joel's prophecy and declared that the spirit is poured out, not upon the flesh of all humankind, but only upon all of Jehovah's servants and handmaids. These are new creatures in Christ Jesus and are yet in the flesh.

Those receiving the spirit are renewed in strength to serve God. These with the powers of young men to discern see the vision of the Kingdom and its establishment in the light of God's Word, and all these prophesy. That is, they publicly proclaim the vision as based upon God's fulfilled prophecy. On the other hand, those not renewed by God's spirit, but living according to the "old man" and remaining inactive and relying on their past, are given to idle and unscriptural dreams that delude themselves and others.—Jeremiah 23: 21-32; Ephesians 4: 22.

To meet the requirements of the prophecy, the spirit's outpouring must be fulfilled upon the remnant of Jehovah's witnesses who are members of Christ's "body". By virtue thereof they are made ambassadors of The Theocratic Government. In Bible times ambassadors were not exchanged between friendly governments, but were sent during times of strained relations or during war. Hence the ambassadors of the Kingdom are sent forth to those needing to be reconciled or to be brought into friendly and peaceable relations with God's King and kingdom, lest they be destroyed in the "battle of that great day of God Almighty". From this standpoint the apostle Paul writes, expressing the position of Jehovah's anointed remnant: "Namely, that God was in Christ reconciling the world to himself, not counting to them their offences; and has deposited with us the word of the reconciliation. On behalf of Christ, therefore, we are ambassadors; as if God were inviting through us, we entreat [sinners], on behalf of Christ,—be you reconciled to God! For him who knew no sin, he made a sin-offering on our behalf, that we might become God's righteousness in him."—2 Corinthians 5: 19-21, *The Emphatic Diaglott.*

Being sent to those living under unfriendly worldly governments, Jehovah's ambassadors for the Kingdom could not expect to be received favorably everywhere or to escape persecution. It is even so. The records in the law courts of the land, and the widely known persecution, mobbings, imprisonments and oppressions of these ambassadors in democratic lands as well as in lands under totalitarian rule prove the Bible to be true as to its prophecies of their experiences from and after A.D. 1914.—Matthew 10: 16-22.

These ambassadors or envoys are but a remnant. Is anything of significance to be attached to the world-wide activity of a despised, persecuted minority like them? Is their message to be taken seriously? Most assuredly, Yes! Their proclamation to the ends of the earth that "the kingdom of heaven is at hand" is in itself an outstanding proof that we have reached the end of the world and that the Kingdom is indeed established. Why? Because, in foretelling the visible evidences of the coming of Christ the King into his kingdom, Jesus said: "And this glad message of the kingdom will be proclaimed in all the inhabited earth, for a witness unto all the nations,—and then will have come the end." (Matthew 24: 14, *Roth.*) It is the good news or gospel, not of the kingdom coming, but of the Kingdom *come!* It is of supreme importance to you, therefore, to verify the truth of the message by other available proofs.

CHAPTER XIX

CONSIDER THE EVIDENCE

HE "kingdom of heaven" is Jehovah's everlasting Theocracy, his royal Government exercised through his anointed King, Christ Jesus. Hence we must rely upon God's Word in order to learn what occurs in the invisible heavens when the Kingdom is set up.

Jehovah is without beginning: "from everlasting to everlasting, thou art God." (Psalm 90: 2) He is the most ancient of all. The scene in the heavens at the time of establishing The Theocratic Government with respect to the earth is revealed in an inspired picture written by the prophet Daniel. He writes: "I beheld till the thrones were cast down [or were set], and the Ancient of days did sit, whose garment was white as snow, and the hair of his head like the pure wool: his throne was like the fiery flame, and his wheels as burning fire. A fiery stream issued and came forth from before him: thousand thousands [millions] ministered unto him, and ten thousand times ten thousand stood before him: the judgment was set, and the books were opened. I saw in the night visions, and, behold, one like the Son of man came with the clouds of heaven, and came to the Ancient of

days, and they brought him near before him.
And there was given him dominion, and glory,
and a kingdom, that all people, nations, and
languages, should serve him: his dominion is an
everlasting dominion, which shall not pass
away, and his kingdom that which shall not be
destroyed."—Daniel 7: 9, 10, 13, 14.

That vision was a preview of the occasion
when the 2,520 years of the "times of the Gentiles" ran out, in A.D. 1914, and Jehovah gave
the Kingdom of a new world of righteousness to
"him whose right it is". Ever since his baptism
in Jordan river as a perfect man that One,
God's anointed King, has held that right. But
he has been waiting until the time for Jehovah
to make his enemies his footstool and to authorize his King to send forth his power from the
capital Zion and down against the enemies at
the earth. The prophecy so said: "Jehovah saith
unto my Lord, Sit thou at my right hand, until
I make thine enemies thy footstool. Jehovah
will send forth the rod of thy strength out of
Zion: Rule thou in the midst of thine enemies.
Jehovah hath sworn, and will not repent: Thou
art a priest for ever after the order of Melchizedek. The Lord [Jehovah] at thy right hand will
strike through kings in the day of his wrath.
He will judge among the nations." (Psalm
110: 1, 2, 4-6, *Am. Stan. Ver.*) This empowering
of Jehovah's anointed King means, therefore,
the birth of the Kingdom, the bringing forth of
the Seed of his "woman" as reigning King. Now
that the period of the uninterrupted rule of Sa-

tan over earth has ended, Jehovah takes to himself his own great power. He invests Christ Jesus with power to wield the rod of The Theocratic Government and to deal with the enemies as these deserve.

That Jehovah should begin reigning with respect to that portion of the universe which has been rebellious is an event of the highest importance to all the universe. The heavenly hosts of holy angels are jubilant thereat. "And the seventh angel sounded; and there followed great voices in heaven, and they said, The kingdom of the world [the new world] is become the kingdom of our Lord, and of his Christ: and he shall reign for ever and ever. And the four and twenty elders, who sit before God on their thrones, fell upon their faces and worshipped God, saying, We give thee thanks, O Lord God, the Almighty, who art and who wast; because thou hast taken thy great power, and didst reign. And the nations were wroth, and thy wrath came, and the time of the dead to be judged, and the time to give their reward to thy servants the prophets, and to the saints, and to them that fear thy name, the small and the great; and to destroy them that destroy the earth. And there was opened the temple of God that is in heaven; and there was seen in his temple the ark of his covenant; and there followed lightnings, and voices, and thunders, and an earthquake, and great hail." (Revelation 11:15-19, *Am. Stan. Ver.*) In due time that information was transmitted to Jehovah's ambassadors on earth, and the Revelation shows this was after the reviving of His "two witnesses".

The thousand thousands whom Daniel's vision shows standing before the Ancient of days, and the ten thousand times ten thousand ministering unto Him, represent Jehovah's faithful universal organization, his "woman". Their bringing the Son of man, God's anointed King, near before Jehovah God on his throne to receive the Kingdom power well pictures how God's "woman" or holy organization brings forth the new government which Jehovah makes to be the capital organization of the universe. In her capacity of bringing forth the capital government God's "woman" is named "Zion" or "Jerusalem" and is the mother organization. Her giving birth to the Kingdom of the "Son of man", Christ Jesus, in the face of the opposition of Satan's entire organization is wonderfully depicted in sign language at Revelation 12:1-5, as follows:

"And there appeared a great wonder [sign] in heaven; a woman clothed with the sun, and the moon under her feet, and upon her head a crown of twelve stars: and she being with child cried, travailing in birth, and pained to be delivered. And there appeared another wonder [sign] in heaven; and behold a great red dragon, having seven heads and ten horns, and seven crowns upon his heads. And his tail drew the third part of the stars of heaven, and did cast them to the earth: and the dragon stood before the woman which was ready to be delivered, for

"Lord, Remember Me when Thou Comest into Thy Kingdom."— Chapter 15.

The Kingdom Sign of the Five Horsemen. – Chapter 19.

to devour her child as soon as it was born. And she brought forth a man child, who was to rule all nations with a rod of iron: and her child was caught up unto God, and to his throne."

Now the Revelation unveils things that took place in the invisible heavens, things which our limited powers of vision could never see. About six thousand years ago, at Eden, Jehovah declared he would put undying enmity between his "woman" and the Serpent, and between her seed and the Serpent's seed; and that, though the Serpent should bruise the heel of her seed, yet her seed should crush the Serpent's head. In A.D. 1914 the dragon organization set itself to spring at the expected new government and to devour it in its infancy. But the newborn Government was safely enthroned at God's right hand. Jehovah's giving power to The Theocratic Government meant immediate war upon the demonic dragon organization in heaven. His King must rule amidst the enemies. Daniel's prophecy calls the King by the title "Michael . . . the great prince which standeth for the children of thy people". (Daniel 12: 1; 10: 21) The name "Michael" means "Who is like God?" and perfectly befits God's Champion, who vindicates the name of Jehovah. The Revelation opens our eyes to see the war he waged (Revelation 12: 7-12):

"And there was war in heaven: Michael and his angels fought against the dragon; and the dragon fought and his angels, and prevailed not; neither was their place found any more in heaven. And the great dragon was cast out, that old serpent, called the Devil, and Satan, which deceiveth the whole world: he was cast out into the earth, and his angels were cast out with him. And I heard a loud voice saying in heaven, Now is come salvation, and strength, and the kingdom of our God, and the power of his Christ: for the accuser of our brethren is cast down, which accused them before our God day and night. And they overcame him by the blood of the Lamb, and by the word of their testimony; and they loved not their lives unto the death. Therefore rejoice, ye heavens, and ye that dwell in them. Woe to the inhabiters of the earth and of the sea! for the devil is come down unto you, having great wrath, because he knoweth that he hath but a short time."

The apostle's inspired words at Hebrews 1: 8, 9 show that Psalm 45 is addressed prophetically to Christ Jesus after his enthronement as King in 1914. This psalm makes clear that the nations of the world are not converted to Christ at the time that Jehovah's Theocracy begins, but that the Kingdom begins in the face of opposition and must fight to put down the Seed of the Serpent and all enemies. Mark its account of the fight, and that, after the fight begins, the marriage of the King to his "bride" takes place:

"My heart overfloweth with a goodly matter; I speak the things which I have made touching the king: My tongue is the pen of a ready writer. . . . Gird thy sword upon thy thigh, O mighty one, thy glory and thy majesty. And in thy majesty ride on prosperously, because of truth and meekness and righteousness: and thy right hand shall teach thee terrible things. Thine arrows are sharp; the peoples fall under thee; they are in the heart of the king's enemies. Thy throne is the throne of God for ever [marginal reading]: a sceptre of equity is the sceptre of thy kingdom. Thou hast loved righteousness, and hated wickedness: therefore God, thy God, hath anointed thee with the oil of gladness above thy fellows. . . . Hearken, O daughter, and consider, and incline thine ear; forget also thine own people, and thy father's house: so will the king desire thy beauty; for he is thy lord; and reverence thou him. . . . The king's [Jehovah's] daughter within the palace is all glorious: her clothing is inwrought with gold. She shall be led unto the king in broidered work: the virgins her companions that follow her shall be brought unto thee. With gladness and rejoicing shall they be led: they shall enter into the king's palace. Instead of thy [the king's] fathers shall be thy children, whom thou shalt make princes in all the earth."—Psalm 45: 1-16, *Am. Stan. Ver.*

The King's bride is the "body of Christ", to whom it is written: "I have espoused you to one husband, that I may present you as a chaste virgin to Christ." (2 Corinthians 11: 2) "For the husband is the head of the wife, even as Christ is the head of the church: and he is the saviour of the body. . . . Christ also loved the church, and gave himself for it; that he might sanctify and cleanse it with the washing of water by the word, that he might present it to himself a glorious church, not having spot, or wrinkle, or any such thing; but that it should be holy and without blemish." (Ephesians 5: 23, 25-27) The bride, "the Lamb's wife," is made up of those begotten of God's spirit and adopted as his children, and hence is the "daughter" of the great King of Eternity, Jehovah God.

Since the mother of these free children of God is "Jerusalem which is above", God's universal organization, she is therefore the mother of the "bride" of Christ. The daughter organization is the chief representative and capital of the mother organization. Therefore the daughter bears the name of the mother organization, namely, "Jerusalem" or "Zion". In ancient times, in the days of Abraham, Sarah his wife was used to typify or foreshadow God's "woman", his universal organization. Isaac, son of Abraham and Sarah, was used as a type of Christ Jesus. Rebekah, whom Isaac married, became a type of Christ's bride, "the Lamb's wife." Rebekah thus held the relation of daughter-in-law to Isaac's mother Sarah, who pictured God's "woman".—Genesis, chapter 24; Galatians 4: 22-31.

Christ Jesus and his "bride", the church, form together the new heavens with respect to our globe. They supplant the old heavens which Satan the Serpent and his demon organization have constituted in relation to the nations of earth. Showing that the daughter organization takes the name of the mother, "Jerusalem," and also showing that the marriage of Christ to his body members or church takes place after Satan and his wicked angels are cast down from their heavenly position, the Revelation says: "Alleluia: for the Lord God omnipotent reigneth. Let us be glad and rejoice, and give honour to him: for the marriage of the Lamb is come, and his wife hath made herself ready. And to her was granted that she should be arrayed in fine linen, clean and white: for the fine linen is the righteousness of saints." "And I saw a new heaven and a new earth: for the first heaven and the first earth were passed away; and there was no more sea. And I John saw the holy city, new Jerusalem, coming down from God out of heaven, prepared as a bride adorned for her husband. And there came unto me one of the seven angels which had the seven vials full of the seven last plagues, and talked with me, saying, Come hither, I will shew thee the bride, the Lamb's wife. And he carried me away in the spirit to a great and high mountain, and shewed me that great city, the holy Jerusalem, descending out of heaven from God, having the glory of God."—Revelation 19: 6-8; 21: 1, 2, 9-11.

From the Scriptures it is evident that the members of the "bride", the members of Christ's "body", did not have part in the war in heaven by which Satan and his demon hosts were cast down to the vicinity of the earth. The reason is clear. The prophecy of Malachi, chapter 3, declared that Jehovah's Messenger of the covenant must come to the temple of Jehovah after the forerunner had prepared the way of the Lord before Jehovah's Messenger. The true temple or palace of Jehovah God the King of Eternity is his royal family. Christ Jesus is at the same time the foundation stone, and the chief corner stone, and the cap or headstone of this temple, for he is its foundation member, its most prominent and exemplary member, and the Head without which it could never be complete.

The members of his "body", the "church", are the other "living stones", which are built upon him and in line with him. To the church "body" God's Word says: "Know ye not that ye are the temple of God, and that the spirit of God dwelleth in you? If any man defile [destroy] the temple of God, him shall God destroy; for the temple of God is holy, which temple ye are. What? know ye not that your body is the temple of the holy [spirit] which is in you, which ye have of God, and ye are not your own?" (1 Corinthians 3:16, 17; 6:19; also 2 Corinthians 6:14-18) "The Lord is gracious. To whom coming, as unto a living stone, disallowed indeed of men, but chosen of God, and precious, ye also, as lively stones, are built up a spiritual house, an holy priesthood, to offer up spiritual sacrifices, acceptable to God by Jesus Christ. Wherefore also it is contained in the scripture, *Behold, I lay in Sion a chief corner stone* [Christ Jesus], *elect, precious: and he that believeth on him shall not be confounded.*" Unbelieving religionists have stumbled over this stone and to them Christ Jesus as King has been a "rock of offence". But to the elect ones who believe and accept him as Jehovah's King or Stone it is written: "Ye are a chosen generation, a royal priesthood, an holy nation, a peculiar people; that ye should shew forth the praises of him who hath called you out of darkness into his marvellous light." —1 Peter 2: 3-9; Exodus 19: 5, 6.

King Solomon, who built the temple in earthly Zion or Jerusalem, laid the foundation stone thereof after having reigned three years, or in the fourth year after being anointed king. (1 Kings 6: 1) Centuries after that, Malachi prophesied about the coming of Jehovah's messenger to the temple for a work of judgment upon all professing to serve and worship there. Mark now the prophecy's fulfillment. Three and a half years after Jesus was baptized at Jordan and was anointed to be King, namely, in the fourth year thereafter, Jesus not only came to the typical temple at Jerusalem and cleansed it from the commercial element, but did more. The Jews tried to destroy the true temple of God by killing Jesus, who is the Foundation, Chief Corner Stone and Head Stone of the temple. But on the third day this all-necessary Stone was raised from the dead, and at once the "living Stone", Christ Jesus, proceeded to build up the spiritual temple of God by gathering together his scattered disciples and then, fifty days later, pouring out the holy spirit upon them at Pentecost.—John 2: 19-22; 12: 12-16; Mark 11: 1-18.

In the grander and complete fulfillment of Malachi 3:1-5, the events must run parallel with the illustrative things both of King Solomon's days and of Jesus' first advent. How? The Gentile times ended in the autumn of 1914, and Jesus was enthroned as Jehovah's Representative in The Theocratic Government. Three and a half years after that would end in the spring of 1918. Then, so all the events fulfilling prophecy indicate, Christ Jesus came to the temple for judgment as the great High Priest upon the throne. "For the time is come that judgment must begin at the house of God." (1 Peter 4:17) Having cast the "dragon" and its angels down from heaven, Jesus came to the temple amid the sound of the great trumpet in heaven that announced: "The kingdom of the world is become the kingdom of our Lord, and of his Christ: and he shall reign for ever and ever."

Then God's wrath came upon the nations; and not only that, but the 'time of the dead to be judged, and the time to give their reward to his servants', came also. It was then, too, that "there was opened the temple of God that is in heaven", and in it was seen the evidence of Jehovah's presence. (Revelation 11:15-19, *Am. Stan. Ver.*) In such way did Christ Jesus "descend from heaven" as Jehovah's Chief Messenger or Archangel and come to the temple; and then it occurred that 'the dead in Christ arose first'. These were the ones that had died faithful and were judged worthy of a place in the Kingdom. As a body those faithful saints sleeping in death were raised from the dead and were united with Christ Jesus at the temple. Thus the "marriage of the Lamb" began. —1 Thessalonians 4: 13-16.

This left alive on earth a faithful remnant, the last members of the body of Christ. (1 Thessalonians 4: 17) Amid World War I they came under a great judgment test as religious forces of "Christendom" closed in on them and "killed" the public witness work in the spring of 1918. Then, as foretold by Malachi, Jehovah's judicial Messenger at the temple judged the consecrated ones on earth to see who of them under test would prove to be his faithful remnant. Those who stood the persecution and then responded to the re-opened privileges of service at the revival of the work in 1919 Christ Jesus united to himself at the temple. On these the holy spirit was poured out in fulfillment of Joel's prophecy, and they were made Jehovah's "faithful and wise servant" class under their Head Christ Jesus. The unfaithful ones were cast out as the "evil servant" class and were cut off from the service at the temple.—Matthew 24: 45-51.

The faithful remnant were then sent forth as Jehovah's witnesses, as His ambassadors of the established Kingdom. They must preach "this gospel of the kingdom" in all the habitable earth for a witness to all nations and must declare the "day of vengeance of our God" against all willful opposers of the Kingdom. Their world-wide witness since then has been the most plain-speaking evidence that "the kingdom of heaven is at hand". That has been the foremost theme of their startling message. Declares God to them: "Ye are my witnesses, saith Jehovah, and my servant whom I have chosen." (Isaiah 43:10, 12, *A.S.V.*) The frightful persecution against them by the religionists is open proof that Satan has been cast out of heaven and angrily makes war upon them. By persecuting them he persecutes God's "woman", they being the "remnant of her seed".—Rev. 12:13, 17.

VISIBLE SIGNS

But hold! What about physical evidences within the nations of the earth themselves? Do the signs show that the Gentile times have run out, the end of Satan's uninterrupted rule is reached, and the final end of his organization must come shortly at the hands of God's established Kingdom? Yes. Let us, then, consider the many evidences and their meaning in the light of Bible prophecy.

Psalm 45, already considered, casts light upon Revelation 6, the second verse of which reads: "And I saw, and behold a white horse: and he that sat on him had a bow; and a crown was given unto him: and he went forth conquering, and to conquer." The rider on the white horse is Christ Jesus, who is thus pictured also at Revelation 19:11-16. The bestowing of the crown upon him shows that the time is the autumn of 1914 and that from 607 B.C. onward "seven times" have passed over the Gentile nations. The terrifying "dragon" organization opposes the horseman's enthronement and his taking power as King. It would swallow up the Government of the New World. Hence the King mounts the "white horse", which clean animal is symbolic of righteous Theocratic warfare, because it is necessary to rule among and in the face of the enemies, Satan the Serpent and his seed. The bow of war which the King takes in hand symbolizes he is able to shoot out destruction to the enemy from afar without needing to be in the exact vicinity of his enemies.

The great Theocrat, Jehovah, sends forth the rod of his King's power out of Zion, the capital organization, saying, "Rule thou." (Psalm 110:2) This action corresponds with that feature of Nebuchadnezzar's dream where 'the Stone was cut out of the mountain without human hands'. It represents Jehovah as setting up the Kingdom, which shall never be destroyed or be succeeded by other governments. (Daniel, chapter 2) The Kingdom is victorious from the start; for it wages war in heaven and ousts the dragon and his demons, and then the conquering King rides on to further conquests.

The consequences of the dragon's opposition to the newborn Kingdom in heaven show themselves in the earth. Satan the Devil is the "god of this world" and of all nations which are a part of this world. (2 Corinthians 4:4) No reason existed to look for the worldly nations to favor the King, for it was prophesied that he "was to rule all nations with a rod of iron":

"Thou shalt break them with a rod of iron; thou shalt dash them in pieces like a potter's vessel." (Revelation 12:5; Psalm 2:8, 9) The anointed David of old well pictured this King, in that when David was enthroned as king he was obliged to rule in the midst of his enemies. When the Philistines heard he had been made ruler over all Israel they massed their armies and came out in force against him. David's victories at Baal-perazim and Gibeon followed. Likewise in 1914, under influence of the "god of this world", the nations ranged up in hostility to Jehovah's newly installed King and determined to hold on to their worldly positions, despite the expiration of the Gentile times. As prophecy predicted: "And the nations were angry."—Revelation 11:18.

To turn their attention away from God's kingdom, and to provide emergency conditions suitable for suppressing the information concerning the Kingdom's establishment, what did Satan the Devil do? He plunged a score of nations into the first world war and taught them total warfare. This took place in spite of the Hague International Conference, which was in operation since 1899. In 1918, at the climax of the struggle, the nations banned the work and literature of Jehovah's consecrated ones, the Kingdom publishers.

Such earthly warfare the Revelation vividly symbolized by what appeared after the King rides forth on the white horse. "And there went out another horse that was red: and power was given to him that sat thereon to take peace from the earth, and that they should kill one another: and there was given unto him a great sword." It was the sword of total warfare, backed by regimenting the people.

Before the momentous year of 1914 the sixth head of the "dragon" organization, namely, the Roman head, had yielded place to the seventh head, namely, the Anglo-American democratic power, with Egypt as its ally. Those two dragon heads had their counterparts on earth in (1) the imperial Teutonic powers, with whom the pope of Rome sympathized to such an extent that the Treaty of London of 1915 debarred the pope from having any part in the peace conference at the close of World War I; and (2) the closely knitted British and American democracies. These two world powers were foretold and symbolized in Daniel's prophecy, chapter 11, as the totalitarian "king of the north" and the democratic "king of the south". The conflict which broke out between them in 1914 for earth's domination, to the exclusion of Jehovah's anointed King, was renewed in 1939; and concerning this Daniel 11:40 prophesied: "And at the time of the end shall the king of the south push at him: and the king of the north shall come against him like a whirlwind, with chariots, and with horsemen, and with many ships; and he shall enter into the countries, and shall overflow and pass over." To show the opposition of "the king of the north" (including the Roman pontiff at Vatican city) against Jeho-

vah's anointed King on Mount Zion, Daniel
11:45 says of the totalitarian "king of the
north": "And he shall plant the tents of his
palace between the sea and the glorious holy
mountain; yet he shall come to his end, and
none shall help him." (*Am. Stan. Ver.*) All such
is proof that the nations have been in their
"time of the end" since 1914.

Such facts fulfilling Revelation 6:4 correspond with that which Jesus said would be the
visible sign of his coming and of the end of the
world, namely: "For nation shall rise against
nation, and kingdom against kingdom." Then,
to forewarn us that other evidence would accompany the total warfare, Jesus quickly added: "*And* there shall be famines, and pesti-
lences, and earthquakes, in divers places. All
these are the beginning of sorrows." (Matthew
24:7,8) They are sorrows upon Satan's organization; but these unmistakable evidences
arouse great joy in those who are looking for
the sign of the end of Satan's world and that
"the kingdom of heaven is at hand". The world's
sorrows that follow in the train of the total warfare the Revelation also pictures in symbolic
vision after disclosing the rider on the red
horse, as follows:

"And when he had opened the third seal, I
heard the third beast say, Come and see. And
I beheld, and lo a black horse; and he that sat
on him had a pair of balances in his hand. And
I heard a voice in the midst of the four beasts
say, A measure of wheat for a penny, and three

measures of barley for a penny [or, modernly speaking, Wheat at a dollar a quart, and barley three quarts for a dollar]; and see thou hurt not the oil and the wine." (Revelation 6:5, 6) Notwithstanding the "victory gardens", the subsidies given to the growers of food, and the lend-lease arrangements between nations, gaunt famine is here prophetically pictured as due to follow upon the hoofs of the total warfare. Food scarcities, whether artificially created or due to natural causes, will raise the prices sky-high and require allocating and rationing of essential supplies to be enforced.

"And when he had opened the fourth seal, I heard the voice of the fourth beast say, Come and see. And I looked, and behold a pale horse: and his name that sat on him was Death, and Hell [the grave] followed with him. And power was given unto them over the fourth part of the earth, to kill with sword, and with hunger, and with death, and with the beasts of the earth." (Revelation 6:7, 8) Here it is foreseen that the efforts of men to establish a global peace and to make it permanent will fail. Death by plague or pestilence and by other causes of wholesale destruction of human life will keep on riding through the postwar "new order"; and "Hell" (or the grave) will ride at its heels to claim death's many victims. "The fourth part of the earth" is merely a symbolic way of saying "the four quarters of the earth", a part representing the whole.

Christ Jesus, "the Lamb of God," warned that his faithful followers and ambassadors would be persecuted in connection with the total warfare, and that "ye shall be hated of all nations for my name's sake". (Matthew 24:9) During the centuries from the days of the apostles down till the "time of the end" the blood of the faithful witnesses of God who have testified concerning his King and kingdom has been shed sacrificially. Their blood has cried to God, as Abel's blood did, for His vengeance upon the religious persecutors that have spilled such righteous blood: "for the life [soul] of all flesh is the blood thereof." (Leviticus 17:14) The Revelation calls attention to this and shows that more deeds of violence against the Kingdom ambassadors would be committed by totalitarian and demonized forces during this "time of the end". The prophecy thereon reads:

"And when he opened the fifth seal, I saw under the altar the persons of those who had been killed because of the Word of God, and because of the testimony which they held. And they cried with a loud voice, saying, 'How long, O Sovereign Lord! the Holy One and true! dost thou not judge and take vengeance for our blood from those who dwell on the earth?' And there was given to them severally a white robe; and it was told them to rest yet for a time, till both their fellow-servants and their brethren, who were about to be killed even as they, should be completed." (Revelation 6:9-11, *Diaglott*) Such blood unjustly shed by intolerant religionists can rest its claims for divine vengeance, because, yet a little season, and the measure of such shedding of the blood of Jehovah's witnesses will be filled to the full. Then the great Universal Sovereign will speedily avenge all his elect ones who have suffered at the hands of the seed of the Serpent.—Luke 18: 7, 8.

In 1918, when Jehovah's Messenger of the covenant came to the temple to judge the house of God, those members of the "body of Christ" that had finished their course in death were resurrected in sign of God's approval of them as members of his royal family. This is the significance of the "white robe" given to each one of them. They were righteous in God's sight, although persecuted and killed under the enemy's false charges of "unpatriotic; seditionist; menace to the state; bigoted heretic". As for the faithful remnant alive on earth since 1918, they do not have to sleep in death when they finish their ambassadorship as Jehovah's witnesses to the Kingdom. The King with power to raise the dead is present at the temple. When the members of the remnant finish their commissioned service "faithful unto death", they have an instantaneous resurrection to life in the spirit with their King. They are "changed, in a moment, in the twinkling of an eye", so that there is no waiting for them to do in a death-sleep. (1 Corinthians 15: 51, 52) They are the blessed ones of whom Revelation 14: 13 says: "Blessed are the dead which die in the Lord from henceforth: Yea, saith the Spirit, that they may rest

from their labours; and their works do follow
them." After their change, no longer will the
persecutors be able to make the Lord's work
laborious for them.

Stability will no more be the lot of the earthly organization of men under the demonic heavens. The "time of the end" having come, Jesus
declared, there must be a general shaking and
unsettlement of man-made organizations of this
old world as by a global earthquake. This is only
the precursor of the final end, when the old
heavens, Satan and his demons now shaken
down from on high, and the old earth of man's
organization will be completely and for ever
removed. Because Jesus so prophesied, it shall
be so; for, said he, "heaven and earth shall pass
away, but my words shall not pass away." (Matthew 24: 35) Foreseeing clearly what would follow the close of the times of the Gentiles, he
further said: "And there shall be signs in the
sun, and in the moon, and in the stars; and upon
the earth distress of nations, with perplexity;
the sea and the waves roaring; men's hearts
failing them for fear, and for looking after
those things which are coming on the earth:
for the powers of heaven shall be shaken. And
then shall they see the Son of man coming in
a cloud with power and great glory. And when
these things begin to come to pass, then look
up, and lift up your heads; for your redemption
[deliverance] draweth nigh."—Luke 21: 24-28.

"The sun" of prosperity in man's selfish sky
is becoming black as in mourning. The "moon"

of man's rule in the darkness of this world is becoming bloody with totalitarian methods. The "stars" which have bedecked man's notions of the higher things and which "stars" man has looked up to to guide him through the night are proving to be false prophets. The religious, political and commercial "bright lights" have no sure guidance for the people and are falling from their high stellar places before the people's eyes. They are as deceitful as the leafy fig tree on which Jesus found no early fruit and which he cursed. (Mark 11:13-21) This crisis must yet be climaxed by the removal of the demonic heavens like a book which has been read and is now laid aside, its wicked record being finished. The visible part of Satan's organization will also be shaken out of existence by the destruction of the human institutions, high and low, great and small, which are of this world. It will be just at the time when all men of this world will be seeking cover because they themselves discern that the end is near.

The apostle John was given a forevision of this and wrote: "And I beheld when he had opened the sixth seal, and, lo, there was a great earthquake; and the sun became black as sackcloth of hair, and the moon became as blood; and the stars of heaven fell unto the earth, even as a fig tree casteth her untimely figs, when she is shaken of a mighty wind. And the heaven departed as a scroll when it is rolled together; and every mountain and island were moved out of their places. And the kings of the earth, and the great men, and the rich men, and the chief captains, and the mighty men, and every bondman, and every free man, hid themselves in the dens and in the rocks of the mountains; and said to the mountains and rocks, Fall on us, and hide us from the face of him that sitteth on the throne, and from the wrath of the Lamb: for the great day of his wrath is come; and who shall be able to stand?"—Revelation 6:12-17.

Jehovah is the One sitting upon the throne as the Possessor of universal domination. In 1914 he took to himself his great power to destroy the old world and to extend his reign to this earth, where Satan has been mankind's invisible overlord for six thousand years. Christ Jesus, "the Lamb," is Jehovah's Executioner and is the enthroned Seed of God's "woman". As such he has enmity for the Serpent and his seed, and in wrath the Lamb will crush the Serpent's head which is now down at the earth since the dragon's ouster from heaven. The issue of universal domination is now the leading question to be settled to God's glory, and the day of wrath against all objectors to His universal domination is nigh at hand.

The religious, political and financial elements of this world, and the common people who have fawned upon those elements for some favors, have disdained to believe the message proclaimed by the remnant of Jehovah's witnesses. Now by the force of events visible to them and painfully felt by them they begin to have their eyes of understanding opened. They discern that Jehovah's King has turned his attention to the earth and to its human organization, and that he comes against it with wrath. The cloud that hides him from their view is the evidence of the storm that brews destruction for the old world. "Behold, he cometh with clouds; and every eye shall see him, and they also which pierced him: and all kindreds of the earth shall wail because of him." (Revelation 1:7) By rejecting His ambassadors and the Kingdom message which these preach, they rejected Christ the King and have chosen no other king than *Caesar*. Thereby they have *pierced* the King, and for the consequences of such antichrist action they shall all wail. They early seek hideouts from divine wrath in the various protective institutions of Satan's visible organization, which they think are as strong as the mountains and the mighty rocks. 'Fall over us, and hide us,' they cry in fear, 'or else this world is lost and the end is come!' And hundreds of millions seek refuge under the religious pontiff of the Vatican who claims to be the *rock* upon which the true church of Jesus Christ is built.

The towering mountain under which mankind seek to hide themselves in the postwar world is the international peace organization, with religion's spiritual guidance. They do not want the Rock or Stone that was cut out from Jehovah's "mountain" without hands in 1914 to smite Satan's organizational image and to become thereafter a great mountain to fill all the earth. The proposers and the backers of international peace machinery for collective security, protected by adequate military police-power, desire this to become the globe-encircling organization. This ten-toe organization, as clamored for by religious leaders, is smeared over with the clay of religion to look "Christian". Underneath, however, is the iron of the feet and toes of Satan's visible organization, both of "the king of the north" and of "the king of the south". It is a counterfeit for Jehovah's mountain of The Theocracy, and therefore it is hateful, abominable to him. It does not have his approval or blessing, but it works desolation and destruction to those who reject Jehovah's King and kingdom and who put their trust in such postwar thing created by men's own hands under demon inspiration.

As one of the most positive evidences that "the kingdom of heaven is at hand" and that the end of the world arrangement is now near, Jesus foretold the setting up of that antichrist organization. It is not an anti-religious organization, but is definitely religious. It piously assumes to fill the holy place which only God's kingdom can occupy with eternal blessings to men of goodwill. Hence it is in opposition to Christ the Rightful King, who has put us on our guard against it, saying: "When ye therefore shall see the abomination of desolation, spoken of by Daniel the prophet [Daniel 11:31; 12:11], stand in the holy place, (whoso readeth, let him understand:) then let them which be in Judæa flee into the mountains: . . . for then shall be

great tribulation, such as was not since the beginning of the world to that time, no, nor ever shall be. And except those days should be shortened, there should no flesh be saved: but for the elect's sake those days shall be shortened."
—Matthew 24:15-22.

The appearing of the man-made organization for international collaboration under religion's benediction makes urgent that all those who seek everlasting life seek shelter, not under it, but under Jehovah's Theocratic Government. The "abomination of desolation" made its first appearance in the form of the League of Nations after World War I. Due to totalitarian aggression in 1939 that creature went into the abyss of suspended animation during the global war. In the postwar period it comes up out of the pit of inaction, in the form of the new international peace-and-security organization. Then religion, the great Babylonish harlot, climbs up on its back and rides it.—Revelation 17:1-11.*

The above-noticed harmony of prophecy with the history-making events since 1914 proves that Jesus was and is a true prophet. It proves more than that. It guarantees that the present-day meaning that Jesus attached to those modern events is the one and only true interpretation. Said he for the sake of his remnant of followers today and their companions of goodwill: "So likewise ye, when ye shall see all these things, know that it is near, even at the doors."

* See the book "The Truth Shall Make You Free", chapter XXVI.

(Matthew 24:33; Mark 13:29) What is near? Luke 21:31, 32 rounds out Jesus' statement for the benefit of this generation, saying: "So likewise ye, when ye see these things come to pass, know ye that the kingdom of God is nigh at hand. Verily I say unto you, This generation shall not pass away, till all be fulfilled."

All the facts put God's kingdom to the fore. Let all those who see these facts with understanding take up the joyous announcement: "The kingdom of heaven is at hand!" This good news that Jehovah God reigns through his King Christ Jesus and that shortly Satan's wicked organization will be brought to its complete end at Armageddon and Christ's own kingdom of a thousand years for mankind's blessing will then begin, this is the gospel that must be published everywhere during the postwar era before the final end comes. This gospel, already being proclaimed, will continue to be preached until the full witness to the Kingdom has been given, and no power of Satan's organization can stop it until then. Jehovah's reigning consort, his King Christ Jesus, will see to it that the prophecy he himself uttered when a man on earth is faithfully fulfilled, namely: "And this glad message of the kingdom will be proclaimed in all the inhabited earth, for a witness unto all the nations,—and then will have come the end." (Matthew 24:14, *Rotherham*) Blessed are all those who see that this Kingdom proclamation is God's will for them now and who unswervingly engage in it unto the end!

CHAPTER XX

SUBJECTS OF THE KING

THOSE who prove worthy subjects of the King of the New World of righteousness must put their trust in him and not in the postwar "new order", so called. They adhere to the Theocratic rule stated at James 1:26, 27 and 4:4: "If any one thinketh that he worshippeth God, and doth not restrain his tongue, but his heart deceiveth him; his worship is vain. For the worship that is pure and holy before God the Father, is this: to visit the fatherless and the widows in their affliction, and that one keep himself unspotted from the world. Ye adulterers, know ye not, that the love of the world is hostility towards God? He therefore who chooseth to be a lover of this world, is the enemy of God." (Syriac Version as translated by Murdock) Religion is the adulteress and idolatress that befriends and commits religious fornication with the political and commercial elements. She is the lover of this world and blesses the world from the balcony of the Vatican and in the pulpits. Religion, whose most powerful representative has ruled from Rome for sixteen centuries, traces her origin all the way back to Babylon of Nimrod's founding, and organized religion deservedly

345

bears the name "Babylon". She has made all nations drink the cup of consequences resulting from her unclean ambition for global domination as a supernational religious hierarchy.

Religion's short-time elevation in the postwar era with reference to the many-headed creature of international collaboration for peace and stability is shown at Revelation 17: 1-6: "Come hither; I will shew unto thee the judgment of the great whore [or idolatress] that sitteth upon many waters: with whom the kings of the earth have committed fornication, and the inhabitants of the earth have been made drunk with the wine of her fornication. . . . I saw a woman sit upon a scarlet coloured beast, full of names of blasphemy, having seven heads and ten horns. And the woman was arrayed in purple and scarlet colour, and decked with gold and precious stones and pearls, having a golden cup in her hand full of abominations and filthiness of her fornication: and upon her forehead was a name written, MYSTERY, BABYLON THE GREAT, THE MOTHER OF HARLOTS AND ABOMINATIONS OF THE EARTH. And I saw the woman drunken with the blood of the saints, and with the blood of the martyrs [witnesses] of Jesus." Organized religion's perch on top of this eighth and last world-power of human history is not the position of the "bride" of Christ, "the Lamb's wife," the true church.

The church's position is by the side of her King, Jehovah's Anointed One with the divine right to rule. She is virgin pure, and is symbolized as "the New Jerusalem". Those who are members of her bridal company are the ones that will reign with her King over the earth. Of her it is written: "And the nations of them which are saved shall walk in the light of it: and the kings of the earth do bring their glory and honour into it."—Revelation 21: 2, 9, 10, 24.

Organized religion, the Babylonish fornicatrix with this world, chooses the postwar creature of international confederation as her king, her Caesar, and she goads its ruling elements on into direct conflict with Jehovah's King on Mount Zion. She deceives them to become antichrist by their international postwar creature or *beast*. These ruling powers, like ten horns, "receive power as kings one hour with the beast. These have one mind, and shall give their power and strength unto the beast. These shall make war with the Lamb, and the Lamb shall overcome them: for he is Lord of lords, and King of kings: and they that are with him are called, and chosen, and faithful." (Revelation 17:11-15) The victorious King is the Rider on the white horse of righteous warfare for the vindication of Jehovah's name: "Behold a white horse; and he that sat upon him was called Faithful and True, and in righteousness he doth judge and make war. . . . and his name is called The Word of God. And the armies which were in heaven followed him upon white horses, clothed in fine linen, white and clean. . . . and he treadeth the winepress of the fierceness and wrath of

Almighty God. And he hath on his vesture and on his thigh a name written, KING OF KINGS, AND LORD OF LORDS."–Revelation 19:11-16.

Let be shocked whoever will, but it is true: Religion leads the rulers and peoples of this earth unto a clash with the King of kings. Those who blindly follow her will be destroyed with her. In the postwar international arrangement, when religion and her lovers are saying "Peace and safety", then sudden destruction will strike them in the "battle of that great day of God Almighty". Religion will save none of them from that battle of Armageddon. In fact, the King of kings will strike confusion into the ranks of the religion-led united nations, and the political elements will turn their horns of power against the religious organization. They will find her a worn-out whore unable longer to satisfy them and serve their purposes. They will "hate the whore, and shall make her desolate and naked, and shall eat her flesh, and burn her with fire". (Revelation 16:13-16; 17:15-18) What their fury leaves of the disorganized religious forces the King of kings will directly consume with the baptism of fiery destruction at Armageddon. Out of no love of God and of his Christ will those ruling elements thus act; for at the same time or immediately thereafter they will whip up their beastly acts of opposition and persecution against the remnant of Jehovah's witnesses and their companions of good-will.

"And I saw the beast, and the kings of the earth, and their armies, gathered together to make war against him that sat on the horse, and against his army. And the beast was taken, and with him the false prophet that wrought miracles before him, with which he deceived them that had received the mark of the beast, and them that worshipped his image. These both were cast alive into a lake of fire burning with brimstone. And the [rest] were slain with the sword of him that sat upon the horse, which sword proceeded out of his mouth: and all the fowls were filled with their flesh." (Revelation 19: 19-21) That means the fiery end of the old "earth" or visible part of Satan's organization.

The apostle Peter discusses the certainty of God's word and writes: "But the heavens and the earth, which are now, by the same word are kept in store, reserved unto fire against the day of judgment and perdition of ungodly men. . . . the day of the Lord will come as a thief in the night; in the which the heavens shall pass away with a great noise, and the elements shall melt with fervent heat, the earth also and the works that are therein shall be burned up." (2 Peter 3: 7, 10) All those on this globe who refuse to become subjects of the King of kings will not survive the battle of Armageddon. At that battle is when the Stone "cut out" of God's "mountain" without hands actually smites the image of Satan's organization on the feet and then grinds the totalitarian thing to powder.

Satan the Serpent and his invisible organization of demons have already been cast down from their former heavenly place. They will witness the destruction of Satan's visible organization or *earth* and its works of postwar construction. The demons and their prince have long acted as the *heavens* to supervise human affairs. But with the old *earth* gone, their own destruction must swiftly follow, at the hands of Jehovah's great "angel" or Messenger. A foreview of this is given, in the next words: "And I saw an angel come down from heaven, having the key of the bottomless pit and a great chain in his hand. And he laid hold on the dragon, that old serpent, which is the Devil, and Satan, and bound him a thousand years, and cast him into the bottomless pit, and shut him up, and set a seal upon him, that he should deceive the nations no more, till the thousand years should be fulfilled: and after that he must be loosed a little season."—Revelation 20:1-3.

The old heavens and earth having thus been disposed of, this wicked world, which has been in its "time of the end" since 1914, will come to its final end. Christ Jesus the King will no longer be obliged to rule in the midst of his enemies. Having now bruised and crushed the Serpent's head, his enmity will have been fulfilled against that wicked one. Then he and his associates, his "body" members or "bride", will reign a thousand years, as kings and priests over the King's obedient subjects on the cleansed earth. Christ Jesus and the 144,000 joint-heirs

will rule as "the kingdom of heaven", Jehovah's
Theocratic Government. As such they will function as "the new heavens" with respect to obedient humankind.

"NEW EARTH"

That which the Bible calls the "new earth"
will be the visible organization on this globe
that represents and acts for the "kingdom of
heaven". After describing the destruction of
this old world the apostle Peter writes: "Nevertheless we, according to his promise [at Isaiah
65:17,18; 66:22], look for new heavens and a
new earth, wherein dwelleth righteousness.
Wherefore, beloved, seeing that ye look for
such things, be diligent that ye may be found
of him in peace, without spot, and blameless.
And account that the longsuffering of our Lord
is salvation." (2 Peter 3:13,15) The "new
earth" or visible organization will therefore be
composed of righteous subjects of the King of
kings who receive their life through him, their
Ransomer and Redeemer.

Not all on earth will constitute that righteous
visible organization. Who, then, will visibly represent "the kingdom of heaven" as princes
thereof? Jesus plainly indicated, saying: "Ye
shall see Abraham, and Isaac, and Jacob, and
all the prophets, in the kingdom of God, . . .
Many shall come from the east and west, and
shall sit down with Abraham, and Isaac, and
Jacob, in the kingdom of heaven." (Luke 13:28,
29; Matthew 8:11,12) In Hebrews, chapter 11,

the apostle Paul sets down briefly the deeds of
faith of those devoted men of olden times and
including John the Baptist. Though sorely tried
as to their faith and integrity toward God, they
abstained from accepting any deliverance from
their enemies by compromise with God's foes,
"that they might obtain a better resurrection."
They died too soon to have a part in the promise of being made members of the spiritual
"seed of Abraham" with Christ Jesus. Hence
the members of the "body of Christ" have a far
higher and *better* reward than do those men of
old by reason of being made joint-heirs with
Christ in the "kingdom of heaven". Nevertheless, those faithful men of old shall be made perfect on earth through the power of the "better
resurrection". Accordingly it is written: "And
these all, having obtained a good report through
faith, received not the promise: God having provided some better thing for us, that they without us should not be made perfect."—Hebrews
11: 35, 39, 40.

Receiving life through the reigning King of
kings, those worthy men of old, a number of
whom were actual forefathers of the King according to fleshly descent, will become his children. This agrees with that which was foretold
of Christ Jesus as a Paternal Ruler: "For unto
us a child is born, unto us a son is given: and
the government shall be upon his shoulder:
and his name shall be called Wonderful, Coun-
sellor, The mighty God, THE EVERLASTING FA-
THER, The Prince of Peace. Of the increase of

his government and peace there shall be no end, upon the throne of David, and upon his kingdom, to [establish] it, and to [uphold] it with judgment and with justice from henceforth even for ever." (Isaiah 9: 6, 7; *Am. Stan. Ver.*) By bestowing eternal life in human perfection upon those faithful men of old, The Prince of Peace becomes their everlasting Father.

In the days of ancient Israel's Theocratic government, when Jehovah God was their invisible King and before they had a human king granted to them, the great Theocrat had visible representatives among that nation. Many of these were numbered among those faithful men of old, from Moses to Samuel. These received communications from the unseen King and transmitted them and executed them toward the "nation whose God is Jehovah". In like manner, during the true and everlasting Theocracy exercised by the "kingdom of heaven", Jehovah will place visible representatives of his kingdom among men. Such representatives will be the faithful men of old who proved worthy of the "better resurrection". As children of the King, they will be princes to represent him. Psalm 45, after joyfully telling of the King and his bride and her virgin companions, then addresses the King with respect to the faithful men who preceded him on earth, saying: "Instead of thy fathers shall be thy children, whom thou mayest make princes in all the earth." (Psalm 45: 16) In their office of princes they will not oppress mankind, but will be as protective shields to the obedient people. Of that time of the reign of Jehovah God through his Theocratic Government under Christ Jesus it is written: "For God is the King of all the earth: sing ye praises with understanding. God reigneth over the nations: God sitteth upon his holy throne. The princes of the peoples are gathered together to be the people of the God of Abraham; for the shields of the earth belong unto God: He is greatly exalted."—Psalm 47:7-9, *Am. Stan. Ver.*

"Behold, a king shall reign in righteousness, and princes shall rule in judgment." (Isaiah 32:1) The resurrecting and installing of the faithful men of old as princes will be the creating of the "new earth". It displaces the wicked visible organization of the Devil. There will thus be "new heavens and a new earth", and the new world will be fully constituted and complete. The world wherein dwells righteousness will thus be recreated or regenerated. This is what Jesus spoke of to his faithful disciples, saying: "Verily I say unto you, That ye which have followed me, in the *regeneration* when the Son of man shall sit in the throne of his glory, ye also shall sit upon twelve thrones, judging the twelve tribes of Israel. And every one that hath forsaken houses, or brethren, or sisters, or father, or mother, or wife, or children, or lands, for my name's sake, shall receive an hundredfold, and shall inherit everlasting life." —Matthew 19:28, 29; also Mark 10:29, 30; Luke 18:29, 30.

The word of the original Greek manuscript here translated *regeneration* is *palingenesia* and is made up of *palin* meaning *again* and *genesia* meaning *genesis, birth* or *a being born.* Hence "regeneration", or *palingenesia,* means a "genesis again" or a "rebirth". Various modern translators render it here as a "new creation" (*Weymouth*) or as a "new world".—*Moffatt; Murdock's Syriac; Goodspeed.*

The original righteous world of which Lucifer and man were a part was corrupted and vanished by the rebellion of those two against God. The birth of the "kingdom of heaven" or Theocracy by the enthronement of God's King in 1914 marked the beginning of the regeneration of the world of righteousness, and the creation of the "new earth" marks the completion thereof. Here, then, *regeneration* has reference to the world of righteousness, whereas at Titus 3:5 the like word applies to individual Christians, as shown on page 288, ¶ 1.

"OTHER SHEEP"

As one of the visible evidences that "the kingdom of heaven is at hand" Jesus declared that, when he comes invisibly "in the clouds of heaven, with power and great glory", then he would use his angels to assemble into unity of action and service all the remnant of his elect ones. "He shall send his angels with a great sound of a trumpet, and they shall gather together his elect from the four winds, from one end of heaven to the other." (Matthew 24:30, 31) This remnant make up the last or "least" of Christ's brethren. It being the time for the trumpet message of the Kingdom, he sends the remnant forth under angelic guidance to proclaim the good news of the Kingdom come. This was prefigured in a vision John saw after seeing the royal Lamb and the 144,000 on Mount Zion: "And I saw another angel fly in the midst of heaven, having the everlasting gospel to preach unto them that dwell on the earth, and to every nation, and kindred, and tongue, and people, saying with a loud voice, Fear God, and give glory to him; for the hour of his judgment is come: and worship him that made heaven, and earth, and the sea, and the fountains of waters." (Revelation 14: 6, 7) The "midheaven" in which the messenger flies seems to picture the time of transition from the old heavens to the new heavens, after Satan and his demons were cast down from heaven and the cry went forth: "Now is come salvation, and strength, and the kingdom of our God, and the power of his Christ."—Revelation 12: 7-12.

The preaching of the everlasting gospel of the Kingdom to all nations and peoples by the remnant of his envoys or ambassadors brings results. All nations are gathered before the King on his throne for judgment as to how they act toward the information that He reigns as King. A division of the people over the Kingdom issue results. It has been taking place since 1918, with the lines becoming more and more sharply divided. This, too, is a sure sign that reads,

"The kingdom of heaven is at hand," Jesus having foretold this sign in his prophecy on the end of the world. He said: "When the Son of man shall come in his glory, and all the holy angels with him, then shall he sit upon the throne of his glory: and before him shall be gathered all nations; and he shall separate them one from another, as a shepherd divideth his sheep from the goats: and he shall set the sheep on his right hand, but the goats on the left."—Matthew 25:31-33.

The *goats* symbolize the seed of the Serpent who curse the name of Jehovah and who oppose his King. They show no sympathy for Jehovah's witnesses who are the remnant of Christ's brethren. They treat them coldly, turn down their message, and offer no aid or relief in their difficulties. They prefer the religious organization and the postwar "abomination of desolation". Therefore the King forces these religionists and antichrists to his left side of adverse judgment and curses them and refuses to admit them into the regenerated new world. "Depart from me, ye cursed, into everlasting fire, prepared for the devil and his angels." Why? Because their attitude and action toward the King's elect brethren has betrayed their heart condition as to the King himself. "And these shall go away into everlasting punishment"; that is, an everlasting destruction or cutting off from life (*kolasin,* Greek). They will not survive the battle of Armageddon.—Matthew 25:41-46; see *The Emphatic Diaglott*.

The *sheep* are beautiful symbols of those who receive the Kingdom message. They manifest their good-will to the King by treating his remnant of ambassadors considerately, and aiding them in their persecutions and helping them in bearing the message to others from house to house. To them the King becomes the Good Shepherd. Looking on them as in addition to his "little flock" of Kingdom heirs He says: "And other sheep I have, which are not of this fold: them also I must bring, and they shall hear my voice; and they shall become one flock, one shepherd." (John 10:16, *Am. Stan. Ver.*) He tenderly gathers them into the fold at his right hand of favorable judgment and bids them enter into the earthly blessings resulting from the established Kingdom, saying: "Come, ye blessed of my Father, inherit the kingdom prepared for you from the foundation of the world." Why? Because what they did to the Kingdom ambassadors they did as unto the King himself.

"And the King shall answer and say unto them, Verily I say unto you, Inasmuch as ye have done it unto one of the least of these my brethren, ye have done it unto me." These are destined for eternal life because accounted righteous through faith and obedience toward the King. A great multitude of these will be hid from the Executioner of Jehovah's vengeance in the battle of Armageddon and will pass through without dying and will survive into the complete regenerated world of righteousness. Then, as Jesus assures us, "Verily, verily, I say unto you, If a man keep my saying, he shall never see death."—Matthew 25:34-40; Zephaniah 2:1-3; John 8:51.

Such "other sheep" do not worship and serve the "abomination of desolation" of the postwar epoch, but flee to Jehovah and his King for protection and salvation. This is pictorialized at Revelation: "After this I beheld, and, lo, a great multitude, which no man could number, of all nations, and kindreds, and people, and tongues, stood before the throne, and before the Lamb, clothed with white robes, and palms in their hands; and cried with a loud voice, saying, Salvation [be attributed] to our God which sitteth upon the throne, and unto the Lamb. . . . These are they which came out of great tribulation, and have washed their robes, and made them white in the blood of the Lamb. Therefore are they before the throne of God, and serve him day and night in his temple: and he that sitteth on the throne shall dwell among them. They shall hunger no more, neither thirst any more; neither shall the sun light on them, nor any heat [of unendurable persecution]. For the Lamb, which is in the midst of the throne, shall feed them, and shall lead them unto living fountains of waters: and God shall wipe away all tears from their eyes."—Revelation 7:9-17.

These "other sheep" engaging in temple service become the associates of the remnant in the proclamation of "this gospel of the Kingdom". They are therefore the same as the companions of the King's "bride", foreseen at Psalm 45: 14, 15 as accompanying her: "The virgins her companions that follow her shall be brought unto thee. With gladness and rejoicing shall they be brought: they shall enter into the King's palace [the temple]."—Psalm 122: 8.

Long ago these were also foreshadowed in a time of world crisis like ours now, the end of the "world that then was" in Noah's day. The three sons of Noah and their wives who were companions of Noah and his wife in the ark during the flood made a picture of the destiny of the "other sheep". Their coming forth from the ark into the cleansed earth and receiving a divine mandate to multiply and fill the earth is illustrative. It shows how a great multitude of the "other sheep" will survive the end of this world under the protection of Jehovah's Theocratic organization and will receive the divine mandate in the new world to be fruitful and fill the earth with a righteous offspring.

Those of the "other sheep" do not hunt for the line of least resistance. They love righteousness and seek it now. The greatest symbol of righteousness is Jehovah's Theocratic Government, because it is the Kingdom which clears the name of Jehovah from all the reproach that Satan's organization has brought upon His name and it fights for Jehovah's rightful universal domination. Hence the "other sheep" take their places alongside the persecuted remnant of Jehovah's witnesses and join with them in the aggressive warfare of divine truth

against all religion. They rejoice to see in the
Scriptures that they were prefigured by those
several hundred Israelites that joined David,
the anointed one of Jehovah, while as yet he

was banned and outlawed by King Saul and obliged to take refuge in cave, or forest, or wilderness. Those adherents of David were bold fighters like the valiant companions of the remnant today, fleet in God's service and with faces filled with the courage of lions, expert at handling the spiritual "weapons of our warfare". They love the remnant with the same unbreakable love and devotion that Jonathan had for David, "passing the love of women." They are willing, with danger to themselves, to stand up for Jehovah's anointed ones in the face of fleshly relatives and the highest authorities of the land. They are content to go down in death now, fighting faithfully against the Philistinian religionists as Jonathan did at Mount Gilboa, for they know that an early resurrection to eternal life in the new world awaits them.

Like the queen of Sheba, they consider no distance too far to come to the Greater than Solomon and to hear His wisdom and to have all their hard questions answered, as to why wickedness is permitted till now, and the destiny of man, and the issue between religion and the true worship of Jehovah God. Like the stranger mentioned in Solomon's prayer at the dedication of the temple, they hear from afar the fame of Jehovah, which has spread to all nations. In honesty of heart they abandon religion, which is demonism, and in the spirit of true worship they come to the temple adorned with His name, which is a house of prayer for all nations, there to adore and serve him and his King forever.

Like that non-Israelite Jonadab, the son of Rechab, they attach themselves to Jehovah's chosen people. Their hearts are right with Jehovah's anointed King, the Greater than Jehu, in his execution of modern Queen Jezebel and all other persecutors and devil-worshipers. They give him their hand and get into the chariot of the King's organization. They ride along with him to see his zeal for Jehovah in destroying the religionists from the earth and wiping out all devil-worship.

In all ways these present-day "Jonadabs", or "other sheep", manifest themselves *now* as loving subjects of the King. They are "men of good-will", of whom the angels sang at the earthly birth of the babe who was to become the King. The peace of God is now theirs on earth. Nothing that may happen in this old world, nothing that demons and men may do to them, can take away that peace. They have heard the King's invitation and have come to the "pure river of water of life" that flows from the "throne of God and of the Lamb". Of it they drink to the fullness of satisfaction. Such draught of truth is a joyous foretaste of life abundant in the new world. Also, unselfishly, they say to others, "Come!"—Revelation 22:1, 17.

GENERAL RESURRECTION

Others, besides the "princes" and those "other sheep" of today, will become loyal subjects of Jehovah's King. In a chapter treating of the resurrection of Christ Jesus and of the members of his "body", the apostle Paul inserts this word of general hope: "Then cometh the end, when he shall have delivered up the kingdom to God, even the Father; when he shall have put down all rule and all authority and power. For he must reign, till he hath put all enemies under his feet. The last enemy that shall be destroyed is death. For he hath put all things under his feet. . . . And when all things shall be subdued unto him, then shall the Son also himself be subject unto him that put all things under him, that God may be all in all."—1 Corinthians 15:24-28.

The death which trails man from Adam's sin in Eden will be destroyed when the due time comes for Jehovah's King to raise the "rest of the dead" that are in the graves. (Revelation 20:5, 11-15; John 5:28, 29) This will be well along in his reign and after Paradise will have been restored and spread over this globe. He reigns for a thousand years. By the end thereof those awakened ones as well as the offspring of Armageddon survivors who become his devoted subjects will have been brought to perfection of humanity.

To test their choice of Jehovah's universal domination through his Theocracy for ever, Satan will then be loosed from the abyss of inaction, for a "little season". Those who selfishly succumb to his deceptions then will be utterly destroyed with him in an everlasting destruction without any hope of reliving. Those who under the test of their integrity continue as uncompromising, devoted subjects of Jehovah's King will be justified to life eternal. They will then live, with the right to endless life on the perfected earth. "And God himself shall be with them, and be their God. And God shall wipe away all tears from their eyes; and there shall be no more death, neither sorrow, nor crying, neither shall there be any more pain: for the former things are passed away. And he [Jehovah, the Universal Sovereign] that sat upon the throne said, Behold, I make all things new. And he said unto me, Write: for these words are true and faithful."—Revelation 21:3-5.

All mankind that then lives becomes a part of Jehovah's universal organization, and all thus become the children of God. Unity of the universe is thereby restored. The reign of Christ Jesus will then have attained its full purpose to vindicate Jehovah's name and word and universal domination. The thousand-year reign of Christ having ended, Satan and all rebels having been destroyed, and all mankind that lives being blessed with the gift of the right to everlasting life, then the Seed of God's *woman* will deliver up the Kingdom to the Author of all sovereignty, Jehovah God, by whose power all this was accomplished. Faithfully Christ Jesus the Son will subject himself to the Supreme One, his Father, to do whatsoever may be the future will of Jehovah God. "That in the ages to come [God] might shew the exceeding riches of his grace in his kindness toward us through Christ Jesus."—Ephesians 2:7.

CHAPTER XXI

"JEHOVAH REIGNS"

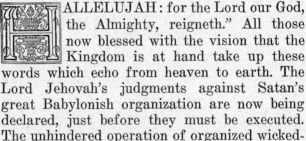ALLELUJAH: for the Lord our God, the Almighty, reigneth." All those now blessed with the vision that the Kingdom is at hand take up these words which echo from heaven to earth. The Lord Jehovah's judgments against Satan's great Babylonish organization are now being declared, just before they must be executed. The unhindered operation of organized wickedness and of oppression upon humankind is swiftly speeding to its close. Shortly the vindicated name of Jah Jehovah will be hallowed by all that are privileged to live, and His perfect and righteous will shall be done in earth as it is in heaven.—Revelation 19:1, 6, *Am. Stan. Ver.;* Luke 11:2.

The uninterrupted rule of Satan the Devil during the "times of the Gentiles" has ended amid the booming of the guns of World War I, and the Omnipotent God of the universe has taken to himself the power to rule with relation to our planet. The Most High God associates with Himself in this reign his beloved Son, and Jehovah reigns through His capital organization, Zion, the Head of which is the glorious King, Christ Jesus. (Psalm 132:13-18) Now is a period of uncontrollable turmoil for mankind on earth. Therefore true thanks are to be rendered that there is an irresistible stabilizing Supreme Power in the universe. He will not fail men of good-will who trust in Him. Let nations rage, the peoples imagine a vain thing for the postwar world, and the political, commercial and religious rulers and monarchs conspire together for world domination against Jehovah and his ordained King. Yet JEHOVAH REIGNS. Laughing at the conceited, totalitarian efforts of the worldly rulers, Jehovah derides them by moving forward with His own righteous purpose and says: "Yet I have installed my king, on Zion my holy mountain." Unwisely refusing instruction from Jehovah's Word, the self-seeking governing powers of earth are toying with destruction for themselves by Jehovah's King at the battle of Armageddon.—Psalm 2:1-12, *Rotherham.*

The nations of earth and their religious and political rulers disdain to recognize "The Higher Powers", and place their own interpretation upon the Bible. God's faithful remnant and their companions recognize that "The Higher Powers" are The Theocrat, Jehovah, and his King, Christ Jesus. They see that it is now important as never in the past to take to heart the inspired words directed to God's organized people: "Let every soul be subject unto the higher powers. For there is no power but of God: the powers that be are ordained of God." At His ordained time Jehovah has taken power and has ordained his Son the governing power of the New World. "For he is the minister of God to thee for good. But if thou do that which is evil, be afraid; for he beareth not the sword in vain: for he is the minister of God, a revenger to execute wrath upon him that doeth evil." (Romans 13:1-4) Hence these true Christians do obeisance to none but "The Higher Powers"; and where there is a difference between the law of God and that of man, they keep integrity to God and say: "We ought to obey God rather than men." (Acts 5:29; 4:19, 20) To God and his King they render first that which is God's. Being for The Theocracy of the New World, they are aliens and strangers to this world. Although being in it, they are not of this world, just as their King and his kingdom are not of this world.—John 17:16; 15:19.

Peter was a man of God. This is what he wrote to those within God's Theocratic organization as an ordinance for order and unity therein: "Submit yourselves to every ordinance of man for the Lord's sake: whether it be to the king, as supreme; or unto governors, as unto them that are sent by him for the punishment of evildoers, and for the praise of them that do well." (1 Peter 2: 11-17) For the benefit of the same organization of God's consecrated covenant people the apostle Paul wrote: "Put them in mind to be subject to principalities and powers, to obey magistrates, to be ready to every good work." (Titus 3: 1) The faithful subjects of The Theocracy readily comply and obey the commandments of Jehovah's great Governor, "The Prince of Peace," and share in his good work of bearing witness to the Kingdom.

With earnestness those who hope in God's kingdom carry out the exhortation which comes to them as another "ordinance of man" from the apostle: "I exhort therefore, that, first of all, supplications, prayers, intercessions, and giving of thanks, be made for all men; for kings, and for all that are in authority; that we may lead a quiet and peaceable life in all godliness and honesty. For this is good and acceptable in the sight of God our Saviour; who will have all men to be saved, and to come unto the knowledge of the truth." (1 Timothy 2: 1-4) All who now pray according to the divine will do pray for all that put themselves on the side of God's organization, that there may be peace and unity among them unto salvation. They cannot pray for the worldly kings who conspire against Jehovah and his Christ, but their prayer is as Jesus taught: "Thy kingdom come." The Kingdom, now established, is like the "stone cut out of the mountain without hands". It must yet *come* against the image of Satan's organization and destroy it at Armageddon. For this coming of the Kingdom we pray. As instructed, we offer supplications and thanks to the King of Eternity, Jehovah God, and we pray in behalf of the interests of the kingdom of his King of kings, Christ Jesus.—Psalm 72:1, 15; 1 Chronicles 29:10-19.

Nothing in heaven or in earth now equals in interest and importance Jehovah's Theocratic Government by his Son. It is His instrument by which He vindicates his holy name and clarifies to his eternal glory the supreme issue of His universal domination. To all seekers of everlasting life who now take their stand and uphold His universal domination this divine command is given in this day when "the kingdom of heaven is at hand": "Praise ye Jehovah. Praise Jehovah, O my soul. . . . Put not your trust in princes, nor in the son of man, in whom there is no help. . . . Happy is he that hath the God of Jacob for his help, whose hope is in Jehovah his God: who made heaven and earth, the sea, and all that in them is; who keepeth truth for ever; . . . Jehovah will reign for ever, Thy God, O Zion, unto all generations. Praise ye Jehovah."–Psalm 146, *Am. Stan. Ver.*

SUBJECT INDEX

NOTE: Numbers refer to pages; Roman numerals, to paragraphs.

371

J

Jacob, 88, I, II; 90, I-92, II
blesses sons, 90, I-92, II
Jehonadab (Jonadab), 162, I
Jehovah, day of, 306, II; 307, I
Founder of Kingdom, 52, II; 53, II
God, Ancient of days, 317, II
King over Israel, 101, I
laughs at opposers, 366, II
lies not nor repents, 127, I, II
makes all things new, 364, II
makes name for himself, 98, II; 153, I-154, I
reigns forever, 98, II; 136, II; 194, I; 324, II; 366, I, II; 370, I
reveals name, 95, I; 96, I
takes power to reign, 318, I; 319, I
Theocrat, 53, I
Universal Sovereign, 52, II
Jehovah's witnesses, 278, I; 329, II
Jehu, 162, I; 362, I
Jeremiah, 166, I; 168, I, II
Jeroboam, 159, I-160, I
Jerusalem, captured, 115, II; 135, I
daughter named, 324, I
doomed, 239, II
made the capital, 135, I
Nebuchadnezzar destroys, 167, I-168, II
New, 324, II
restored, 194, I-195, II
rewalled, 191, I
Romans destroy, 307, I
Jesus, age of; at baptism, 41, II
angels minister to, 28, I
anointed, 212, I-217, I
antehuman existence of, 46, II-48, II
ascension of, 261, I
at Nazareth synagogue, 217, I; 218, I
baptism of, 19, I-20, II; 212, I, II
before Pilate, 246, I-250, I
before Sanhedrin, 245, II; 246, I
begetting of, 214, I-215, I; 259, II; 260, I
betrayed, arrested, 244, I-245, I
birth of, 78, II; 208, I-210, I
Bridegroom, 322, I-324, II
burial of, 255, I
casts Satan out of heaven, 321, I, II
cleanses temple, 237, I
conceived immaculately by Mary, 42, II-45, I; 207, II
death of, 253, I-254, I
discusses Kingdom covenant, 243, I
draws first disciples, 34, I-36, II; 218, II-219, II
empowered to rule, 318, I-320, II
fights as King, 322, I, II
firstfruits of dead, 256, II; 258, I; 263, I
foretells death, 231, I
High Priest, 214, I; 260, I
human genealogy of, 38, I-42, II; 50, II
institutes Memorial, 242, I, II
Jehovah's Associate on throne, 340, I; 344, I; 366, II
King on Zion, 366, II; 370, I
made a curse, 255, I; 256, I
meaning of name, 46, I
Nazarene, 211, I
not Jehovah God, 47, I; 48, I; 50, I
offers self for sacrifice, 214, I; 245, I
on the tree, 250, I-252, II
ordains twelve apostles, 219, II
pioneers to homes, 223, I-225, I
prays for unity, 244, I
preaches Kingdom at hand, 31, I; 37, I; 216, I
preaches Kingdom truths, 220, I-222, I
prefigured by Zerubbabel and Joshua, 196, I-198, I
promises spirit, 260, II; 261, I
proved worthy to rule, 29, I, II
raised from dead, 256, II-259, II
religionists reject, 236, II-239, II
resists Satan's temptations, 24, I-27, I
rides into Jerusalem, 235, I
sheds forth spirit, 270, I
shows self alive, 259, I; 260, II
Son of David, 39, I-42, I; 139, I
Son of God, how, 36, I; 38, I; 41, II-50, II
Son of man, 317, II
studies in wilderness, 23, I
subject to parents, 212, II
subjects self to Father, 363, II; 365, I
transfigured, 232, I-234, I
true Christ to be followed, 50, II; 51, I
true Prophet, 343, II
unhurt in wilderness, 22, I
waited at God's right hand, 262, I
witness, 216, I; 218, I; 245, II; 248, I
Jezebel, 161, I, II
John Baptist, advises inquirers, 15, I
announces Kingdom, 15, II; 306, I
announces Lamb, 33, I; 34, I
baptizes Jesus, 20, I
began preaching, when? 18, II
birth of, 206, II
decreases, 32, I; 36, II
denounced religion, 14, I
disciples of, 33, I
food, clothing of, 10, I
foretold baptism of spirit, 14, I
fulfilled prophecy, 12, I
identified self, 32, I, II
imprisoned, 36, II; 37, I
like Elijah, 31, I; 306, II; 307, I; 309, I, II
looked for Messiah, 18, I
meaning of name, 13, I
not in Kingdom, 222, I
preached repentance, 11, II
prophecies as to mission of, 31, I
sees Jesus coming, 19, I
sees spirit descend, 20, II
why called Baptist, 11, I
why not priest, 13, I
Jonadabs, 362, I; 363, I
Jonathan, 124, I; 129, I, II; 131, II; 133, I, III; 360, II
Joshua, high priest, 197, I, II; 199, I-200, I
judge, 106, I-107, I; 108, I; 111, I-115, II
Jubilee, 104, I; 115, I
Judah, 91, I-92, II; 115, II
Judas Iscariot, 230, II; 241, I; 242, I; 244, I; 246, I
Judges of Israel, 116, I
Judgment, at temple, 327, I-329, I; 337, I
of nations, 356, I
Justification, 286, II; 287, I
at end of 1000 years, 364, II
of called ones, 265, II; 292, II

K

Keys of the Kingdom, 268, I; 269, I; 271, I; 275, I, II
King, Abimelech becomes, 118, II
  Gideon refuses to be, 118, I
  Israelites ask for, 118, I; 120, I-122, II
  law ordained no, 101, I
  not at first in Israel, 119, I, II
  of kings, 280, I; 346, II; 347, I
  of north and of south, 166, II; 167, I; 177 I; 186, II; 187, I; 333, I
  presence of, 226, I-229, I
  requirements for, 157, I
  time of installing, 123, I
Kingdom divided after Solomon, 158, I; 159, I; 171, II
  meaning of, 226, I
  of Israel, 159, I-162, I
  of Judah, 159, I; 163, I-168, I
  of priests, 100, I, II; 273, II; 282, I
  of world becomes God's and Christ's, 319, I-321, II
  prayer for coming of, 369, II
  reigning line of; interrupted, 155, I; 170, II; 171, I
  right to, 170, II; 171, I; 213, I
  saints receive, 305, I
  Theocratic, 156, I-157, I
  within you, 227, I
Kingdom Covenant, disciples taken into, 264, II; 299, I
  faithfulness required in, 154, II
  Gentiles taken into, 273, II; 275, II
  in Eden, 53, II; 61, I
  Jesus discusses, 243, I
  not cast away, 155, I; 170, II; 171, I
  not with Saul, 129, I
  with Abraham, 75, I-77, I; 80, I; 81, I
  with David, 138, I-140, I
Kingdom of Heaven, advertising of, 312, I-316, I
  begins against opposition, 321, I-322, II
  birth of, 318, I; 320, I, II
  foremost doctrine, 306, I
  given to Son of man, 317, II; 318, I
  is come, 321, II
  Jesus preached, 220, I-223, I
  manner of, 15, II; 37, II
  not of this world, 248, I
  of grace? 262, I
  publicity due the establishment of, 306, I, II
  requirements for, 220, I-221, II; 231 I; 232, I; 234, II; 283, I; 299, II-302, I
  source, founder of, 52, II
  steps to enter, 283, I-305, I
  stone pictures, 179, I; 182, I; 189, I-190, II
  subjects of, 345, I; 351, I; 363, I-364, II
  The Theocracy, 317, I
  visible representatives of, 351, II-354, I
  without successor, 182, I; 189, I-190, II
Kingdom of Heaven Is at Hand, announced, 9, I; 31, I; 37, I; 216, I
  evidences, signs that, 240, I; 330, I-344, I; 355, III; 356, I

first time preached, 9, I; 15, II
  message of; silenced, 228, I; 271, II
  not announced to Gentiles, 306, I
  not mistaken message, 226, I-229, II
  now again announced, 307, II
  proof that, 309, II-316, I; 329, II
Kingdoms, first of worldly, 72, I-74, I
  Jesus refuses worldly, 25, II-27, I; 215, II
  not founded by God, 53, II; 72, I
  pictured by dream-image, 180, I-189, I
Kings, of Judah, 163, I; 165, I-168, I
  prayers for 369, II
  Table of Contemporary, 171, II-175

L

Law Covenant, safeguard against religion, 109, I; 164, I
  with Israel, 99, I-105, I; 256, I
League of Nations, 343, I
Levi, tribe of, 101, II; 106, II; 114, II
Life with Christ, 299, II; 302, I
Lucifer, cherub, rebels, 56, I-59, I; 183, II; 184, I
  like gold head, 183, I

M

Magi, 209, I, II
Malachi, 205, I-206, II
Malefactor befriends Jesus, 252, I-253, I
Marriage of Lamb, 324, II; 328, II
Mary, bears Jesus, 208, I
  conceives, 43, I-45, I
  Heli's daughter, 42, I
  not God's mother, 46, II-49, I
  not "the woman", 60, II; 79, I
  of tribe of Judah, not immaculate, 42, II; 43, I
Melchizedek, blesses Abraham, 84, I-85, II
  priest after order of, 85, II-87, I; 260, I; 318, I
Memorial, 242, I, II
Men of Good-Will, 132, I; 208, I; 363, I
Messiah, appearing of, 200, III; 212, I-213, I
  cut off, 253, II; 254, I; 272, I
Michael, 321, I, II
Moses, at transfiguration, 232, II-234, I
  did not enter Canaan, 108, I-110, I
  in Egypt, 94, II-98, I
  leads out of Egypt, 98, II; 99, I
  mediates at Mt. Sinai, 100, I-101, II
  Prophet like to, 109, I
Mountain, stone becomes, 179, I; 190, II
  stone cut out of, 179, I; 188, II
Mountains called on for protection, 338, II-341, I
Mystery of woman's seed, 279, I-280, I

N

Name, people for Jehovah's, 277, I; 278, I
Name's Sake, Jehovah acts for, 123, I; 195, I
Nations, angry at Christ's reign, 331, II-334, I; 366, II
  hate Jehovah's people, 315, II; 336, I
Nebuchadnezzar, dreams of image, 177, II-179, I

INDEX TO SCRIPTURES CITED

"The Truth Shall Make You Free"

reveals how simple and understandable the Bible truth is from Genesis to Revelation. It is a fascinating story, with the vital Bible doctrines explained without interrupting the flow of the story from God and his creation of all things clear through to the end of the 1000-year reign of his King Christ Jesus.

"THE TRUTH SHALL MAKE YOU FREE" has a violet binding, with gold-stamped title and design. Printing is in large type. The 30 chapters are replete with many color illustrations. A complete index of all Scripture references builds up its contents to 384 pages. Publishers send it, postpaid, to any address on a contribution of 25c a copy.

The New World

safeguards against delusion by the misleading propaganda of the postwar "new order" promised by religion and politics. It sets forth truthfully the regeneration or rebirth of the world of righteousness and peace, which world Jehovah God establishes.

THE NEW WORLD is published in peach-colored binding, with artistic cover-embossing. Numerous color illustrations adorn its 384 pages. The comprehensive subject index and the complete Scripture index are most valuable features for study of this book. It is mailed, postpaid, on a contribution of 25c a copy.

WATCHTOWER　　　**117 Adams St.**　　　**Brooklyn 1, N. Y.**

WATCHTOWER SCRIPTURE EDITIONS

THE HOLY BIBLE

Authorized or King James Version of 1611.

The text thereof is unaltered but this special edition appends a unique Theocratic Concordance for quickly locating important Bible passages, besides other handy Bible-study and Kingdom-witness helps. The edition is in flexible binding of maroon color, and measures $7\frac{3}{8}'' \times 5\frac{1}{8}'' \times 1\frac{3}{8}''$. It is sent postpaid on a contribution of $1.00 a copy.

THE HOLY BIBLE

American Standard Version of 1901.

Its modern text, with footnotes, is printed unaltered, in boldface type. The WATCHTOWER edition thereof is the first to annex thereto a 95-page Cyclopedic Concordance of words and expressions found in this valuable version. The edition is published in flexible binding of light-brown color, and measures $7\frac{3}{8}'' \times 5\frac{1}{8}'' \times 1\frac{3}{8}''$. Mailed, postpaid, on a contribution of $1.50 a copy.

THE EMPHATIC DIAGLOTT, presenting in parallel columns both the Greek text of the Scriptures from Matthew to Revelation and an emphatic modern English translation of it. The Greek text is also supplied with a sublinear word-for-word translation in English, and there are copious footnotes. Other convenient Bible helps fill up the rest of the *Diaglott's* 924 pages. Bound in blue leatherette, gold-embossed, it is sent, postpaid, on a contribution of $2.00 a copy.

Remit to

WATCHTOWER   **117 Adams St.**   **Brooklyn 1, N. Y.**

Chief Office and Official Address of

WATCH TOWER BIBLE & TRACT SOCIETY
WATCHTOWER BIBLE AND TRACT SOCIETY, INC.
INTERNATIONAL BIBLE STUDENTS ASSOCIATION
is
124 Columbia Heights, Brooklyn 2, N. Y.

Address of factories and publishers:

America,	117 Adams St.,	Brooklyn 1, N. Y.
Argentina,	Calle Honduras 5646-48,	Buenos Aires
Australia,	2 Homebush Rd.,	Strathfield, N.S.W.
Brazil,	Caixa Postal 1319,	Rio de Janeiro
British Guiana,	5 Croal St.,	Georgetown, Demerara
Chile, Avda. Buenos Aires 80 (Blanqueado),		Santiago
China,	Box 1903,	Shanghai
Costa Rica,	Apartado 709,	San Jose
Cuba,	Padre Varela 55,	Habana
Denmark,	Sondre Fasanvej 54,	Copenhagen-Valby
England,	34 Craven Terrace,	London, W. 2
Finland,	Vainamoisenkatu 27,	Helsinki
Greece,	Lombardou 44,	Athens
Hawaii,	1228 Pensacola St.,	Honolulu
India,	167 Love Lane,	Bombay 27
Jamaica, B. W. I.,	151 King St.,	Kingston
Java,	Post Box 59,	Batavia Centrum
Mexico,	Calzada Melchor Ocampo 71,	Mexico, D.F.
Norway,	Inkognitogaten 28, b.,	Oslo
Philippine Islands,	1736 M. Natividad,	Manila
South Africa,	623 Boston House,	Cape Town
Straits Settlements,	Post Box 566,	Singapore
Sweden,	Luntmakaregatan 94,	Stockholm
Switzerland,	Allmendstrasse 39,	Berne
West Africa,	71 Broad St., Box 695,	Lagos, Nigeria
Yugoslavia,	Dalmatinska ul. 59,	Beograd

All communications for literature should be addressed
Watch Tower Bible & Tract Society, at the above
addresses respectively.

Announcing JEHOVAH'S Kingdom

Ever since
March 1, 1939,

THE WATCHTOWER

has carried the subtitle "Announcing Jehovah's Kingdom" in place of the former "Herald of Christ's Presence". This was befitting to the fact that Christ Jesus has been present in the throne of Jehovah's kingdom since 1914, and the Kingdom is at hand, and it is Jehovah's means to vindicate his name.

NO OTHER MAGAZINE on the earth, devoted to Bible study, is announcing Jehovah's Theocratic Government as having come and as constituting The Higher Powers. To the announcement of that kingdom *The Watchtower* stands committed, without compromise, for the postwar period, no matter what the developments then. All instruction to be found on the 16 pages of this magazine will faithfully accord with this all-important annunciation. For bold, straightforward explanation of the Scriptures respecting Jehovah's glorious kingdom, all "men of good-will" everywhere need the regular visits of this journal.

THE WATCHTOWER appears semimonthly, without commercial advertising, and with its leading articles supplemented with pointed questions suitable for private and group Bible study. A year's subscription, 24 issues, is just $1.00, in America. Remit to

WATCHTOWER   **117 Adams St.**   **Brooklyn 1, N. Y.**